HUSTLE
HARDER,

HUSTLE
SMARTER

HUSTLE HARDER,

HUSTLE SMARTER

CURTIS "50 CENT" JACKSON

AMISTAD

An Imprint of HarperCollinsPublishers

HarperCollins books may be purchased for educational, business, or sales promotional use. For information, please email the Special Markets Department at SPsales@harpercollins.com.

FIRST EDITION

Designed by THE COSMIC LION

Library of Congress Cataloging-in-Publication Data is available upon request.

ISBN 978-0-06-295380-3

20 21 22 23 24   LSC   10 9 8 7 6 5 4 3 2 1

This book is dedicated to the memory of my mother,
Sabrina Jackson, and my nana, Beulah Jackson.
They might have departed in their physical forms,
but their love, support, and guidance
continue to inspire me every day.

CONTENTS

Introduction   ix

1. Finding Fearlessness   1

2. Heart of a Hustler   21

3. Constructing Your Crew   55

4. Knowing Your Value   87

5. Evolve or Die   123

6. Power of Perception   155

7. If We Can't Be Friends   197

8. Learning from Your Ls   227

9. The Entitlement Trap   239

Acknowledgments   283

INTRODUCTION

For years people have been encouraging me to pen a self-help book. Even waved a couple of big checks in my face.

I always passed.

Not that I didn't come close a few times. I even got as far as coauthoring one (*The 50th Law*) with the great Robert Greene, but I still never felt totally comfortable writing one on my own.

I just didn't like the idea of presenting myself as an expert on life.

That might sound strange coming from the one who has never been shy about telling you how much money he has, how many records he sold, or the TV shows he's produced.

Yes, I've been comfortable sharing my successes publicly, but privately I'm sensitive to the fact that those accomplishments haven't made my life all the way right. There are many things I've fucked up: money, relationships, opportunities, friendships . . . you name it.

I've absolutely failed as many times as I've succeeded.

Which, ultimately, is the very reason I finally decided to write a book.

There aren't many people who have experienced success on the level I have. Within that elite group, even fewer had to pull themselves up from the bottom like I had to.

It's a story I've told many times before but is worth repeating here: my mother had me when she was just fifteen. As a single mother, she was forced to turn to selling drugs to support me. For several years she prospered on the streets, but as they do with almost everyone, those streets eventually caught up with her. She was killed when I was eight years old, and I was forced to move in with my grandparents, who were already raising nine children of their own. By the time I was twelve, I was selling drugs on the same streets that had claimed my mother.

It was the kind of circumstances that knock most people down and keep them there. But I never stopped pushing. I got into hip-hop, made a little noise, and then got shot nine times over a neighborhood beef. That would have been the end of the road for most people, but I was just getting started. I recovered, kept working on my music, and ended up releasing one of the bestselling debut albums in history. By the time I hit thirty, I'd sold tens of millions of albums, produced and starred in my own biopic, and become one of the first hip-hop artists to create a mainstream brand.

I figured I'd left the struggle behind me once and for all, but I was wrong. Over the next few years, my manager/mentor Chris Lighty died under tragic circumstances, I became a target for lawsuits, and most of the money in the record industry literally streamed out the door as MP3s replaced CDs.

In my unprecedented success, people couldn't get enough of me. Even when things became complicated, I grew in popularity, but for the wrong reasons. The forces that built me up were now taking pleasure in my potential destruction. It was never a true rock bottom—very few rock bottoms are lined with Gucci wallpaper and have Lamborghinis in the garage—but my life felt like it was headed in the wrong direction.

So what did I do?

I rethought my approach and shed people and excess baggage like a snake sheds skin. I hustled harder and smarter. And, in dedicating myself to building a relationship with my youngest son, Sire, I would like to think I also became a better person.

Within a few years, I made a series of moves that led to some of the greatest successes of my career. I created and executive-produced a hit show for Starz, *Power*. Soon I was dominating shows in the ratings the way I used to dominate other rappers on the charts. But *Power* was just the start of my master plan. This past October, my company, G-Unit Film and Television, Inc., signed a four-year deal with Starz/Lionsgate that is said to be the biggest deal in premium cable history. And that's just one of the many projects I have in the pipeline.

The most accomplished and lucky ones achieve success once; I've managed to make it to the top *twice*. In many ways, I'm prouder of my second trip to the summit than my first.

A lot of people wrote me off. Said that I was done. Even, to borrow a phrase from one of my albums, self-destructed. I saw all of the headlines. Heard all of the talk. Caught all of the celebrations of my failures.

Which has only made my success in the television field even sweeter. It's also what finally spurred me to write this book. I need people to understand that there is no such thing as "making it." That no matter how much money you stack, fame you achieve, or success you taste, there are going to be more struggles in your future. More drama to deal with. More obstacles placed in your path.

The goal is not just to be successful. It's about learning how to sustain that success, too.

A skill I had to learn the hard way. And one I'm going to teach you in this book.

Today I'm forty-four years old, an age I once thought I'd never come close to reaching. Hell, just making it to twenty-one seemed like it might be too much to ask at one point. Yet here I am in my fourth decade, with a few grays peeking through my beard and the wrinkles starting to set in (still got a six-pack and strong hairline, though). But I'm comfortable where I'm at. It's a more mature age, one that allows me to look at my life and accurately assess what's made me who I am. And when I try to sum up my ability to keep finding ways to stay on top, I can see it comes down to two main characteristics:

I've got the heart of a hustler.

And I'm fearless.

My primary goal for this book is to help you develop those same characteristics. But before we get into how, I want to talk about those words: "fearless" and "hustler." Coming from me, those words probably make you think of 50 Cent the Gangsta. The guy who openly bragged about selling drugs. Who got shot nine times and didn't seem to mind. Who got into beefs with some of the most feared names both on the streets and in hip-hop and never once backed down.

Those exploits all belonged to 50 Cent, a persona I adopted in order to help deal with the chaos and insanity that I saw all around me growing up. But this book isn't designed to turn you into the next 50 Cent.

Don't get it twisted: 50 Cent was, and still is, a real part of who I am. But if that persona was all there was to me, I never would have been able to maintain the success I've achieved.

That's why, in this book, I'm going to share the thinking of both 50 Cent *and* Curtis Jackson.

I didn't start going by "50 Cent" till I was older, but ever since I was a kid, I've always felt like there were two sides to me. Two identities I had to be comfortable with. The side that allowed me to exist in my grandmother's home, where cussing wasn't tolerated and Sundays were for church, and the side that allowed me to survive on the streets. I needed both of those sides to get by.

There were times when I would actually wonder if there was something off about me. Did everyone else have that sense of duality inside of them? Or was I slightly off in the head?

Today, I can see that there was nothing off about it. Just the opposite. My ability to harness both personalities has been one of my greatest strengths. 50 Cent propelled me to the top. Curtis Jackson is the man who has been able to keep me there.

At this point I've been moving in corporate America longer than I was hustlin'. I was only making dirty money from the age of twelve to twenty-four. I've been earning legal, corporate cash from twenty-five to forty-four. That's almost twice as long.

Not surprisingly, at this point, the streets and the business world often don't seem that different to me. Neither play fair. Both are ultracompetitive. They're both ruthless. And you can still dominate each one if you follow several basic principles:

> **Be fearless.** Most people run from what they're afraid of. I run toward it. That doesn't mean I think I'm bulletproof (I've learned the hard way that I'm not) or that I'm unaware of danger. I experience fear as much as the next man.
>
> But one of the greatest mistakes people can make is becoming comfortable with their fears. Whatever is worrying me, I meet it head-on and engage it until the situation is resolved. My refusal to become comfortable with fear gives me an advantage in almost every situation.
>
> **Cultivate the heart of a hustler.** Hustlin' might be associated with selling drugs, but it's actually a character trait that's shared by winners in every profession. Steve Jobs was as much of a hustler at Apple as I was when I was on the streets.
>
> The key to building up that trait in your own personality is accepting that you're never hustling toward

a certain goal. Hustlin' is a motor that's got to be running inside of you each and every day. And its fuel is
passion. If you can keep that motor running, it will
take you everywhere you want to go in life.

Build a strong crew. You're only going to be as strong
as the weakest person in your crew. That's why you have
to be extremely conscious of who you have around you.
Betrayal is never as far away as you'd like to believe.

That's why it's imperative to find a balance between
establishing trust and discipline in the people you work
with and giving them the freedom to be themselves. If
you can establish that equilibrium, you will be in the
position to get the very best out of your team.

Know your value. One of the cornerstones of my
sustained success is that I don't rush into deals. Even
though I've become synonymous with "getting paid,"
I never chase money. I evaluate every new venture
based on its long-term potential, not on what the first
check I get is going to look like.

The reason I do that is I have supreme confidence
in my own value and ability. I'm secure that as long as
I'm betting on myself, I'm always going to win.

Evolve or die. If I'd been unwilling—or unable—to
evolve as an individual, I'd be dead or in jail right now.
One of the keys to my success is that at every stage of
my life, I've been willing to assess any new situation
I find myself in, and make the necessary adjustments.

While I'll always draw from the lessons I learned
on the streets, I've never been limited to them. Instead,

I'm always looking to absorb new information from as many sources as possible. I don't care where you come from or what you look like—if you've created success, I want to learn from you.

Shape perception. Everything you share with the world—your words, your energy, what you wear—tells a story. You must make sure your narrative always presents you as the person you want to be seen as, even if your reality tells a slightly different story.

One of the secrets to getting what you want in life is creating the perception that you don't need a thing. That can be a difficult energy to project—especially when you're struggling—but committing to that perception will make you more attractive professionally, personally, and even romantically.

Don't be afraid to compete. Some people try to portray me as a troll, or a bully, but that's not accurate. My first instinct is always to build positive and mutually beneficial relationships with people. But if someone isn't interested in being friends with me, I'm more than comfortable being enemies with them.

The reason is I believe competition is healthy for all parties involved. Whether it's taking on established rappers or hit TV shows, I've always experienced my greatest success when I've met my rivals head-on and without any hesitation.

Learn from your Ls. As many victories as I've racked up over the years, I've experienced many more losses. That doesn't make me the exception among successful

people—it makes me the rule. I don't know an affluent rapper, mogul, executive, or entrepreneur whose
losses don't far outweigh their wins.

What separates those people from the pack is that
instead of complaining about or hiding from their
losses, they actively seek to learn from them.

Avoid the entitlement trap. Nothing was ever given
to me in life. I've had to fight for everything I've
earned. That's why the concept of entitlement has
never seeped into my mentality. But almost everywhere I look—from the streets to the boardrooms—I
still see a lot of entitled people.

You're never going to find lasting success until
you take full responsibility for what happens in your
life. No one owes you anything. Just as you don't owe
anyone else. Once you accept that fundamental truth
and accept that you control your journey, so many
doors that seemed closed are going to open up in front
of you.

G rowing up, reading was often seen as an assignment that must be
endured, instead of a tool that can help improve your life.

Because of that mentality, no matter how many secrets I share in
this book about happiness, business, and improving your life, there are
a lot of folks in the hood who still won't ever find them. They simply
don't sit down and read books. They might walk past a book like this
a thousand times, until it's covered in dust, before they even *think* of
cracking it open.

It's not entirely their fault, either. A lot of books aren't written in a
language that feels accessible to everyone. Personally, I didn't get into

reading until I found writers like Donald Goines and Iceberg Slim who wrote in a voice that felt familiar to me. Their style made me comfortable, and once I had that, it gave me the confidence to start exploring authors who didn't come from the same background as me. Writers like Don Miguel Ruiz, Paulo Coelho, and one who has even become a close friend and collaborator, Robert Greene.

Even if you're not from the streets (and given how diverse my audience has become, there's a good chance you're not), you've still made an important step just by picking this book up. These days a lot of folks have replaced reading with clicking. They'll skim the surface of a topic—maybe watch a short video, maybe read a Wikipedia page—and feel like they've put in work.

Sorry, but a few clicks or scrolls just aren't enough. I've found that you need to learn about multiple examples and read about multiple scenarios before certain principles start to sink in.

After you finish this book, you might only take a few of the principles with you. Even just one. That's fine. That was the case when I read Robert's *48 Laws of Power*. Ask me today what that book was about and all I can really tell you is, "As the student, never outshine the master."

There were forty-seven other laws in that book, but that's the one that stayed lodged in my brain. And because it's never left me, I've been able to apply it so many times over the years. I've literally made millions by remembering to follow that principle.

My hope is that you'll leave this book with at least one fundamental principle lodged in your brain, too. Maybe it will be about fearlessness. Maybe it will be about controlling perspective. Or the importance of evolving.

Whichever principle it is that resonates with you, hold on to it. Carry it with you until it becomes a part of your life.

———————

When you get to the top of the game, when you have all the money, then your perspective shifts, and you start to look at what really matters. How you help people.

I'm not someone who is comfortable resting on their laurels. If I'm around at seventy, I still want to be contributing and participating. It may require less of me, but I'll still be a part of the culture. Helping push it forward. I might not be jumping around anymore, but I'll still be there, trying to help.

I've helped people in ways that maybe you haven't seen or heard about before. But this book is one of the most effective and far-reaching ways that I can do it.

For every reckless tweet or wild lyric from 50 Cent, trust that there's a method to how Curtis Jackson is moving. A strategy behind each action that is battle-tested and proven to work.

This is my chance to share those strategies with you so you can move with purpose and confidence in your own life.

I'm excited that you're joining me on this journey.

HUSTLE
HARDER,

HUSTLE
SMARTER

CHAPTER 1

FINDING FEARLESSNESS

I wouldn't give a tinker's damn for a man who isn't sometimes afraid. Fear's the spice that makes it interesting to go ahead.

—**DANIEL BOONE**

A few years ago I hired a French guy named Corentin Villemeur to run my website. When he wasn't working for me, one of Corentin's hobbies was to take selfies in spectacular settings—standing precariously on the edge of a cliff or sitting on the roof of a high-rise with his legs dangling over the sides.

When he'd show those pics to the guys in my office, they would shake their heads and laugh, saying, "Only a white guy would do that." To them it was like skydiving or trying to pet wild animals. An unnecessary risk that only someone who had never experienced real danger would take.

I saw it differently.

I saw an opportunity for freedom.

So one day I took Corentin up to the roof of my old offices in Times Square to take some pictures of my own. But instead of just dangling my legs over the side, I decided to up the ante.

On the roof was a water tower, a wooden, barrel-like structure rising several stories above us. Without any hesitation, I climbed up its rickety ladder and took a seat on its edge. I must have been forty stories up in the air. Below me, the people on the streets looked like ants at a picnic. If I slipped, it would have been a long trip down to the sidewalk.

The stakes (and me) were very high, but I didn't experience any fear. Instead, I took in the spectacular view. The New York Times Building towered over me to my left, and the Hudson River sparkled behind me. I felt incredibly alive. Seeing my hometown from a bird's-eye view filled me with the same ambition I'd felt as a younger man. New York City was literally at my feet. The city of dreams. And I was going to keep hustlin' my hardest to realize every one of them!

I leaned back and Corentin snapped a spectacular shot for IG. When I got back down to my office, I posted it with this caption:

> *I live on the edge. I'm only free because I'm not afraid.*
> *Everything I was afraid of already happened to me.*

A lot of people loved the post. "That's real," one wrote, with another adding, "Man, what a powerful word." But not everyone appreciated it. About a week after posting the pic, I received a letter from my insurance company explaining that if I knowingly risked my life like that again, they would immediately cancel my policy.

The insurance company shouldn't have been surprised, though. If there's one trait that has defined me since an early age, it's fearlessness.

A lot of people probably think I was born fearless.

I might project that energy, but it's not true.

I was scared of the dark as a child. Just like I was definitely terrified of being killed when I was on the street, or petrified of failing when I started rapping. I've experienced anxiety and angst of all kinds.

The difference is I refuse to allow myself to grow comfortable in those fears. Comfort, I've learned, is a dream killer. It saps our ambition. Blinds our vision. Promotes complacency.

The number one thing most people are comfortable with is fear. Not that most of them would admit it. Ask someone if they're living in a constant state of fear and they'll probably say, "Of course not." That's just pride talking, though. Fear dominates most people's lives. Fear of loss. Fear of failure. Fear of the unknown. Fear of loneliness.

I don't think there's anything shameful about experiencing fear. A little bit of paranoia is actually extremely helpful. There are a lot of real dangers out there. A lot of people with bad intentions. Being aware of those possibilities makes it easier to avoid them.

What you cannot do is become complacent with any of those fears. If you fear loss, you can't spend your life avoiding intimacy and love (something I've struggled with). If you fear failure, you can't stop taking risks. If you fear the unknown, you can't stop trying new experiences. "It is not death that a man should fear," said the Roman emperor and philosopher Marcus Aurelius, "but he should fear never beginning to live."

I can trace the root of my own sense of fearlessness back to one specific event: the death of my mother. That's a special kind of fear, one that's hard to describe. More than getting shot nine times, losing my mother was the most significant thing that ever happened to me. Even in middle age, I can still feel her loss.

But through her death, my mother managed to give me a rare gift: the seed of fearlessness.

It would take a lot of time for that trait to fully blossom in me. I would, unfortunately, have to experience a lot more difficult and dangerous moments until it became second nature.

In this chapter, I'm going to share some of the experiences and situations that helped encourage that sense of gutsiness in me. That allowed me to accept that what lives on the other side of fear isn't danger, or even death, but freedom.

I want to show you that fearlessness is a strength you can develop, too. A muscle you can build, hopefully without having to experience the trauma that made mine so jacked. You don't have to lose your mother, or survive getting shot nine times, to develop the belief that you can survive anything that happens to you. That the only thing you can't overcome is never taking risks in the first place.

DON'T BE AFRAID TO GET HIT

Team sports weren't my thing as a kid. Didn't matter what we were playing—football, basketball, or baseball—if we lost, I'd always be quick to point out whose fault it was. "Yo, we got blown because you can't guard your fuckin' man!" I might tell a teammate who got burned on defense in basketball. "He kept bustin' your ass. We lost because of *you*, bro!"

It wasn't that I was trying to evade responsibility. If I made a bad play or couldn't guard my man, I'd be the first to admit it. It was more that I didn't like having my success ride on someone else's ability or inability to perform. It's a feeling I haven't been able to shake to this day. I always say that if I were ever going to bet on a horse at the track, then let it be me, goddammit. Because I know I'm going to run as hard as I can.

I was smart enough to accept I wasn't emotionally suited for team sports. I needed a sport where if I lost, it was my fault alone. Individual sports like golf and tennis weren't sports anyone I knew played. (I only lived about twenty minutes from where the US Open is played in Flushing, but it might just as well have been in another state.) And in my hood, you usually only find yourself running if someone was chasing you.

There was, however, a Police Athletic League boxing gym near me, run by a local fighter named Allah Understanding. He was from the nearby Baisley Projects and came up in the days when having a strong knuckle game was something people respected, aspired to, and feared. I training with Allah when I was around twelve years old, and I knew almost right away that boxing was the right fit for me.

One day I was hanging out at the gym when a street dude named Black Justice stopped by, accompanied by one of his boys. Blackie, as we called him, was one of the most respected dealers in Baisley, a top lieutenant for the Supreme Team, the biggest drug crew in Queens at the time. His boy was essentially his muscle, a constant presence to make sure a rival would have to think twice before trying him. They were probably only eighteen or nineteen years old themselves, but already their reputations were well known around the neighborhood. The kind of young guns you didn't want *any* problem with.

The gym got quiet as we all watched Blackie and his boy walk around. Then, without a word, Blackie's boy stopped in front of one of the heavy bags and started laying into it.

Bam-bam, bam-bam-bam.

As the youngest kid in the space, common sense would dictate I keep my mouth shut and just observe. But, maybe because I was the youngest, I felt a little bolder and my big mouth got the better of me. As soon as the guy was finished on the bags, I called out to him.

"Hey man, you look good hitting that bag," I said, loud enough for everyone in the gym to hear. "But that bag doesn't hit back."

Blackie whipped around. "What you say, young boy? You talkin' to me?"

"Naw, you a big nigga," I quickly replied. "I'm talking to him," I said, nodding toward his man.

Most guys in their position might have whooped my ass—or worse—on the spot. But these guys took my shit-talking in stride (Blackie had a generous spirit, free of the greed that infected a lot of his peers). Instead of taking offense, they both respected my outsize courage.

"Yeah, I like this kid," Blackie said, gesturing to me. "We gonna have some champions come out of here, because these little niggas crazy."

That recognition alone would've made my whole day. Instead, Blackie did us one better. "This gym could use some work if we gonna get the most out of these fighters," he announced, looking around at the shabby setting. "What kind of stuff do y'all need? Write it all down."

Two weeks later the gym was completely refurnished. Blackie had gotten us boxing shoes, trunks, new ropes, punching bags, and a new set of weights to replace our old rusty set that probably hadn't been updated since the sixties. From then on, Blackie took care of us. Whatever we needed, he got us. Although it was technically the Parks and Recreation Department's building, after that it was Blackie's gym.

I hadn't opened my big mouth just to get it fed, but that's what ended up happening. It was an important lesson for me to learn. You need to bend fear into moments of action at every opportunity, because the fearless not only recognize but also often reward one of their own.

I entered Allah's gym as a chunky twelve-year-old, the 150 pounds I was carrying making me seem older than I was. You ever heard the expression "punching above your weight"? Well, in that gym I had to punch above my weight *and* age from my first day. There were no other kids my age in the program, so Allah Understanding had me fight whoever was in my weight class, which usually meant opponents four to five years older than me. That might not seem like a big deal, but there's a massive difference between a twelve-year-old and a seventeen-year-old. Those seventeen-year-olds were basically men, whereas I was still waiting on my balls to drop. I might have been in the same weight class, but I lacked their strength and maturity. It was intimidating as hell to step into the ring with those guys.

I never gave in to that fear—mostly because Allah Understanding refused to let me. One of the best things he and the other coaches did was refuse to coddle me. If an older boy hit me in the face while we were sparring, they didn't stop the proceedings and ask if I was okay. They were going to teach me to keep fighting no matter how scared or hurt I was.

The lesson I learned from those ass whippings would be twofold.

First off, I learned that I could survive them. Yes, getting hit in the face wasn't pleasant. It would leave you disoriented. It would hurt. It might leave your eyes watering. But those blows didn't kill me. Hell, they didn't even knock me out. Once I realized I could absorb them and then keep moving forward, most of the fear I had felt evaporated.

Second, and I'm forever indebted to Allah Understanding for teaching me this, I learned that if I didn't like getting hit, then I needed to *do something* about it. "Keep your fucking hands up!" he'd yell if I let down my guard and my opponent tagged me. If my opponent started laying into me with body shots after trapping me in a corner, Allah would holler, "Get back into the center of the ring!" Punishment, Allah Understanding taught me, wasn't something I had to accept. I could always do something about it.

They knew I was outsized and often overmatched, but they refused to coddle me. You ever see a kid fall down and scrape his knee? How he reacts largely depends on the parent's reaction. If the parent runs over and worriedly asks, "Oh baby, are you okay?," the kid is probably going to cry. But if the parent assesses the situation, figures the kid is fine, and doesn't ask if he's okay, the kid is just going to brush his knee off and get back to whatever game he was playing. That's the kind of parent Allah Understanding was to me. He taught me to brush off being hit and get back to what I was doing.

He wasn't being heartless—he was trying to condition me to brush off the inevitable blows life was going to rain down on me and keep moving forward to where I was trying to go, instead of where I was being pushed.

Once I learned not to be afraid of getting hit, I became a much better boxer. Instead of constantly staying on my heels, worried about what my opponent was going to do *to me*, I brought the fight to my opponent. I learned how to dictate the terms of the confrontation. If I lost, it wasn't because I'd been backed into a corner and beaten down. It would be because I'd gone for what I wanted and had simply come up against someone with more skill.

It's been a long time since I've gotten popped in the face inside the ring, but I've tried to keep that attitude in everything I do. I refuse to be afraid to take a punch. I know the blows are going to come, and some of them are going to stagger me, but I'll be able to take them.

A lot of y'all are like the kid who fell off his scooter and waited for his mommy to come over and say, "Baby, are you all right?" Not me. When I fall off, I'm not waiting for a sympathetic word or someone to check in on me. I'm getting right back on my feet and continuing my journey.

I've accepted that the punches are going to come in life, and some of them are going to land. But I'm always going to survive and keep fighting for the things I want. That has to be your attitude, too.

FACING FEAR HEAD-ON

As I've said, my mother's death is what forced me to build up my immunity to fear. Learning how to get punched in the face only increased my insensitivity. For a while, it seemed like fear might be an emotion I'd never have to deal with again.

It wasn't to be the case, though. Getting shot definitely reawakened that sensation in me.

First and foremost, in the weeks that followed the incident, I found myself very afraid of the people who'd shot me. I knew that they were still out there, not very far away and eager to finish the job they'd started.

In addition to the emotional anxiety, the physical pain of getting shot also reacquainted me with fear. Not in the moment I got hit—the adrenaline stops you from feeling too much of that—but in the months that would follow.

Once the adrenaline wears off and the doctor tells you that you're going to make it, you start to acutely *feel* the effects of bullets ripping through muscles and pulverizing bone. I felt pain everywhere—where lead went through my thumb or through my cheek. For months it was like I had headaches throughout my body: a relentless and deep throbbing I didn't know you could feel in your leg or your hand.

Every time I had to go to physical therapy and put weight on my leg, or break through the scar tissue in my thumb, it hurt like hell. I realized I was scared of having to go through that process again. Maybe even more so than dying.

But as my rehab continued, I also came to understand another important truth: I wasn't comfortable being scared. That might sound like an obvious thing to say, but I think it's actually what makes me unique. Most people are extremely comfortable with their fears. Afraid of flying? Stay off of planes. Afraid of sharks? Don't go snorkeling on your Caribbean vacation. Afraid of failure? Well, then don't even try. A lot of people live their entire lives that way.

Not me. I *hated* being scared. I hated looking over my shoulder. I couldn't stand the idea of staying off the block till things cooled down. To me, hiding would have almost been worse than getting shot.

In some ways, the physical pain I endured was my friend. It pushed me further than most people are willing to go. Trust me, when you get hurt that bad, there's a shift. You *want* to approach the problem instead of run from it. Which is exactly what I did.

———————————

After several weeks in rehab, I went back to my grandmother's house in Queens. Literally back to the scene of the crime. That in itself was a big step for me psychologically. The easy—hell, the sensible— thing would have been to move far away. A place where no one except my closest friends would know how to find me. It didn't even have to be far in terms of mileage. I could have moved to the Bronx or Staten Island, and it would have been like going to another country. I was determined not to give in an inch to my fear. I was going to go back to where I wanted to be, which was my grandmother's house.

When I left rehab, the doctors told me to start jogging to build up stamina and strength in my injured legs. I was committed to their plan, but almost immediately I hit an obstacle. One morning I took a peek out my grandma's window and saw someone I didn't recognize in front of her house. To me, he was trying too hard to look inconspicuous and blend in. I was admittedly in a very paranoid state, so it could have been nothing. But paranoia sharpens your senses the way an antelope's acute sense of smell can identify a lion from hundreds of yards away. Maybe I was sensing my own predator.

I canceled the jog I had planned for the day. And the next day, too, after I saw the same guy lurking on the street again. By this point I was experiencing a lot of confusion. Were my heightened senses tipping me off to unseen danger? Or was I imagining menace that wasn't really there? I couldn't tell. All I knew for sure was that fear was starting to consume me.

I decided that if I stayed in that house and didn't follow my rehab plan, then I had already lost. When fear interrupts your routine, or makes you rethink it in any way, it's gotten its hooks deep in you and will hold you back forever. "Cowards die many times before their deaths," wrote Shakespeare. "The valiant never taste of death but once." I wasn't trying to go out like a coward.

The best way to get past a fear that's holding you back is first to acknowledge it and then come up with a plan to get past it. So that's what

I did. First, I accepted that I was afraid. Then I gathered my most trusted friends in my grandmother's living room and explained that I was going to need them to go jogging with me the next morning. "No doubt," everyone said. "We'll be back tomorrow." When the next morning rolled around, however, only one of them actually showed up: my guy Halim. I don't think the rest of them were scared of any potential drama—they'd proved themselves in that realm too many times already. I think they were more afraid of the idea of having to do some cardio in the morning. *That* wasn't something they were comfortable with.

I decided to head out with just Halim, even though he wasn't the ideal candidate: he was in even worse shape than I was. More important, I had serious doubts about how he might react if a threat did present itself. In a crew full of dudes just looking for any excuse to let one fly, Halim's nature was to look for a way to avoid confrontation.

As for Halim, since he was out of shape, I gave him a bike so he could keep pace alongside me. As for my second concern, I opted to take matters into my own hands, literally.

I found a small pistol, put it in my good hand, and then wrapped it with medical bandages. Everyone knew me as a boxer, so to the casual eye, it just looked like I'd busted my hand in the ring. I used so many bandages that the gun disappeared into my "cast" almost completely, with only the barrel peeking out. I told Halim to pedal alongside me and keep an eye out for anyone who looked like they wanted to jump out of the bushes and take a shot at me. All he had to do was sound the alarm, and I'd take it from there.

Halim and I performed this routine every morning. I was committed to getting my strength and stamina back, and wasn't going to let a threat—perceived or actual—get between me and my goals. Was I actually scared on any of those runs? At first I was, but I took comfort in knowing that each time I set out, I'd done all I could do to take the necessary precautions. I had both a lookout and protection, which was at least more than I had when I'd been shot.

It was an extension of what Allah Understanding had taught me: instead of being afraid of getting hit and just giving up, do the things that make you a difficult target. In the ring, that meant staying on my toes, moving constantly, and keeping my hands up. On the street, it meant jogging with a bodyguard and a pistol up my sleeve.

No one ended up challenging me, and I was able to get myself back into shape through those runs. But looking back, I can see that I didn't have to be so aggressive in confronting my fears. I didn't *have* to run through the same streets where I'd just been shot—I could have just as easily gone to a local gym, or even put a treadmill in my grandmother's basement.

I was just so uncomfortable that anything less than jogging outside, in full view of the whole neighborhood, would have felt like a complete concession to fear. A concession I wasn't willing to make.

Today, I'm a little less likely to be so aggressive in confronting things head-on. In fact, if I'm being completely honest, there are still some fears I've barely confronted at all.

THE ONE THING I'M STILL AFRAID OF

We can spend our entire lives—and many people do—trying to ignore something we're actually carrying around with us every day. But you can't hide from something you never put down.

To give you an example, when I look in the mirror and take an authentic assessment of where I'm at in life, the thing I'm most afraid of is family.

It's a fear I haven't wanted to admit, because I know for the vast majority of people, family brings incredible comfort. Security. A sense of well-being and connection.

I've never had that feeling. Family makes me uncomfortable as hell. It doesn't make me feel safe. It makes me feel extremely vulnerable.

That's probably not a surprise given my background. The number one fear every child experiences, no matter where they live or what their circumstance, is losing a parent. It's built into our DNA. You don't have to download that app onto your phone; it comes pre-installed. Psychologists say the fear of losing a parent is especially acute between the ages of four and eight. Every kid in that age range is going to start worrying when their parent is late coming back from the store, or goes away for a couple of days. Of course the parent always comes back, and in time the kid stops obsessing over the possibility that they won't. Well, my mother never came back. So when every child's worst fear actually came true for me, it made it very, very hard to open myself up to the type of love I had for my mother with anyone else.

As you've probably gathered, things didn't get much easier once I went to my grandparents' house. Their love was unquestionable, but the environment was chaotic even in the best of times. There was never enough money, attention, or stability. But there was plenty of drug and alcohol abuse. A lot of dysfunction. My grandparents' house was not the ideal place to mourn my mother.

But they were the only family I had. I've never met my father. I don't even know who the guy is. A lot of people who have grown up fatherless have a desire to reconnect when they're older, but I've never felt that way. In fact, I'm glad he hasn't come forward. The things he could have helped me with—the lessons he could have taught me—those moments have all passed. I don't think there's anything positive he could add to my life now.

Like many people do, at first I continued the cycle of dysfunction that began with my mother's death. When my son Marquise was born, right around the time my rap career was blowing up, I thought I'd turned a corner. I remember telling an interviewer, "When my son came into my life, my priorities changed, because I wanted to have the relationship with him that I didn't have with my father."

That was my pure intention, but it's not what happened. Instead, Marquise's mother, Shaniqua, and I got caught up in an extremely dysfunctional relationship of our own. I'll talk about some of my frustrations with Shaniqua and Marquise later in the book. But for now I'll admit a lot of criticism I've received for how I've dealt with that situation has been justified.

I'm someone who's incredibly honest and transparent, and the things I've said publicly about my older son are the same sorts of things a lot of parents who are stuck in bad relationships also think and feel. They just don't articulate it. That doesn't make it right, but it might make it a little bit more relatable.

If I have done one thing right when it comes to family, it's that I've tried to break that cycle of dysfunction with my younger son, Sire. His mother and I aren't together, but I've tried to be much more present in his life. He lives with his mom, so I go see him whenever I get the chance. We'll hang out at the pool, play video games, and watch sports. The normal things fathers and sons do. Most important, there's no tension when I see him. His mother and I are on the same page and do a great job coparenting. So when Sire sees me walk up for a hug, it's nothing but love.

It brings me a lot of happiness to know that I'm always going to be a big part of his life and be there to help him navigate the inevitable peaks and valleys. To make sure that Sire doesn't have to make the same mistakes that I've made. That's what I wanted for Marquise, but neither his mother nor I was emotionally mature enough to create that foundation for him. The truth is, I was scared of having a family. Maybe she was, too. Our son suffered for it. And now my relationship with Marquise is just a reflection of the negative energy between his mother and me.

My relationship with Marquise is the area in my life where I've got the most work to do. There have been times, even recently, when I've thought about writing that relationship off forever. I don't want to do that, but sometimes when you've been hurt a lot—and you've done your share of the hurting, too—it feels best to walk away.

I came extremely close not long ago, after I unexpectedly bumped into Marquise at my jeweler's store in Manhattan. I didn't even know he was in the city at the time, so I was shocked to see him. I tried to start a conversation, but he immediately accused me of having him followed. I told him that was crazy, but things only went downhill from there.

The energy between us was terrible. Marquise even said, "What, am I supposed to be afraid of you?" That really messed my head up. This was my firstborn son, my own flesh and blood, and we couldn't even speak to each other, let alone hug and laugh at an unexpected encounter. Finally, without a word, Marquise basically fled the store, leaving me dumbfounded.

A couple of my guys went down to the street to try to catch up with Marquise and say, "Why are you bugging? This is your father. Come and talk with him," but Marquise had already disappeared. He didn't want to be found. I couldn't even follow them into the street—my mind was fuzzy and I couldn't think straight. I had to take several minutes to compose myself.

There are very few times when I'm knocked completely off-kilter, but when they happen, they always involve family. Let me bump into a rapper who dissed me, or a CEO I've had a tense negotiation with, and I'm good. In fact, I'm great. Those moments don't faze me—they're what I live for. Only family seems to faze me.

It's not just my relationship with Marquise, either. I don't even like going home for holidays anymore because seeing my family makes me so tense. I'll stop by my grandmother's old house a day before Christmas to kick it with my grandfather. But I won't come back on the actual holiday. Even if I bring only positive vibes into the house, someone is inevitably going to bring their negativity toward me. An aunt or a cousin will end up saying, "I'm tired of everyone kissing his ass because he's 50 Cent. Shit, he ain't *that* special." Instead of a celebration, the entire night will be about what I did for one person but didn't do for everyone else. That sort of energy makes me extremely uncomfortable.

I know my fear of family isn't healthy, and I'm working on it. It may take years, but I'm committed to the process. So by the time I'm my grandfather's age, I hope I'll have a solid relationship with my children, and maybe their children, too.

RAISE YOUR HAND!

I know I have a reputation as a hothead, but in reality, no matter what private jet I'm flying on or corporate boardroom I'm seated in, I'm always relaxed. The person operating under the *least* amount of fear. I'm confident nothing that gets said, threatened, or promised in any of those conversations is going to hurt me. Sure, I'd like to seal that $30 million distribution deal or land the role of a lifetime. But I'm not afraid they might go away. Why would I be scared? I've already been through some of the scariest shit life has to offer.

So how do you harness the same sort of confidence I have? To keep cool where most people would be sweating through their shirts? It's not rocket science. The only way to access that kind of confidence is by putting in the work. That's it.

Have you truly dedicated yourself to learning everything that you can about your field? Do you give 100 percent every time you walk in the office, sit down in the classroom, or step onstage for an audition? If the answer is yes, what do you really have to be afraid of?

You've already done everything you can do. Now you just need to make sure the world recognizes it.

That can be a challenge, especially if you're not someone who's been raised from an early age to think that you belong in those meetings. If you're not a white guy or didn't get into the "right" prep school, you might have to go a little harder to get the credit you deserve. It shouldn't be that way, but it's what it is. For now.

You're going to have to project the confidence that you belong, that you've got the answers, even if the people you're talking to aren't giving you the credit. All your hard work isn't going to be worth shit if you're not ready—no, determined—to share it with the world.

I'll give you an example. A guy in the music industry who I've known for years hasn't been able to translate his hard work and talent into the success he deserves. I won't say his name because he's a great dude and I don't want to hurt his confidence. (See, I am maturing.)

He started as a street guy, but thanks to his charisma, intelligence, and work ethic, he was able to make real inroads in the music biz. He became close to several moguls, myself included, who really trusted his judgment and taste. He made good money and was respected in the industry, but he was never quite able to reach the mogul level himself. And I knew that frustrated him.

He'd ask me for advice, but I couldn't honestly put my finger on what was holding him back. Then one day we went to a meeting with some big executives at a record label. Smooth guys in suits with good haircuts and nice leather shoes. Guys who were extremely self-assured.

They were confident, but they also didn't really understand the project we were there to discuss. My guy did, though. Up and down. Back and forth. We'd spent hours talking about it, and he understood it both factually and instinctively. That's why I brought him with me, because he could articulate what needed to be done better than I could.

I expected him to blow them away, but when those executives started asking questions and spitballing ideas, he just sat on his hands. Didn't make a peep. You would have thought he was just a buddy of mine along for the ride, instead of what he was, which was the one true expert in the room.

At first I couldn't understand what he was doing (or not doing). Then it dawned on me: He's afraid. He's scared to raise his hand because he doesn't want to give the wrong answer. He'd put in the work, but in the presence of those executives' self-assurance, he lost faith in himself.

And that meant the executives never noticed him. Never made a mental note that he was a guy to keep an eye on. Never offered him the platform he was looking for—and deserved.

Instead, he stayed stuck in place. It was a pretty good place, one that a lot of other folks would have liked to reach, but not where he aspired to. He was stuck at a level that wasn't equal to his skill.

When the money in the music business started to dry up, he found himself in a very vulnerable spot. If he had made it to that mogul status, he would have been okay. He would already have put away his rainy-day money. Instead, the rain came and he got soaked. He was one of the first to lose their jobs. (It's great to be a highly paid exec, but when things start to go south, those are the first people to get the ax. Sometimes it's better to be a little underpaid.) Today, he tries to do consulting work, but he's on the outside looking in, becoming an old man in a space that prioritizes youth.

Don't make the same mistake. If you've put in the work, and know your shit, raise your damn hand! Every single time. There's nothing worse than being someone who's spent hours—even when you're off the clock at home—studying your company's reports, but when your boss asks for that information, you always let someone else provide it first.

That person probably hasn't put in nearly the work that you have, but they're also not afraid to be wrong. So when your boss looks at that person, she sees someone who is active. Who is participating. Who seems passionate. When she looks at you, she doesn't know what to think. Maybe she doesn't think anything at all.

It's not fair, but that person with their hand always up is going to get promoted before you. They're going to get an office before you. They're going to leverage their promotion to a better-paying job at a competitor before you even get a raise. You were better trained, better prepared. But you didn't let the world see that because you were scared. That fear is going to stop you from getting full value for your work. Don't let it happen.

On the other side of this coin is the person who's *too* quick to raise their hand. They're doing it because they're fearful that someone else is going to get props before they do. So even if they don't know the answer, they're going to say something anyway.

I knew a guy like that, too. We'd go into a meeting, and he'd be shouting out a solution before anyone had even identified the problem. He just wanted to be heard. Whenever he'd start doing that, I'd just shake my head and think, "Yo, what is wrong with you, bro?" It got to the point where I had to tell Chris Lighty, my manager at the time, not to bring this guy to any more meetings. It was unfortunate, because he was smart and talented. But he was doing too much. He was so fearful of someone else getting to shine that he ended up costing himself opportunities.

Being fearful can trip you up in so many ways, in both your professional and personal lives. That's why it's so critical that you identify the things you're afraid of and put in the work to get past that fear. In your personal life, letting go of all that baggage will be such a relief. You won't know how heavy the load you've been carrying around all these years has been until you finally put it down once and for all. The moment you do, you're going to feel nothing but freedom.

CHAPTER 2

HEART OF A HUSTLER

Things may come to those who wait, but only the things left by those who hustle.

— ANONYMOUS

I n 1978, a young Brazilian woman named Maria das Graças Silva received an internship at Petrobras, the country's largest oil and gas company. It didn't pay, but the internship was a major accomplishment for Graças Silva. She had been born in one of Rio's notorious favelas, the city's desperately poor neighborhoods that make the Southside of Queens look like Beverly Hills. She had spent her childhood picking rags and collecting scrap metal to help her family pay for her education. The internship represented a way out of the slums and into a better world. She was determined to give it everything she had.

Graças Silva (later known as Graças Foster) ended up spending over thirty years at Petrobras. It wasn't easy to climb the corporate ladder—Brazil has a notoriously macho culture, where women regularly face discrimination and harassment. She didn't let any of that slow her down. She'd already experienced much worse growing up in the favela and was determined to outwork all of the men who were her competition. She was so driven that she earned the nickname "Caveiaro," which is the term Brazilians use for the iron cars police use to periodically clear out criminals from the favelas. In other words, she was like a tank. Slow, steady, and strong. A relentless worker who just kept moving ahead no matter what obstacles got put in her way.

When Graças Silva started at Petrobras, she didn't enjoy any advantages. She was from the slums, not from one of the country's fancy neighborhoods. She was never going to be part of the boys' club at Petrobras. The odds were absolutely stacked against her. She overcame them by outworking her competition. It took her over thirty years, but her work ethic got her to the absolute top of her industry.

In 2012, she was named Petrobras's CEO, becoming the first woman in the world to lead a major oil company. *Forbes* would name her the sixteenth most powerful woman in the world, while *TIME* magazine would put her on its list of the hundred most influential people in the world. From a childhood spent picking trash, she has managed to become one of the most powerful people—man or woman—in the world.

When asked how she managed to overcome so many obstacles, she said the answer was simple: "It has been a very long story of hard work and personal sacrifice."

It sounds cliché to say that hard work is the most critical ingredient for success, but it's a fundamental truth that has to be repeated over and over again. If you're not hustling your absolute hardest, you're never going to reach your full potential in life.

None of the strategies in this book that involve hustling smarter—like building a strong crew, embracing evolution, knowing your value, or controlling perception—can be successfully implemented without also hustlin' your hardest first.

A strong work ethic is the one trait *all* successful people share. I've never met anyone at the top of their industry who wasn't fully committed to their job, who was willing to give anything less than their best.

Yes, there are some people who find success through talent, luck, circumstance, or even inheritance. But those same people never hold on to it.

You might see a picture of my new car or a view from my apartment on IG with the hashtag #workhardplayharder. The cars and the view are real, but the hashtag is fake. The truth is that I work much harder than I play. That's because I enjoy the work more. My attitude toward my career is "whistle while you work." Every eighteen-hour day on the set is fun for me. Every all-nighter in the studio is a joy. Every 4:30 a.m. wake-up call is a blessing, the signal that I'm getting another chance to do something I love.

I get bored easily when I'm not working. I have places I like to go on vacation, like Montego Bay, Miami, and Dubai, but the first thing I pack isn't my swimsuit—it's always my computer. I know after the first day of jet skiing or hanging out in a spa, I'm going to be ready to get back to work. Figuring out the next deal, working on the next script, or planning the next album is more exciting to me than any beach or five-star resort.

My work ethic can be hard on the people around me. There have been many times when, after a long day in the office followed by a night in the studio, my driver has dropped me off at home at 3 a.m. And I'll still tell him, "Yo man, come back and pick me up for the gym at 5 a.m." I know that means he's not going to be able to grab more than an hour nap in his car, but if you are rolling with me, you have to be prepared for nights like that. I just don't know any other speed to go at. It's why a lot of people who work with me compare me to a robot or a machine. I'm made of flesh and blood just like everyone else, but I want it more. What really separates me from the pack is that I'm willing to hustle harder and make more sacrifices than 99 percent of the population.

Think about it: I have a good ear and a catchy style, but I admit I'm not the most talented rapper out there. I'll never be as lyrical as Nas or as funny as Biggie. And while I pride myself on staying in shape, I know I'm not the best-looking entertainer out there, either.

Even though I'm proud of *Power*, I know I have a long ways to go before I'm mentioned in the same breath as some legendary TV producers.

So, despite not being the most talented, best-looking, or most experienced, how do I keep finding success in so many different fields? I hustle as hard as I can, day in and day out.

Plenty of people might be willing to outrap, outperform, or even outsmart me, but no one—and I mean no one—is ever going to outwork me.

COMMITTING TO A CLEAN LIFESTYLE

It's not enough just to say you *want* to work hard. You have to commit to lifestyle choices that allow you to have the energy, focus, and stamina to actually *do* the work, too. So many people prioritize lifestyle over work and then wonder why they can't get ahead.

There is a reason I can get up and go to the gym after only a couple of hours of sleep. Or have the stamina to work consecutive eighteen-hour days: I prioritize leading a very clean lifestyle.

Unlike most of my peers, I largely abstain from alcohol. I will have a rare drink from time to time, but that's it. I have never missed a session at the gym, a meeting, or an early morning flight because I had too much to drink the night before.

That doesn't stop me from going out and partying. I'm still in the clubs. I just don't need booze to enjoy myself. If I'm at an event promoting Branson Cognac or Le Chemin du Roi Champagne or one of my other alcohol brands, I have a routine I always follow: First I'll pour drinks from a bottle of champagne for everyone who is in VIP with me.

When the bottle is empty, I'll give it to one of my guys and have him quietly refill it with ginger ale. For the rest of the night I'll have that bottle in my hand. I'll take swigs every now and then just to keep the vibe right, but I'm not drinking anything but Canada Dry.

My energy is the same as everyone else's. I'm smiling, and laughing, maybe even doing a little two-step to the music. I'm also checking out everything that's going on around me, making hundreds of little calculations in my mind.

A lot of artists want to stay away from the clubs once they get famous. That world begins to feel too chaotic, too dangerous, to them. They'd rather stay home than find themselves in a hot, sweaty space where the energy is turned all the way up. Where something bad could always pop off. That's never an issue for me. I always have my head on straight, and my judgment is never impaired. I can see issues coming from a mile away and be long gone before a situation gets serious.

Being able to still hang out with people is the real advantage for me. The clubs always have been, and always will be, the incubators of whatever is coming up next in hip-hop. It's very hard to stay relevant and keep your finger on the pulse of the culture if you're afraid to go out and absorb the music in the club setting.

Staying sober in a setting where everyone else is drinking can open up all sorts of opportunities for you. Let's say your boss invites you and all your co-workers out for drinks on a Friday night. Normally you might take full advantage of the company credit card and get trashed. It's understandable—you've been working hard all week and want to let off some steam. Doing it on the company's tab makes it that much more appealing.

But next time you get that offer, as tempting as it might be to let your boss buy you that beer or vodka and cranberry, just get a seltzer instead. You don't even have to announce what you're doing. Stick a lime in there, and it will look like you're enjoying a gin and tonic of your own.

As the evening progresses, you'll probably start to notice how sloppy everyone else is getting, how they're starting to let down the facades they've worked so hard to keep up at the office. If there's information you've been looking to get out of your co-workers—or even your boss—this is the time to get it. Your normally tight-lipped co-workers will be more than happy to tell you what projects they're working on or what they overheard your boss saying about the future of the company. Put a couple of drinks in most people and they will tell you almost anything with a little coaxing.

Outside of the competitive advantage you can gain from not drinking, I'm also hyperaware of the damage alcohol abuse can cause. I've seen it firsthand. When I moved into my grandmother's house after my mother died, a few of my aunts and uncles were full-blown alcoholics.

I had one uncle in particular who was a cool guy most of the time, but put a few drinks in him and all of a sudden he became Marvin Hagler. Every comment, no matter how innocent, was taken as an insult, and he'd want to put hands up. Even with a nine-year-old.

My reaction was to stay out of his way as much as possible, but even from that distance it was still very clear to see that all booze did was bring out his weakness and render his character unstable. And it wasn't just him; across the board, it seemed that the people in my immediate family were prone to alcoholism.

There is a lot of evidence out there that alcoholism is hereditary. If it seems to run in your family, sticking with ginger ale might not just be about getting a competitive edge—it might be about keeping yourself out of a lifelong state of dysfunction and addiction.

Another advantage I have over my competition, especially within hip-hop, is that I also don't mess with drugs.

To hear some rappers tell it, drugs open up a pathway to creativity. They claim they do their best work when they're high. They might feel that way but, in my experience, drugs ultimately become a crutch. Something rappers can lean on when they're feeling insecure or lacking focus. They might be helpful when you're getting started, but you're never going to get too far when you need a crutch to move forward.

I witness this all the time in the studio. I know so many rappers who honestly don't believe they can make good music without being high in one way or another. They wouldn't dream of getting in the booth if there's no liquor to sip or weed to smoke. They're completely fearful that, without that support, they can't perform or properly connect with the music they're trying to make.

My thought has always been, "Suppose that crutch isn't available?" What if you're at the studio and suddenly get the call that Dr. Dre is coming through and wants you to record a verse for him? Or that Just Blaze, Timbaland, or Mustard is coming through? You're gonna tell one of these guys you can't record until someone runs out and gets you a bottle or until your weed man rolls through? That opportunity might have passed by the time your man comes back.

If you're a true creator, you have to be able to practice your craft in any situation. It's imperative that you can create your own comfort zone without depending on any substance for help. Yes, you might believe the weed makes you a better writer, or the liquor makes it easier to be yourself, but you also need the confidence to know that you can do it without them. Otherwise, you're never going to be in total control of your own situation.

No matter what situation or setting you find yourself in, you don't ever want to depend on anything—or any other person—to make you feel in control and comfortable. That sense of confidence should always come from within. Not from an external source.

To be clear, I don't judge people who do like to drink or smoke. In fact, I'm happy to sell you a bottle of Le Chemin du Roi to help you celebrate the next time you're out partying. All that I'd ask is that you are honest in your appraisal of the role drugs and alcohol play in your life. Some people are able to truly be "social" drinkers or smokers. They enjoy participating in social settings, but they can also just as easily go without. They could have a bottle of booze in their kitchen, or a bag of weed in their dresser, and never feel the urge to consume it.

I can have cases of Branson Cognac or Le Chemin du Roi Champagne in my office and never think about them until it's time to do an event. Someone else might be tempted to crack open a bottle every single time they walked by. Or they might start drinking a whole bottle every day on the sly.

If alcohol or drugs have that sort of pull on you, it's important that you address it head-on. It's going to require a lot of discipline and focus, but you can build a lifestyle for yourself that doesn't need to be fueled by booze and drugs to get things done.

I also understand that it can feel very overwhelming when you're the one person in your circle who doesn't drink or smoke. It can be hard, but I've been that person for years, and I always manage to abstain, so it is possible.

I doubt there's anyone in the history of the world who has said no to more blunts or booze than me. I've spent hours in cafes in Amsterdam where everyone in G-Unit was blowing ruler-size blunts in my face. I might have gotten a contact high, but I never took a hit. Snoop Dogg, B-Real, Redman, Method Man, Wiz Khalifa—I've hung with all those dudes. I have a great time with them, but I choose not to smoke with them. And please don't say, "Well, they probably leave you alone because you're 50 Cent." Nothing could be further from the truth. Everyone wants to be the one to finally get me to smoke. I'm like the pretty girl who won't date anyone, so everyone wants to ask me out, but I just keep saying no.

For example, I recently hosted my Tycoon party in NYC, and Snoop was one of my special guests. So when he tried to pass one of his blunts my way, everyone around us started cheering for me to hit it. Not wanting to kill the mood, I took a big hit . . . and then just let the smoke swirl around in my mouth before I blew it back out. That's as far as it went. Bill Clinton has probably inhaled more weed smoke than me.

Everyone was excited that I'd taken a hit, but there was no way I was actually inhaling that weed, especially something as strong as the stuff Snoop smokes. The very few times I've smoked it's made me extremely paranoid. So why would I get high surrounded by a thousand people all pushed up together, and I'm the one in charge of the entire event? I wouldn't have been enjoying the music if I'd inhaled—I would have been freaking the fuck out over all the things that could be going wrong at my event. I'm always at my most comfortable when I'm in complete control of my surroundings. And that's very hard to do when you're high.

In order to truly be in the position to hustle your hardest day in and day out, it's not enough to only avoid (or at least cut way down on) booze and weed. You also, especially as you grow older, need to proactively try to preserve your body. The best way you can do that is through eating right and working out.

My diet is pretty straightforward. I avoid carbs and processed food whenever I can and focus on eating as many whole foods and veggies as possible. I'm not really a breakfast guy, so just a smoothie or protein shake of some sort will do. For lunch, it's usually a salad. If I'm eating out for dinner, which is hard to avoid for me, I'll order something like a chicken and lettuce wrap or a steak with asparagus. Maybe it's not the most exciting diet, but it's simple enough that I'm able to follow a version of it almost every day, and it features ingredients that are on most American and European menus. Consistency and availability are important when you spend a lot of time on the road, dealing with its constant temptations to cheat.

While I might cheat on my diet from time to time, I'm absolutely religious about working out. No matter how late I might have stayed at the studio or club the night before, I'm going to hit the gym the next morning. Sometimes I'll switch up gyms (I actually have memberships to two near my apartment) just so things don't get repetitive or feel stagnant. If I'm on the road, I'll hit the gym in my hotel or rent a private studio. Doesn't matter if I'm jet-lagged, having trouble adjusting to the time zones, or not sleeping well because I miss my own bed. No excuses. I'm still getting that workout in.

Most days I'll do a session with my trainer that might include non-weight work like pushups and pull-ups, jumping rope, sledgehammer swings, and hitting a heavy bag.

Then once my training session is over, I'll stick around the gym and hit some weights on my own.

My go-to routine is lifting light weights with very short breaks for rest between sets. That helps me get toned and get a cardio workout at the same time. If I'm preparing for a film role where I have to look really cut, then I'll also work with heavier weights to add bulk.

If I'm trying to lose weight for a role or photo shoot, I'll incorporate running into my routine. Generally I try to go between three and four miles per run. If I'm at home, I'll usually work out on a treadmill in the gym. But if I'm on the road, a lot of times I'll go jogging on the streets around my hotel. It's a good way for me to get outside without attracting too much attention. There have been times when fans have been lining up outside my hotel waiting to see me and I've jogged right past them without anyone recognizing me. They're all expecting me to pull up in a limo, not jog past them in sweatpants and a hoodie.

Unlike a lot of people, I don't look to caffeine to enhance my energy. Coffee has never really been my thing, and you won't find me knocking down Diet Cokes during the day (though I do enjoy a ginger ale with my salad). I get my energy from working out, and that hour or two in the morning carries me through the rest of the day.

Working out is not only good for my health, but is a critical business tool as well. I absolutely do some of my clearest thinking in the gym. I'm not looking at my phone, being distracted by calls or someone walking into my office with a question. The time in the gym gives me a chance to think about everything that's in front of me for the day. Instead of coming into the office wiping sleep out of my eyes and feeling scatterbrained, when I get in I'm already feeling fully in control, energized, and mentally prepared. It's the only way to show up at the office if you want to make things happen.

One aspect of my lifestyle where I know I need to improve is getting as much sleep as possible. When I'm locked in on a project, I do become that robot. I can go eighteen hours straight and barely feel fatigue. I love knowing that I'm outworking my competition, but I also realize that I need to find a way to make sleep a bigger priority. Like a lot of Nas fans, I got gassed up when he rhymed, "I never sleep, 'cause sleep is the cousin of death." It sounded so deep and mysterious that a lot of people began to associate staying up all night and burning the candle at both ends with the hustler's lifestyle.

I contributed to that misconception for many years. I used to say things like "sleep is for broke people" or "I don't like to sleep because I might miss the opportunity to turn a dream into a reality." The basic motivation behind those messages was correct—that you have to be willing to hustle harder than your competition if you want to win. But I shouldn't have connected hustling harder to sleeping less. In recent years, I've learned that some of the most successful people out there are also big sleepers. Jeff Bezos says he prioritizes sleeping eight hours every night because it makes his thinking much clearer. Facebook's COO, Sheryl Sandberg, also makes getting enough sleep a priority, saying that staying up all night might help you get more things done in the moment, but in the long term proves to be very "counterproductive" because it makes people "anxious, irritable and confused." It's a strategy echoed by former Google CEO Eric Schmidt, who says, "The real secret is the most successful people have awareness of what their body needs and sleep whenever necessary."

I'm trying to learn from those leaders and adjust my own approach. Maybe I could get away with skimping on the sleep when I was younger, especially because I don't drink or smoke, but now I understand it's a shortcut I can't take anymore.

One way I've tried to improve my approach is by going to sleep around midnight every Saturday night. Then I allow myself to sleep late on Sunday—till around nine or ten—since it's the one day I never have anything scheduled in the morning. My goal moving forward is to get those nine hours in another two or three times a week. I'm confident if I can get those extra hours in, I'm going to be even more productive than I already am. Good luck to my competition keeping up!

A lot of the steps I'm prescribing in this chapter—sobriety, working out, eating right, and getting enough sleep—can feel very daunting if they're not currently part of your lifestyle.

Don't let that deter you. I'm a firm believer that no matter how formidable they might feel, there are very few negative habits you can't break in thirty days. Whenever I'm trying to improve an aspect of my life, thirty days is the goal I set for myself. And I've always been able to meet my goal in that time frame.

The key is how you approach adjusting the habit. Let's say you're trying to improve your diet, cut down on how much you drink, or reduce the time you spend on social media. It's not helpful to make a sweeping generalization like "I'm not smoking weed anymore" or "I'm going vegan." Those sorts of statements might sound good in the moment, but they also can feel so ambitious that you give up before your transformation ever truly gets started.

Instead of saying "I'm not smoking weed anymore," just say "I'm not smoking for the next month." Then just focus on the first *week* in front of you. If you see that you're supposed to be going to a party where you know everyone is going to be lighting up, choose not to go. Do something with your non-pothead friends instead that night.

Then take a look at what you have planned for the following week. Is getting high before going to the club one of your rituals? Then plan a week where you have other things to do during the evening. Or just stay home and watch TV if you think being around smokers is going to be too tempting. Catch up on some shows you've been meaning to watch. Or better yet, go work out every night. Before you know it, you'll already be halfway there.

If you can have that confidence in your commitment, by week three you're going to be coasting. Your evolution is going to have some momentum behind it. Instead of constantly saying "Damn, I want to light up right now," you're going to be able to take an accurate assessment of what your life is like without getting high. It might feel so natural that you're ready to make a more permanent adjustment in your lifestyle. Or you might say "I don't need to give up weed entirely. I just need to set some boundaries about how and when I consume it."

That's a conversation that's going to be much more productive at the thirty-day threshold than at day one. Whatever it is you want to improve or correct, commit to it for thirty days, and see how it changes your perspective. Give yourself the opportunity to identify with something different. You're going to find that some of the things you "couldn't live without" were actually standing between you and your best life. When you break those habits, you're going to be amazed by how much you can accomplish when you free up your focus and put everything you have into your work.

FINDING YOUR FOCUS

Hard work and dedication are two of the characteristics found in all true hustlers. Another is focus. Because if you're not able to focus and direct your hard work, you might be hustlin' hard, but you won't be hustlin' smart.

One of my favorite examples of someone who was able to combine hard work and focus is a gentleman named Isaac Wright Jr. In the early 1990s, Isaac was wrongly imprisoned on a life sentence in New Jersey for being an alleged drug kingpin. In fact, he was one of the first people convicted under that statute in New Jersey. The one problem with that was he was actually innocent.

Isaac refused to accept his sentence and began looking for ways to get it overturned. Even though he didn't have any legal training, he set about learning the law in the prison's library. He became so skilled that he began working as a paralegal on other prisoners' cases, helping several of them get their sentences overturned.

Eventually he was able to get his own life sentence overturned, but he still had several other convictions on the books that threatened to keep him behind bars for seventy years. Isaac *still* wouldn't give up. He eventually managed to find a police officer who had testified against him who was willing to admit that he'd participated in misconduct and cover-ups. No one gets cops to snitch on themselves, except for Isaac. It was an incredible victory—unprecedented, really—and after nine years behind bars and the suicide of the prosecutor involved in his case, Isaac was finally set free. Today he's a practicing attorney in New Jersey, the state that wrongly locked him up. Isaac's story was so compelling to me, I developed a hit scripted project called *For Life* on ABC based on his story.

There are a lot of people—way too many—who've been wrongly locked up but never came close to fighting their injustice the way Isaac did. The only hope for most guys in that situation is finding a prisoner's rights foundation or big law firm to take up their case pro bono. Isaac wasn't willing to wait for someone else to decide if his life was worth fighting for. He took his fate into his own hands.

So what allowed Isaac to achieve what all those other inmates couldn't? His combination of hard work and focus. When Isaac got locked up, he didn't spend his time debating who were the best rappers with other inmates, or writing to old girlfriends in his cell, or bullshitting out in the yard. He spent every single free moment he had teaching himself the law. He refused to allow any distractions to get between him and his goal. There was no confusion in his mind about what he was doing with his time: if he wasn't eating, sleeping, or on work duty, he had his head in those law books.

At first it was hard. Those books are not written for amateurs—you're not supposed to be able to understand them unless you've had training. But in time, the language started to flow more easily. As Isaac began working on briefs and seeing them help other prisoners, he started getting excited. That created its own momentum, which made him hit the books even harder. He ended up doing four years of law school in less than two years because he was so locked in (no pun intended). Once he had all that information at his disposal, he was able to set the process in motion that eventually led to his release.

None of that could have happened if Isaac had allowed himself to feel defeated. If at any point in the process he had become confused about what he was trying to do, he wouldn't have been able to write his own ticket out of jail. It only happened because he was so determined to save himself. The story behind Isaac's journey was a natural fit for television. When we tested the pilot episode it received one of the strongest positive audience reactions in the network's history. I'm not surprised—Isaac's hustle to get his life back is that inspiring.

Keep in mind that Isaac wasn't hustling for jewelry, cars, or houses.

He was hustling for the most important goal: freedom. And thanks to his focus, he was able to achieve it in spite of a corrupt system aligned against him. Yes, Isaac was a hustler. A kingpin even. But not in the way the government had tried to paint him. He was hustling for freedom.

The one question Isaac's story should make you ask is "What could I achieve with the same level of focus in my own life?" What if you spent seven or eight hours a day working toward something without any distractions? Without guards telling you to turn the lights off at 10 p.m.? Without your stomach hurting from lousy prison food and your back aching from a lumpy prison mattress? Without someone in the next cell keeping you up all night screaming out their demons? Or loudly jerking off with mayonnaise from the prison mess hall? What could you accomplish without *those* kinds of distractions?

Then consider the distractions that are probably keeping you from hustling your hardest. Right now. Bullshitting on social media? Arguing with your boyfriend? Feeling like you need to roll up a blunt? Sleeping late because you were out drinking the night before?

If you were able to apply only a small fraction of the focus Isaac was able to tap into, after even just one month you'd start to experience the same momentum and excitement Isaac did. That wave could pick you up and help carry you to whatever goal you're aiming for.

PASSION MAKES PERFECT

One thing I always try to assess in new business partners is what I call their "passion stance." Just how passionate are they about making this thing happen? Someone with a weak passion stance will probably get knocked over the first time they meet a little resistance. I'm not interested in being around that sort of energy.

Someone with a strong passion stance, on the other hand, will really dig in. Get their feet planted and shoulders squared up. So no matter how hard the world pushes back, or how much negativity gets thrown their way, they ain't budging an inch. *That's* the sort of energy I want to work with. The type of people I'm willing to put my money behind. A strong passion stance is what separates the hustlers who win from the people who always seem stuck in place.

Passion is what allowed me to lose more than fifty pounds to play a football player dying of cancer in the movie *All Things Fall Apart*. In nine weeks, I went from 214 to 160 pounds by going on a liquid diet and running on a treadmill for three hours a day. Now that might have been a little bit easier for me than the average person—I was more comfortable with a liquid diet because I'd been on one after I was shot—but it was still an extremely challenging two months. I was dropping weight like crazy, but every day when I looked in the mirror, all I could think was "I need to get smaller." I was passionate about nailing that role.

Part of it was personal. The story was based on an actual close friend of mine, and I needed to do his story justice. But it was also professional. I'd never received the accolades as an actor that I'd gotten in the music business. As a result, I didn't have the same confidence as an actor that I have as a rapper or entrepreneur.

My passion for acting, however, is just as strong as it is for music or business.

There's something about the craft that's always fascinated me and captured my imagination. Like a lot of people from my era, I've been particularly inspired by actors like Robert De Niro and Al Pacino in their gangster roles. I loved how they were able to convey a certain type of aggression through their body language. I wanted to bring that sort of energy to the screen.

I knew I didn't have—and would probably never have—the same sort of acting ability as De Niro. That wasn't going to stop me from putting in the work. I'd read about how he gained forty pounds for his Oscar-winning role in *Raging Bull*. So when I saw that my role in *All Things Fall Apart* called for my character to lose weight as he underwent chemo, I decided to commit physically to my role the same way De Niro did for his in *Raging Bull*.

I didn't win an Oscar—or any award—for *All Things Fall Apart*. I also didn't care. I'd proved to myself that I was passionate enough about acting to do whatever it took for the role. I saw some folks try to clown me—"Clown thinks he's De Niro or something. Fuck outta here"—because I'd put in so much work for a movie that ended up going straight to video. Those jokes don't slow me down for a second. I know damn well I'm not De Niro. I'm still going to work to get to that level. And even if I never win an Oscar, my movies have made over $500 million at the box office. Fair to say that's a number a lot of other actors would dream about putting alongside their names.

De Niro was actually one of the people who taught me just how important passion is to acting. In 2008 I was supposed to star in a film with him called *Streets of Blood*. He invited me to meet him at his apartment and asked me point-blank if the movie was something I was serious about. He wanted to know whether I was only doing it for the money or the look. I told him I was absolutely serious about it—if I just wanted money, I could easily make more touring for two months than being on a movie set. I took the opportunity to share with him how I'd always loved his work and was honored by the possibility of working alongside him.

De Niro ended up not being able to do the movie because of a scheduling conflict (and was replaced by Val Kilmer, another actor I have a lot of respect for), but we became friends after that call. We'd finally get to work together, alongside Forest Whitaker, on the movie *Freelancers*.

However, that call with De Niro left an impression on me. He was one of the biggest names in the history of film, and *Streets of Blood* would have been a minor film for him, but he still took the time to call me to make sure I was truly passionate about what was in front of us. That's one of the reasons he's an all-time great. He understands that if even one person in the cast is just showing up to collect a check, the film won't be a success. Everybody on the set has to share the same passion for the project.

Music is another space where passion is paramount. Take Tupac. No disrespect, but he was not an all-time great MC if you judge him strictly by his skills. He wasn't able to articulate street life like Nas, talk slick like Jay-Z, or be funny like Biggie. He couldn't spit as hard as Eminem. What he had—in abundance—was passion. When he rhymed, his passion just poured through. Even if he was actually an art student playing the role of a thug, he delivered his lines with so much intensity that you felt every word that he said. *That's* what made him an all-time great.

A lot of rappers have tried to become stars by taking on the thug persona—Ja Rule, for example—but they just weren't as committed as 'Pac. Yeah, Ja growled a lot and called himself a "murderer," but he wasn't believable. He didn't have the same hunger that 'Pac did.

'Pac committed to his passion the way De Niro committed to his role in *Casino* or *Goodfellas*. You could say that 'Pac was so committed that he ultimately paid for it with his life.

I'm looking for the same kind of passion in the people I work with. Maybe not putting your life on the line, but at least being willing to consider it. Might sound dramatic, but that level of commitment is often what it takes.

WHAT ARE YOU HUSTLIN' FOR?

Not too long ago, after a hectic morning full of meetings, contract negotiations, and a photo shoot, I left my office in Manhattan to head to a movie lot across the river in Queens. As my car crawled through traffic on FDR Drive, I noticed a solitary man playing handball on a court near the road. The guy was just smacking that rubber ball against the wall over and over while the hectic city buzzed around him. The scene struck me so much that I picked up my phone and posted this on IG:

> *Yo I just saw a grown man listening to music and play-*
> *ing handball by himself in the middle of the day. I been*
> *on the phone working, his life might be better than mine*

Of course, the internet accused me of trolling, as it's quick to do. How could 50 Cent sit there in his air-conditioned, chauffeur-driven luxury vehicle and be jealous of some guy playing handball?

I could see why some might have felt that way, but I promise I wasn't trolling. When I saw that guy, I saw someone getting in a good workout, listening to the music he liked, breathing fresh air, and enjoying himself—all without spending a dime.

I mean, who knows? That guy could have been out there because his wife kicked him out of the apartment and he had nowhere else to go. Or maybe he'd just lost his job and was smacking that ball off the wall over and over again to try to get his mind off it.

All I know is that in the brief moment I saw him outside my tinted window, the only energy I felt coming from him was contentedness. It made me legitimately ask myself, "Yo, is this guy fuckin' beating me in life?"

I felt that mixture of envy and competitiveness because he seemed to have what I've always wanted above all else.

Freedom.

The freedom to do what I want, when I want, and how I want.

All the jewelry, watches, cars, and mansions you've seen in my videos or on my IG—that was never what I was truly working for.

What I was hustling for, and what I'm still hustling for today, is freedom.

To be an effective hustler you must be able to identify what you want. It doesn't have to be a big concept like freedom. There might be something much more specific you have your sights set on. Your goal might be to be the first person in your family to graduate from college. Or to open your own restaurant. Or to save up enough money to travel the world.

I have a friend who lives with his family in an apartment in Brooklyn, and his goal is to make enough to buy them a house with a backyard. Nothing too crazy, just enough space to let a dog run around and to sit outside with a cup of coffee when the weather is nice. When he's working late at night or on the weekend, the image of that little backyard is always in his mind, pushing him forward when he's tired or when things don't seem to be going his way. When he feels like he's adrift on the seas of his career, the image of that little backyard is his North Star that gets him back on course.

You need to set a goal for yourself. Ask yourself: What is it that I want? Be honest. It might be something that will help a lot of people. Or it could be something incredibly selfish. It might be a seemingly impossible goal. Or something that's almost within your reach.

It might be a plan you're proud to share with the world. Or something you're never going to tell more than a handful of people about.

Any of those scenarios is fine, as long as *you* are crystal clear about whatever *it* is. Without that clear vision, your hustle is never going to take you anywhere significant.

It's also important to accept that your vision can—no, make that *should*—change. When I first started selling crack, my goals were very simple. First I needed fresh sneakers. Not the KangaROOs my grandmother got me, but Adidas and FILAs. Once I got the sneakers and clothes I wanted for myself, I set my sights on jewelry. Once I had the right chains, I focused on a set of wheels. At first, I just wanted a car so I wouldn't have to pay a cab to wait for me when I took a girl to the movies. A basic Honda would do. But soon, I needed a flashy ride to announce to the entire neighborhood that I was a force to be reckoned with. So I kept working on the streets until I was pushing a 400 SE Benz. (I've probably bought a thousand more cars since then, but I still miss that one.)

Once I'd collected all the typical drug dealer status symbols, I turned my sights on signing a record deal. Once I had that, I wanted a hit record. That was my wish. And it came true. In a very big way.

Still, I couldn't settle. Even with Grammys and platinum records under my belt, I set my sights on making my own movie. And so on and so on, all the way up to my work in television today.

I'd say my biggest goal now is to give back. When you reach a certain pay grade, you become more conscious of what's happening back in the communities you came from. Instead of worrying about what you're about to do, you shift to focusing on your legacy and how people are going to remember you. Am I going to be remembered for making popular songs and selling flavored water? Or positively impacting the world? I hope that it will be for the second. That's why, on a local level, I put my money behind projects that clean up playgrounds and promote healthy living for young people. On a global level I've developed projects that promote conscious capitalism (more on that later), and support the United Nations World Food Programme, which is going to provide a meal with every energy drink that is sold through our project.

Being able to cop a new pair of sneakers is a much different goal than trying to make a dent in world hunger, but in my journey they've both taken on the same significance and inspired the same amount of focus and hard work.

A lack of clarity about what people really want is what's holding so many folks back. They don't even know how to ask for what they want when they have an opportunity. It is not enough to say you want someone to "put you on," or even worse, to tell someone that your goal is to "be famous." In order to get the most out of your hustle, you have to be able to clearly define what you're working for.

For examples of how *not* to do it, take a look at my IG: you won't have to scroll far to find dozens of people pleading, "Yo Fif, sign me to a record deal!" or, "Man, you need to let me jump on *Power*. I can act!" Sorry, but those sorts of ridiculous asks do not constitute hustlin'.

It's even worse in person. People will stop me on the street, or even approach me on TV and video shoots. They think they're putting in work, or taking advantage of an opportunity, by stepping up to me and asking me to "put a brother on." But the second I hear those sorts of vague asks, I know I'm dealing with someone who isn't worth any investment. If you can't even articulate to me what you're trying to do, why would I try to help you?

It might sound out of character for me, but I believe vision boards are a very powerful tool in calcifying what you're working toward. When you force yourself to articulate your vision in words, you set a powerful energy in motion. You give something that was just a thought, or maybe even just a feeling, a real presence in the world. You make it a real thing.

It's easy to get started on your computer. Go to Google Images, and type in everything you think you'd like to have in your life: "beach-front property," "Range Rover," "pit bull puppy."

But what if your dream isn't a physical thing? If you want a promotion at your job, google an image of a corner office. If you want to design your own streetwear, google a picture of Ronnie Feig or Virgil Abloh. If you want to go to college, google Harvard's graduation ceremony—you should always aim high on your boards. If you want to fall in love, google an image of your favorite celebrity couple. Or even put up a picture of your grandparents if they've been together for fifty years.

I think vision boards are even a great way for couples to get on the same page. Put together your own board, and have your significant other do the same. Then compare notes. The things that show up in yours, but not your partner's, are the things they're going to have to learn to accept about you. And vice versa. Making boards with each other is a great way to get a lot of unspoken things out in the open. I once told a journalist from *GQ* to make one with his girlfriend. He did and wrote that when he looked at hers "it had more babies than an orphanage." They hadn't talked about having kids yet, but that vision board put what she wanted front and center.

I've seen vision boards make a real difference in people's lives, and the stats back me up. A study by Dominican University found that you're forty-two times more likely to achieve your goals if you write them down. And a study in *Psychological Bulletin* found that people are 90 percent more likely to achieve goals that are challenging and specific.

That's not to say that the universe is going to just drop a bag into your lap because you said you wanted one. You still have to put in the work. A lot of it. But by identifying your vision and giving it a name, you're taking a big step toward realizing your goal.

If you're feeling even a little bit of uncertainty about what you want, take the time to make a vision board. The power of vision boards is real and very accessible.

NEVER BREAK YOUR STRIDE

As you probably realize, *hustling* can also mean selling drugs. My mother was a hustler in that sense. I was, too. As were a lot of my friends—and enemies—back in Queens.

I'm not going to give you a crash course on drug dealing here. I've talked about that stuff in my first book, my movie, and a lot of my songs. Chances are you've already heard those stories.

What I want to address here is the *attitude* you have to develop to be a successful drug dealer. The mentality that no matter what happens to you on the street, you're not going to break stride. Let's say you bought some coke you thought was pure but was actually cut with laxatives. Instead of bitching and moaning, you have to address the situation and say, "It's cool. I'll get my money back on the next pack." That has to be your constant attitude on the street. "I'll get it back on the next one."

In what I'll call the "civilian world," a lot of times when people encounter setbacks, they dwell on them. Instead of moving on to "the next one," they get stuck. If a deal they were working on falls through, or they don't get a promotion they thought they deserved, they let it slow their momentum. They start to feel sorry for themselves. They blame other people. They say the system was rigged against them. That their boss had it in for them, or that their teachers were biased against them. The list of excuses and rationalizations goes on and on. If they hit one little bump on the road of life, they pull their car over, do a U-turn, and head home.

The streets don't allow you the luxury of excuses. If something goes bad and your reaction is to point the finger at someone else, hey, that's cool. Until that person hears what you've been saying and decides to blow your head off!

You want to complain that the system is rigged against you? You can yell about that at the top of your lungs, but no one on the streets is going to give you a break because of it. No shit! Of course it is! Who didn't know that? Rather than complain about it, get to work outsmarting all those cops, POs, judges, and politicians who would like to keep you locked up.

There's no time for a defeatist, woe-is-me mentality on the streets. Your daily mind-set *has* to be "I'll get it back on the next one," or you'll wind up one of three ways: broke, dead, or locked up.

We spend a lot of time talking about privilege in this country, about how certain people are handed things and put in position to win. There's a lot of truth to that, but we're not looking at the other side of the privilege coin. Those boys and girls who get sent to the best schools and best colleges, and then are walked into the best companies, certainly have a lot of opportunity. But what they lack is *resiliency*. They've never truly been tested. Okay, they've been tested in the literal sense—they better get a good score on their SATs or else they won't get into their top college choice. But how does that really compare to overhearing your single mother say "Damn, how are we going to keep the lights on this month?" or hearing your father say "They said if we don't pay the last two months' rent, they gonna evict us." That's a different level of struggle. (And to be fair, there are levels in other countries that we can't imagine. "They're gonna turn the lights out" isn't shit compared to "If ISIS makes it over that mountain, they're killing this whole village.")

If you've spent your childhood worrying about past-due bills, family members in jail, or gunshots on your corner but are still out here trying to make it happen, you possess real resiliency. Acknowledge that about yourself. And then use that to your advantage.

Contrast that with your co-worker who's been at an advantage their whole life, whether they realize it or not. Maybe they got the job because their prep school classmate's father runs the place.

That guy is comfortable with success—hell, he expects it. What he's much less comfortable with is adversity. Even just a little bit of it. If his picks start coming up dry, he won't know what to do. He might start drinking heavily or start to blow his money on coke because he's so confused. Losing was not in his playbook. I've seen Wall Street guys and high-powered lawyers take an unexpected loss and literally be ready to jump out of their office window. One loss and they're ready to end it all.

Coming from where I've been, I would never let a defeat or setback have that sort of effect on me. And if you come from a similar background, you shouldn't either. If I somehow lost it all tomorrow, I promise I would not be fazed.

I'm sitting at my desk in my office as I write this. Looking out my window I can see a guy on the sidewalk selling peanuts. If I lost everything tomorrow, I'm not jumping out *this* window. Nope, the next day I'd be out there on the opposite corner setting up my own peanut stand. Let's call it 50's Nuts. Maybe to make my cart stand out, I'd introduce chocolate-covered nuts and some cherry-coated ones, too. Because I'm offering more selection than my competition, I'd create a little buzz on my block. Then I'd figure out a way to use that buzz to get 50's Nuts over to Yankee Stadium and sell them in the stands. And after that, open up a restaurant in the concourse. And then another one back in Manhattan. And before you know it, I've got a chain. And with that, I'm back in the game, baby!

Having a hustler's mentality, I would never allow myself to think, "Shit, I just lost everything. My enemies are going to clown me. My critics are going to have a field day. I don't think I can do this anymore." No. If it all goes away, I'm confident I'm getting my money back. And then some.

This mentality is why people like me, Jay-Z, Puffy, Nas, and so many others have all done so well in corporate America. We keep finding success because we don't get thrown by life's inevitable setbacks. We've already experienced the type of lifestyle that a so-called loss might bring. We know it's not going to break us forever. So we keep our momentum going.

Look at Puffy. The popular perception is that he's been on top for the last twenty-five years, but he's actually experienced plenty of setbacks during his career. In 1991, nine people were trampled to death at a concert he threw at City College in New York. That was supposed to end his career. It didn't. Then he got fired from Uptown

Records—where he'd launched the careers of artists like Mary J. Blige and Jodeci—for being a hothead. That would have been the final chapter for a lot of people. Not Puffy. He started Bad Boy Records and took that label to the top. Then Biggie, the artist he'd built an entire movement around, was murdered. A blow like that would have slowed a lot of folks all the way down. Puffy didn't stop for a second. A few years later he got Jennifer Lopez, one of the biggest pop stars in the world, caught up in an attempted murder case. The same case that got his top artist at the time, Shyne, sent to jail for ten years. That would have been the final straw for most people. Not Puffy. He swallowed all those Ls, probably washed them down with a shot of Pink Grapefruit Cîroc, and kept it moving. Bad Boy doesn't have hits anymore, people don't wear Sean John, and Cîroc is losing its market share, but Puffy is still looking ahead. Now that his kids are grown, he's trying to put them on. When Puffy says "Can't stop, won't stop," that dude really means it. And I respect his hustle.

Here's the bottom line: whether you're a rapper, stockbroker, scientist, schoolteacher, or drug dealer, you're going to experience peaks and valleys. Even when you think you've been through it all, you're going to find out there's still more shit to go through.

One of the most important realizations I came to early in my business career is that I'm running through an endless tunnel. What I mean by that is I came to understand that there's no "happily ever after." No matter how many records I sell, cases of liquor I move, and hit TV shows I create and executive-produce, there's never going to be a moment where I say, "Okay, this is the end of the road. I've finally made it," and then take my foot off the pedal.

I know there's going to be another challenge right around the corner. And then another one after that.

Some people might find the endless-tunnel idea overwhelming or even depressing. They spend their entire lives working toward finally seeing the "light at the end of the tunnel," so it can be difficult to accept that there won't ever be one. But there isn't.

I actually find it liberating to know that I'll be hustling for the rest of my life. Accepting that I'm going to be working just as hard (though maybe a little bit slowly) at seventy as I am now makes me happy. In many ways that knowledge gives me the freedom that I've always been looking for.

I hope you'll be able to understand the hustler attitude I've developed in the streets and then apply it in your life. To have that sort of resiliency and positive outlook, but without having to go through the heartbreaks and violence I experienced. To move like the type of hustler 50 Cent used to be, but in the types of settings Curtis Jackson is in now.

TRUST YOUR INSTINCT

Another advantage I've gained from being active in the streets is learning how to trust my instinct. Was another dealer going to rip me off? I had to go on my instinct. Is the corner I'm about to set up on going to be targeted by the cops? I have to go on my instinct. Could I trust someone not to talk after they got busted? I had to trust my instinct.

I've noticed that a lot of people who weren't raised in street environments have lost that connection with their instinct. They'll go to business school and study how to move in the professional world. Maybe they'll internalize what their professors teach them long enough to pass midterms. And then promptly forget it all in a couple of months.

Even if they end up retaining what they've been taught, they're still learning to rely on instruction, rather than intuition. A business professor might have some good tips, but nothing he or she can teach will ever outweigh simply listening to your own instinct.

The neighborhood teaches you to always follow the most instinctive route. It's an invaluable power to possess. If you weren't blessed by having to develop your instinct on the streets, don't worry. It's still a skill you can develop.

Whenever you feel confused about a situation, it's imperative that you find a way to turn the volume down and reconnect with what you're truly feeling. For me, working out definitely helps quiet that noise. At some point in the workout, the physical exertion I'm putting myself through seems to wash all the BS out of my system. I can literally feel myself breathing the distractions out of my mind. When they're gone, the only things left behind are my good ideas. My true instincts. The thoughts I need to listen to more closely.

It's very important that you have something similar in your own arsenal. Some people can access that state through taking a walk in the park. Or gardening. Or even painting. Whatever it is, you have to incorporate some activity into your lifestyle that allows you to disconnect from the noise of both the past and present and reconnect with whatever you're feeling in your gut in the moment.

A final word on hustling: just because I'm encouraging you to trust your instinct doesn't mean I don't believe there's a strong role for strategy in hustlin'. When people hear hustlers say things like "Make it happen" or "Scared money stays home," they think it implies that there's a certain recklessness to the hustler's mentality. That's not the case.

You might have even thought this if you listened to 50 Cent the rapper. People loved it when I rhymed:

> *Have a baby by me, baby, be a millionaire*
> *I'll write the check before the baby comes*
> *Who the fuck cares*

I'm stanky rich,
I'ma die trying to spend this shit

Sounds like I'm just throwing money up in the air, right? But those lines simply created a *perception*. The *reality* is that *Curtis Jackson* is not reckless with his money at all. In fact, I'm only putting my money behind things that (a) I'm passionate about and (b) I've done *all* my homework on. Even though hustlers are always aggressive, they're not always gambling. A skilled hustler will always strategically assess *all* the risks and rewards before he commits to something.

I have to understand something completely before I'll write a check to back it. I'll spend hours online researching the industry, tracking its history, and figuring out who the most important players are. Then I'll call any smart person I know who has experience in that space and try to pick their brains. Do you think there's room for growth? Or is the space flooded? Am I going to meet resistance if I make a move? What's that resistance going to look like? Who do I need as an ally?

Once I have those answers, I'll read gossip sites, blogs, and any other sources that can help fill me in on what's not being reported in the mainstream press.

After I have all that information, if I still feel like I can make an impact, I'm going all in. To me, that's not really gambling. That's making a bet on a sure thing.

When I feel that mixture of passion and understanding, I'm operating with supreme confidence. So much so that I don't even bother to put together a plan B. Why would I need a plan B when I'm dead certain that plan A is gonna work?

The only time I'll get involved with something that I don't have a complete understanding of is when I'm not putting up my own money. If someone approaches me to executive-produce a project, or lend my name to it in exchange for equity, I'm okay with a slightly bigger risk. If there's already a strong team in place and all they need is a little boost from me to put it over the top, I'll be a little more willing to fly blindly into something.

Even then, I'll get involved only if I feel a passion for what I'm doing. I'm not signing up for anything just for a check. That's the easiest way to dilute your brand and lose your money. Your fans will know that there's nothing organic about what you're doing and won't support it.

And if you're not passionate about the idea, you're not going to be emailing for updates. Checking in with your partners for any changes. You're basically just hoping that you can write a check and wake up one day to find that someone has dropped a big bag of money in your lap. That's not gambling. That's basically asking to lose your money.

The only time I got close to embracing gambling was when I was hanging out a lot with Floyd Mayweather. He would bet on everything—$250,000 on if someone would make a half-court shot during halftime of a basketball game, a million dollars on a preseason football game—because he fed off that sort of adrenaline.

When he'd win one of those bets, he'd ride that energy for days. All-night parties followed by trips to the auto dealership in the morning. But when he lost, it was a different story. If his team lost at 8 p.m., he could have thirty people in his suite ready to party, but he'd be in bed by nine. The loss sucked all the life out of him. Then the depression would lift a few days later, and he'd be back betting stacks on something crazy.

I'm not built that way. I'd put little bets down, maybe $20,000 here or there, just to try to keep him company, but I just didn't have the stomach for it. First off, betting on things that I can't fully research gives me anxiety. Why would I do that to myself? The other thing is, team sports have never been that important to me. I don't really care who wins the Super Bowl. I don't bleed orange and blue for the Knicks. There was no emotional attachment to those bets.

The one exception is boxing. I did all right when I bet on Floyd to win. But then I lost $20,000 when I bet on Adrien Broner to beat Pacquiao in 2019. After that, I was pretty much done with gambling.

At the end of the day, I like betting on sure things. And the only sure thing you can always count on, 100 percent of the time, is yourself.

CHAPTER 3

CONSTRUCTING
YOUR CREW

If you don't have the right people around you and you're
moving at a million miles an hour, you can lose yourself.

—DAVE CHAPPELLE

A sk any successful entrepreneur what their greatest attribute is
and you might be surprised by their answer.

It's not their negotiation skills, strategic planning, or ability
to understand new technology.

No, they're all going to tell you the same thing: their greatest skill
is being an astute judge of character.

Nobody, not even a rapper, makes it on their own. Yes, I'm alone
in the booth when it's time to spit my rhymes, but outside of the booth
there's a small army supporting me. Managers, attorneys, agents, engineers, producers, roadies, assistants, stylists, publicists, and friends I
trust to keep it real with me (probably the most valuable members of
my crew).

People like to make fun of rappers' entourages. (I'll admit having your own weed carrier is ridiculous. I don't smoke, but if I did I'd
damn sure roll my own blunts. Why would I want someone touching
and licking something I'm about to put in my own mouth?) But you

must surround yourself with people who can help support, grow, and articulate your vision.

Pick the right people and you can build a team that will take you to the top.

But pick the wrong people and it can derail your vision before it ever fully gets on track.

You can recover from blowing a lucrative deal, missing out on a change in the marketplace, or failing to upgrade your operation. Blowing those kinds of opportunities will hurt, but you'll recover—provided you have the heart of a hustler.

But if you pick the wrong person for a job, especially a critical one, the results can be catastrophic. This is true for every kind of business.

Back when I was slinging rocks, one of the jobs that needed to be filled in every crew was the "steerer." This person wouldn't have any money or drugs on them, but would direct customers to someone who did. Lots of dealers wouldn't even think twice about who they hired for that job—it was an entry-level position, and anyone who approached them was viable. If you weren't a cop, congratulations: you're hired. There was zero consideration about the person's character or who could vouch for them.

Nonetheless, steering presented an extreme liability to the operation. Since steerers usually had the shortest tenure, *they also had the least invested in the crew.* Which meant that if they got busted, they had little reason not to name names to the cops.

Understanding this vulnerability, instead of grabbing whoever happened to cross my path, I tried to pick people who seemed to possess a strong character. Who seemed like they'd be able to stay cool under pressure and have confidence that I'd bail them out (more on that later).

A lot of my steerers did get busted, but because I'd considered their character before hiring them, they usually didn't flip on me. Dealers who hired without much thought? They generally didn't last too long.

The ability to recognize character—or the lack thereof—is just as critical on the corporate level. Let's say you're the CEO of a Fortune 500 company and you hire a new guy to be your CFO. Everything can be fine for years. You become very comfortable with the guy. He's proficient with numbers, maybe more so than you are. You get to know his family outside of the office and go to his kid's sweet sixteen. He's so capable that you're able to increase your distance from the day-to-day financial details and start focusing on the bigger picture: mergers that are going to make you a legend, and gala events with celebs as you build your brand.

Then one morning you wake up to find out the CFO has looted the company's accounts and flown off to Dubai with his new girlfriend. Time to kiss your legendary status good-bye. Maybe even your job, too. Sure, a true hustler can survive that sort of blow. They're always going to figure out a way to make more money, because they know the frequent lurches between feast and famine. But they'd also much rather put the right person in that position and sidestep any potential drama than have to deal with the betrayal.

The importance of judging character is especially important in marriage. If you look at the guys who end up on the cover of *Fortune*, the column that shows where they took their biggest losses is always the same: divorce.

Billionaires don't lose the bulk of their money to competitors or to new technologies; they lose it to their exes. Jeff Bezos of Amazon reportedly had to pay his wife, MacKenzie, *$38 billion* when they split up. I don't care what happens with Amazon down the road, but there's no way the company itself is going to lose that much money for him.

People get divorced for all sorts of reasons, but a lot of wealthy individuals marry without knowing the true motive of their partners. I can promise you that *every* millionaire who has had to pay out a huge settlement has wished they were a better judge of character when they said "I do."

RATHER BE ROBBED

I've never had to file for divorce, but I'll be the first to tell you I've got a lot of issues in my personal life. And at the top of the list are trust issues.

A few years ago I was talking with a woman who'd taken some psychology classes in college. We were discussing a situation where I'd become convinced someone close to me was going to stab me in the back.

When I was done venting, she looked at me and asked, "You ever hear of the word 'pistanthrophobia'?"

"Nah, what's that?"

"It's what you have. Look it up."

I typed it into my phone and got the following definition: "The fear of trusting people due to past experience and relationships gone wrong."

Can't lie, it sounded exactly like me.

I think everyone is a little afraid of being too trustful, but I'm definitely worse than most. In my life, I feel like I've been betrayed by people I deserved better from: people I've given money to, opportunities to, love to, even life to. Because of that, for a long time the only thing I had faith in was money. I only trusted the paper that said "In God We Trust."

This is one of the reasons the theme of betrayal is so prominent in my show *Power*. It's an issue that's always on my mind, so much so that I even called the last season "The Final Betrayal."

I'd rather be robbed at gunpoint than be betrayed (not that I'd suggest you try it). At least getting robbed is exciting! There's an undeniable rush when someone pulls out their piece and growls, "Get on the fucking floor!" Once it's over (provided you don't get shot), you can go back and tell your friends, "Yo, they just stuck me up!" Your pockets might be lighter, but you'll be much stronger overall for having survived the experience.

Getting betrayed is different. You don't get a great war story out of it. I've never heard of someone getting hyped to tell their friends, "Yo, you won't believe this, but I just got backstabbed by my mans!" There are no stripes earned for that shit. When you open yourself up to someone, either financially or emotionally, and they go left on you, it's a different kind of pain, even more dramatic than a stickup kid physically taking something from you. Like Malcolm X said, "To me, the thing that is worse than death is betrayal. You see, I could conceive death, but I could not conceive betrayal."

B ecause I find betrayal so painful, I put incredible thought and consideration into the people who surround me. As I detail in this chapter, when I was first coming up, I made the mistake of confusing loyalty and location. It's a miscalculation a lot of people make—wanting to believe that just because someone is from the same streets as you that they're going to have your back forever. I learned the hard way that that's not the case. Sure, when you share a common experience with someone, there's a greater chance for loyalty and understanding, but it's far from guaranteed.

To achieve lasting success, you have to strive for balance when building your team. If you only surround yourself with people from your past, then chances are the past is where you'll be stuck. But if you abandon the people who were in the trenches with you for people you've just met—the ones who might be charismatic but have never proved anything *to you*—you're probably going to get burned.

If you look at my team today, you'll find a mix of old and new blood, weathered soldiers alongside impressive people I've met since my initial success. Walk into the G-Unit Records office and you might see guys who were right there with me on the streets of Southside, proving that they could remain cool under fire.

Some people form that bond going to school or playing on a sports team together. Definitely from serving in the military. When your life is on the line and the bullets are flying, you form a very deep connection with the people who have your back.

This is why I believe that you can learn more about what someone is made of in two minutes on the streets than twenty years in the boardroom.

In business it takes a long time to get a gauge on true nature. Instead of having the luxury of watching someone in action, you'll have to rely on instinct more. But once you do feel confident about someone's loyalty and work ethic, that's a person you need on your team. It's a rare combination in the business world, but one that's extremely valuable.

That's why, in addition to those day one veterans, I've tried to round out my roster with smart businesspeople who I feel I can trust—despite my hang-ups. Like my general counsel, Steve, who oversees my legal and business matters. Or my publicist, Amanda, who doesn't freak out every time I post something on social media and cleans up when I make a mess. Or my book agent, Marc, who helped put this project together. None of them have set foot in the Southside, but they've all been critical in keeping my brand expanding and moving in the right direction.

A great example of someone I've only met in the last five years but who has really helped me evolve is Chris Albrecht, the former CEO of Starz Networks. Chris built HBO into what it is today before taking over at Starz. He's taught me a tremendous amount about how TV works while giving me the freedom to be myself. Plus, he's from Queens, too, so it's almost like our relationship was meant to be.

Chris's number is one I'm never deleting from my phone. I don't care where he goes; I'm going to try to do business with him. I consider television to be my second career after music, and I would never have reached the level I'm at today without establishing a relationship with him. Yes, we're from different parts of Queens and have pretty different backgrounds, but we've clicked since day one and have really been able to help each other. Chris might not be one of my day one homies, but we've been through some wars of our own, and we know we have each other's back.

If I hadn't been open to bringing new people like Chris, and their knowledge, into my life, there wouldn't be a second stage in my career. Or whatever comes after this.

If I had kept my circle exclusive to my day one homies, things would have stagnated. I'd be yet another rapper who fell off after a couple of albums and was never really relevant again. Maybe I'd make the rounds on TV shows and podcasts, spending my time complaining that the rappers today can't really spit. Maybe I'd even appear on a reality show or two.

But I've avoided that fate. The key was finding the right balance of old and new, to keep moving forward, but without losing my footing.

In this chapter I'm going to share my strategies for assembling that resourceful, dedicated, and trustworthy crew that can help you build on what you've already grown and create new opportunities.

BRINGING THE HOOD WITH YOU

Growing up in the Southside of Queens, I knew that once I made it, I was going to bring my neighborhood with me. In the streets, you are taught from a very early age that the stronger your crew is, the stronger *you* are. The streets are a jungle, and you want to be perceived as being part of a strong pack. Not as prey.

This is why almost all the top rappers in the nineties made a point of championing their neighborhoods. Nas got on and brought Queensbridge with him. Biggie got a deal and brought Bedford-Stuyvesant with him. In LA, N.W.A. put Compton on the national map, and Snoop repped Long Beach a few years later.

I was determined to do the same with Southside. For the first several years of my career as a rapper, everywhere I went, the Southside came with me. Tony Yayo and Lloyd Banks of G-Unit weren't guys I met at some industry conference—they grew up around the block from me. You saw the neighborhood in my videos and during my live shows, and most important, you heard it in my music. I wanted that energy near me at all times. Today, I call that energy "the homeboy complex": when you feel the need to keep your homies as close to you as possible.

My "homeboy complex" was the main reason I bought Mike Tyson's mansion in Connecticut. When I came off my first tour for *Get Rich or Die Tryin'*, suddenly I had $38 million burning a hole in my pocket. Around the same time, I did an interview with a journalist who casually mentioned that Tyson was selling his home. "Oh, I'm going to buy that," I replied.

I had just been talking shit, but a couple of weeks later I found myself in Hartford, Connecticut. I consider Hartford a music mecca. It's close to New York, but just far enough away that it has its own energy and taste. I've found that if a song from a New York artist creates a buzz in Hartford, there's a good chance it can break in the rest of the country. So I try to stop through as often as possible and take the pulse of what people are listening to.

On this trip, I realized I wasn't too far from Tyson's place, so I had someone call up the broker and then went over to check it out. Once I was there, the vibe and scale seemed right for me. The money wasn't an issue. I bought it outright with a wire transfer the next week.

There was no family living with me at the time, so I didn't really need a house with eighteen bedrooms and twenty-five bathrooms (not to mention a movie theater, indoor and outdoor pool, indoor and outdoor basketball courts, a nightclub named TKO, and seventeen acres of land). But I bought it so that the Southside would literally be under the same roof as me!

There would be nights, out in the middle of the country (the closest city, Hartford, Connecticut, was ten miles away), where if you closed your eyes, you'd swear you were standing on a corner of Sutphin Boulevard. There was music playing, people dancing, and dice rolling. The same people I grew up with eating Chinese takeout on the stoop were now being served by waiters at *my* dining room table. And instead of watching a bootleg DVD on a grimy couch, I was able to show a first-run movie in my own movie theater. Doing things like that for the people I came up with gave me more validation than selling millions of records.

At the time, it seemed like a necessary move. Today, I've come to accept that it was one I didn't have to make.

First off, that house cost *waaay* too much money to maintain. I was spending close to $70,000 a month on maintenance alone. I don't care how rich you are, you never get comfortable paying a $70K utilities and maintenance bill every *month*—especially when you're on the road most of the time. Bill Gates would look at a bill like that and say, "Do we have to run the AC *every* night?"

It was great to be able to have eighteen bedrooms at my disposal, but I could only sleep in one of them at a time. I had to concede that I wasn't using that home correctly.

In many ways, the estate came to serve as a metaphor for my relationship with the hood. Yes, it served a purpose for me initially. I got a lot of support from my roots. And I gave a lot of people opportunities they would have never had otherwise.

But it was time to cut the cord.

I didn't cut everyone off—the core group I mentioned is still very much part of my life and business pursuits. But a lot of folks who had been with me for a long time got let go.

The eighteen-bedroom mansion has been downsized to an apartment (though a pretty damn nice one). My two-hour commute is down to twenty minutes.

I'm not sure why I even waited so long to make the move. At first, money was part of it. At one point I'd been talked into listing the house for over $15 million, which was an unrealistic price. When someone puts a number in your head, every time you move off that number, it feels like a loss. You can't get tricked into thinking that way.

I might not have gotten what I wanted for the property, but in the end I didn't care about losing money (and I ended up giving my proceeds to charity anyway). I had won by moving on with my life. I'd cleared my plate and refocused on the future, instead of being held down by a relic of the past.

BACK IN THE BARREL

Another mistake people make time and time again is that after they've found success, they feel they still owe something to the place they came from. This is especially prevalent in the African American community. When a black person from the hood reaches a certain level of success, they seem to feel obligated to maintain their roots.

You don't see this nearly as much in other communities. If a Chinese immigrant works his ass off for years and builds a chain of his own stores, he'll probably move to a big house in the suburbs the first chance he gets. He won't feel like he owes anything to his fellow immigrants back in Chinatown. He'll do what they'd do if they came into money, too—move to the biggest house in the safest neighborhood with the best schools that they could.

Same with a Mexican woman who grew up in the barrio. If she ends up, through her hard work and hustle, becoming a real estate magnate, she's probably not looking to stay in her old hood. Nope, she's getting that big house in the nice, safe neighborhood, too. Without any guilt.

When the Irish, Italian, and Jewish immigrants started making money, the first thing they did was beat it out to the suburbs.

It seems like it's only in the African American community that we have a hard time walking away from our struggle. If we don't stay connected to that struggle, we'll somehow lose whatever it was that made us successful.

I know that feeling very well. Being afraid to cut the umbilical cord to the hood is why I bought Mike Tyson's place. But at least I had the sense to bring the hood to me, instead of staying in the hood itself. I've known a lot of people who made that mistake, and some have paid the ultimate price for their unwillingness to walk away.

A tragic example was my friend and mentor Jam Master Jay, who was from Hollis, Queens. As a member of Run-DMC, Jay personified the pinnacle of success in our neighborhood. He sold millions of records. He toured the world, rocking stages from Europe to Asia. As part of the first breakout hip-hop group, he was an inspiration to millions of black kids in Queens and around the country.

Once they hit the big time, the rest of Run-DMC left Queens and never looked back — Rev Run and DMC went to New Jersey, and their manager, Russell Simmons, set up shop in Manhattan. But Jay stayed in Queens his entire life. He opened a recording studio in Jamaica, where he taught aspiring local rappers — myself included — the finer points of constructing a song.

It seems like a great story. Local DJ becomes famous, tours the world, and comes back to his old stomping grounds to share his gift with the next generation.

In reality, it was a death sentence.

By staying in Queens, Jay never separated himself from the negative elements close to hip-hop, especially in our hood. In Queens, the drug dealers were the first people to have real money. Hip-hop was a hobby, just something to do with your homies on the stoop or in the park. The cash was in selling drugs. Jay's generation was inspired by what the drug dealers had — nice clothes, fly cars, and beautiful women on their arms. The peacoats and godfather hats that Jay helped make famous with Run-DMC? That's what he saw the dealers wearing. Same with the gold chains Run-DMC and later LL Cool J helped popularize. They represented drug dealer fashion before they became hip-hop.

Today, the opposite is true—rappers can make way more money than drug dealers, thanks in no small part to the path early pioneers like Jam Master Jay helped blaze. Jay's mistake was that he didn't keep moving forward. If he'd followed Run, Russell, and DMC to Jersey, Long Island, or Manhattan, I have no doubt he'd still be alive today.

Instead, he stayed too close to the wrong kind of people—people who not only didn't have his best interest at heart but were actually jealous of his fame and success. They didn't celebrate him for staying in the neighborhood and mentoring aspiring MCs. They actually hated him for it. By staying around folks like that, he made it inevitable for sucker shit to happen.

It was a similar situation with Nipsey Hussle. I didn't know Nipsey as well as I knew Jay, but he seemed like a stand-up guy. When I agreed to shoot the video for YG's "Toot It and Boot It," which Nipsey was featured on, I told the guy at the record company, "Hey, make sure you bring that kid who looks like Snoop." That's how we met in person. Nipsey was a great dude who seemed focused on both his community and his family.

Sadly, the same sucker shit that got Jay also got Nipsey. When Nipsey was killed, people started pointing fingers at everyone *except* those suckers. On Twitter or IG, the first thing you'd see was "The government killed Nipsey!" The logic was Nipsey had been working on a documentary about Dr. Sebi, the famed Honduran herbalist who some people felt had been jailed and later killed because of his controversial views on Western medicine. Dr. Sebi's teachings were a threat to the pharmaceutical industry, so Nipsey had to be killed before he could help spread them to the world.

To hear other people tell it, Nipsey was a threat to the government because he was teaching the hood about financial empowerment and social justice. If too many poor young people became enlightened because of Nipsey's work, it would threaten the status quo in Los Angeles. So he had to go for that.

There's no doubt Nipsey was doing great work in his hood, especially with Vector90, a co-working space and STEM training center that taught tech skills. And though I don't have any strong feelings on Dr. Sebi's teachings, I wouldn't be shocked if there were some elements in the pharmaceutical field who wanted to keep that work under wraps.

But when people say the government killed Nipsey, they're just not being honest or realistic. The government didn't kill Nipsey. Allegedly, a sucker named Shitty Cuz killed him. That's the depressing truth.

He didn't kill Nipsey because Nip was a threat to any status quo. And no one paid him to kill Nipsey to protect Pfizer or Johnson & Johnson. No, Shitty killed Nipsey because he was a hater, plain and simple. He was a snitch, and when Nipsey called him on it, Shitty reacted with violence. He couldn't stand that someone as successful and beloved as Nipsey didn't want someone as unsuccessful and untrustworthy as Shitty around.

The crab-in-the-barrel mentality is what killed Nipsey, just like it killed Jay and so many other successful black folks who stayed in their community after they found success. That's why, when I started making legitimate money, I left the hood and never looked back. Sure, I'll visit from time to time. But I'd never move back permanently. If I did, there's zero question I would have been negatively impacted.

Understanding that mentality is why I don't have any second thoughts about not sticking around. Do I give a lot of money back to the streets through my charities? Absolutely. Do I work to make sure those kids have better legal opportunities than I had? No doubt. I'm not living under any illusions, though. On the streets, there just isn't enough space for both success and suckers. The quicker you understand that, the quicker you'll get the most out of your journey.

DEMAND DISCIPLINE

I'm not suggesting that you drop all your day one homeboys the second you taste a little success. Those are the people who know you best, and if they're true friends, they'll keep it the most real with you. They'll tell you when your verse is wack. Or your shirt is too young. Or that "influencer" who is promising big things actually seems like they're full of shit.

Those are some of the positive qualities that your day ones can add to your team. But they can also bring some of the negative qualities of the hood: beefs, dramas, and clashes of ego. To make sure that doesn't happen, you have to first instill—and then demand—a sense of discipline in your team.

That became clear to me early in my career, when I was supposed to perform with Nas at a concert in Central Park. Getting to share a stage with him was a big deal to me. As a superstar coming out of Queens, Nas was someone I really looked up to.

When I got to the venue, Nas was already there. And it looked like he'd brought all of Queensbridge with him. There must have been a couple dozen guys from the Bridge standing backstage, drinking, smoking, and hyping themselves up for Nas's set. I realized they didn't know what to do with the energy they were creating. It was like they were starting a fire they couldn't contain. Sure enough, they started fighting each other. It was Queensbridge versus Queensbridge. Even though his crew was turning on itself, Nas was either unwilling or unable to put out the fire. Soon the cops got called and the concert got shut down before Nas even stepped onstage.

In my eyes, Nas had mishandled the moment. I understood why he'd brought so many guys from Queensbridge with him—Central Park is no-man's-land and there's no telling who he might have run into there. A crew from Brooklyn. A couple of guys from the Bronx. Or maybe a rival crew from another neighborhood in Queens. It was smart to make sure he was surrounded by his own people.

What wasn't as strategic was his failure to keep them in check. By failing to control the energy he'd brought with him, he'd lost the chance to perform that day. It probably cost him money down the road, too. When promoters hear there was a problem at a high-profile venue like Central Park, it will make them think twice about booking you. So while the impulse to bring Queensbridge with him was understandable, their presence came at the expense of his overall growth.

Watching those Queensbridge dudes fight each other, I vowed to myself that when my crew and I hit the road, I would have *zero* tolerance for internal conflict. I knew that if I couldn't control my own people, there would be a pretty low ceiling on how high I could build my brand.

Plus, I understood that there are no "minor" fights when you're living together on the road. Let's say two guys get into it over a girl. One of them ends up smacking the other one in the face. Whoever got touched is going to feel humiliated long after the physical sting subsides. Every time he sees that other guy on the bus, backstage, in the hotel lobby, waiting for a plane—he's going to want to reassert himself. That sort of resentment can boil beneath the surface until it explodes. And the fallout from a serious enough explosion can take down an entire tour.

That's why, as soon as G-Unit hit the road, I was very clear about my policy on guys getting into it with each other. I told them, "We're going to encounter a lot of people who are jealous of our success. If you have some steam you need to let off, fight one of them. I'll have your back no matter what happens. Shit, I'll have your back if you end up punching some random stranger in the face. But if any of you guys fight *each other*, you're going home the next day. Period!"

For a while, everyone obeyed my edict. Yes, there were moments when it looked like something might pop off, but I was always quick to remind the would-be combatants, "I'm not playing. You're going home if you step to him!"

Then in the quieter moments I would pull guys aside and explain my motives. I wasn't trying to police them, just trying to help them win. "We're trying to build something with G-Unit," I'd say. "This tour, and the attention it's going to create, are going to be the building blocks for something special. But if those blocks keep shifting, whatever we try to build is going to come crashing down. Then we're going to be back on the corner, instead of out here eating lobster, staying in nice hotels, and meeting girls in every city!"

That little pep talk would usually get through to people, and I didn't have to send anyone home. That is, until we got to Philadelphia.

The problem started when Mitchell & Ness, the legendary Philadelphia sports clothing company, sent some complimentary throwback jerseys to our hotel. This was the era when a Mitchell & Ness jersey was basically the official uniform of hip-hop. Everyone wanted to be seen in one, and some of the rare editions were worth thousands of dollars.

Even though the shirts were meant for me, the package ended up in the hands of a guy named Marcus, who was our tour manager. He knew I always buy my own clothes, so he decided to take a couple of the jerseys for himself. He felt that since he was the tour manager, they were some of the "spoils" he was entitled to.

Bang 'Em Smurf didn't see it that way though. Bang 'Em was someone from Southside that I was considering signing to G-Unit, so I'd taken him on the road to help him get some exposure. Bang 'Em had potential, but he made the mistake of thinking that just being on the road meant that he'd already made it. He started drinking his own juice before he'd proved anything. He didn't have a single. He didn't have any buzz. The girls didn't look at him and say, "Who's the cute one?" To the world, he was just another dude onstage shouting the end of my lines. That experience alone got him so gassed that he thought the rules didn't apply to him.

The morning after the Philly show, we were scheduled to get on the bus at 5 a.m. and head to the next city. But instead of my alarm clock, I got an early morning wake-up from the sounds of a fight taking place under my window. I pulled back the shades to see an unexpected sight: Marcus and Bang 'Em rolling around in the streets, trading blows over a Mitchell & Ness jersey. "It's mine," I could hear Bang 'Em shouting. "Nah, that ain't yours!" yelled Marcus. "Yours had a piece of gum stuck on the side. This is mine!"

Apparently, Bang 'Em had decided one of those jerseys was his. And when Marcus wouldn't hand it over, Bang 'Em was just going to take it. Not what I wanted to deal with at the crack of dawn. I went outside and immediately broke them up. Then I asked Bang 'Em what the hell he was thinking. "Nah, Fif," Bang 'Em started to explain. "He's trying to take my shirt. I had to check him." I wasn't trying to hear it. "Man, you know I told everyone no fights on this tour!" Then I looked at Marcus and said, pointing to Bang 'Em, "Get this punk a bus ticket. He's going home."

It wasn't until that moment that Bang 'Em realized I wasn't playing. When I said "zero tolerance," I meant *zero*. If you're going to maintain control of your team, you must make people respect the repercussions. Even if it means ending a relationship.

So Bang 'Em got sent home right then and there. He'd have plenty of time to drink his own juice back in Queens. Bang 'Em thought he was bigger than the crew, but it turned out he didn't know how to move on his own. He started working with some other local rappers and from time to time would try to get me to support them, but nothing really caught my ear. Without my support, no one wanted to give him a break. Instead of being on the road with me, making legal money and seeing the world, he eventually caught a case back in Queens. He asked me to bail him out, but I explained to him that wasn't my job. He eventually got deported back to Trinidad, where he was born. To this day, he blames me, not himself, for his situation.

Whenever you find success in life, there will be people who believe some of it belongs to *them*. Bang 'Em was that sort of person. When you remove them from your life, instead of looking in the mirror, they get angry at you.

If I had let Bang 'Em slide with a warning, I would have lost my authority. All the other egos on the tour—and there were plenty of them—would have started to bubble, too. Soon they wouldn't just be fighting over Mitchell & Ness jerseys; they would've been beefing over girls, who got the most time onstage, or who was getting paid what. That kind of dissension has ground many tours—before and since—to a premature halt. I wasn't about to let that sort of energy mess up our momentum.

Almost twenty years later, I'm still touring the globe. I've performed in countless countries to millions of people. Recently, someone flew me overseas to do a concert for several million dollars. Not a bad little check for a flight on a private jet and one day's work. But it was also the kind of check that comes only after you've established yourself as a seasoned, profitable, and *reliable* touring act—the kind of reputation that I was focused on building all those years ago back in Philly.

Those choices don't have to be as dramatic as getting someone a bus ticket home. If you're a supervisor at a company, it could just mean transferring them to another department. If you're the manager at a retail store, maybe it means moving that kind of person to another location. If you run your own small business, it probably means firing their ass immediately. You won't have the luxury of carrying anyone giving you anything less than their best.

No matter what position you're in, when you make rules that benefit the collective good, you need to enforce them. Don't let someone who's focused only on themselves ruin it for everyone else. They can be hard rules to live by, but doing so will always pay off in the long run.

HANDLE INTERNAL PROBLEMS FIRST

No matter how high you build your empire, you'll never be able to maintain it if your house isn't in order. Just like I told Bang 'Em back in the day, if the blocks on the bottom aren't solid, it's just a matter of time before everything crashes down.

A classic example of this is what happened to the Brooklyn rapper Tekashi 6ix9ine. Tekashi is a half-Mexican, half–Puerto Rican rapper from Brooklyn. His multicolored hairdo and over-the-top energy won him millions of fans across the country—especially white kids. They might not be able to dread their hair like the Migos, but they could definitely put in all the colors of the rainbow like Tekashi. He went from being a virtually unknown SoundCloud rapper to one of the biggest stars out there in not much more than a year.

Tekashi's image was of a tough, reckless instigator, but he was actually a sweet kid at heart. Much closer to a WWF wrestler playing a role than an actual gangsta. So to reinforce his image, he started surrounding himself with street dudes.

But those guys were not playing a role. They were the real deal. Once they realized Tekashi wasn't, they started seeing him as food. And food is *never* what you want to be perceived as by real street dudes.

As his star rose, Tekashi and I began to build a friendship. I liked that he was brash. That he didn't seem to be afraid of the moment. A lot of people even said that Tekashi reminded them of a young me.

One day he called and asked if he could come to my office. He'd had some run-ins with the law, and promoters were starting to get nervous booking him. He needed advice.

When he arrived, I didn't see a brash young man. Or an arrogant rapper. I saw a scared kid.

Settling into a chair in my office, Tekashi got right to the point: "50, what am I supposed to do?"

I had to give him credit. He acted wild in public, but in front of me he was willing to be vulnerable. He was smart enough to know he was in over his head. He and I had never had any conversations about what was going on, but as an experienced observer, I had a good guess where the root of his problems lay.

"Your biggest issue is going to be internal," I told him. "You've got too many people around you, and they're not really supporting you. They're supposed to be your team, but they don't have your best interest at heart. If you don't get that situation together, it's going to be a problem."

I told him this because I'd been hearing he was switching up crews a lot. One month he'd have one bunch of guys around him; the next month they'd be replaced by a new group. He was swapping crews the way some guys swap cars. Ride one for a while, then trade it in for another.

He probably thought that was all part of the act, but I knew it was a serious miscalculation. When you bring people around as a rapper, there's an expectation that you're going to provide them with opportunities. Help them get noticed as an artist themselves or get established as a behind-the-scenes player. Introduce them to brands they can get checks from.

You only have a limited amount of time to make good on that expectation. If you don't, confusion will set in. It will grow faster if they see you suggesting the opportunities to other people. When that happens, the original crew will start feeling disposable. You never want anyone around you feeling that way.

When someone perceives themselves as disposable, any sense of loyalty will vanish. Instead of waiting for an opportunity, they're going to aggressively come after you for what they think is "owed" to them. They're going to extract that debt however they can.

Being a smart kid, Tekashi saw the value in my advice and conceded that he was in a precarious spot. He even started to make moves to replace the guys he knew had it in for him. But it was already too late.

Not long after our conversation, Tekashi was arrested on federal RICO and firearms charges. In the indictment, the government even alleged that several members of his crew had plotted to kill him. I'm sure that was a scary realization for a kid who thought he was a WWF wrestler, not someone who was actually playing with life-and-death stakes. As I'm writing this, Tekashi has just finished testifying against his own crew and was sentenced to two years behind bars.

I believe one of the things that tripped up people like Tekashi and Ja Rule is that they grew up on the outskirts of the hood. They weren't from the hood, but they had been exposed to it. It tricked them into thinking they were equipped to handle situations they weren't actually built for.

Contrast them with someone like Drake, who isn't from even the outskirts of the hood. He's from a completely different environment. I never see Drake associating too closely with the artists he puts on. He always keeps a good deal of space between himself and whoever he's associated with at the time. He's smart enough to judge his own character and concede that there are some forces he won't be able to harness.

Tekashi was a great judge of what white kids wanted to listen to in order to piss off their parents, but he wasn't as good at assessing people's characters and intentions. Sadder still, I really think Tekashi is a perceptive kid. If he had slowed down and taken the time to study the people around him, get a feel for their energy, he would have recognized that they weren't the right fit for him. Instead, he was in a rush. The Instagram likes and retweets were coming so fast that he probably started confusing social media with reality.

On social media, the guy throwing up signs next to you is your man until the end. Your ride or die. In real life, things are never that simple.

Jealousy and envy grow very easily, especially when they start getting a taste of success. If you bring a bunch of wolves into your circle, you better be damn sure to feed them. Otherwise, it won't be long before the pack turns on you.

If you want a textbook example of the *right* way to replace an existing crew with a new one, consider what Jay-Z did while president of Def Jam Recordings. At the time, a lot of people couldn't understand why an artist as successful as Jay-Z would want to switch up roles and take a job sitting behind a desk.

I'll admit I didn't quite understand it at first, either. For a while I was running G-Unit Records, and I found that incredibly stressful. No matter how hard you work for artists, they are never happy. As an artist himself, Jay would know that.

But as I observed his tenure at Def Jam, it began to dawn on me what he was up to. He wasn't there to run the label. He was there to construct a new team! Before taking over Def Jam, Jay's crew had largely comprised Philadelphia rappers he'd recruited and groomed under the State Property franchise, artists like Beanie Sigel, Freeway, Chris and Meek, and Omillio Sparks.

Those guys were certainly (and still are) respected artists, but none of them broke out commercially the way Jay had hoped. His plan was for one of them to turn into the next Jay-Z (just like I was hoping for Tony Yayo to be the next 50 Cent). But it never happened.

By taking over Def Jam, Jay positioned himself to make that label's preexisting superstars his new crew. Instead of being closely associated with Beanie Sigel and Freeway, he became associated with Kanye and Rihanna. It was a major commercial upgrade. And unlike when he was running Roc-A-Fella Records, Jay didn't have to put in any work grooming them or investing money in their careers. Def Jam had *already* done that. It was like moving into a fully furnished home. And better still, after he stopped running Def Jam, Kanye and

Rihanna still saw Jay as their boss. He got to take all that furniture with him when he moved out!

I salute Jay for a sophisticated strategy. There was nothing unethical or disloyal about it. He gave those Philly artists plenty of opportunities when they were on Roc-A-Fella Records.

But when they never quite became what he had set them up to be, he was savvy enough to move on. A lot of people hesitate to make those moves. They'd rather stay connected with the same group of people, even if those people aren't getting them any closer to success. Jay didn't fall into that trap. Still hasn't.

PROVIDE ENCOURAGEMENT

In addition to maintaining discipline and stability within your crew, to be a truly effective leader you also have to be able to motivate people with encouragement.

As tough as I can be on people who get out of line, I also pride myself on being able to deliver heartfelt pep talks when they're needed. If you're primarily known as a disciplinarian, the moments when you step out of that role and show that you have real concern about someone will carry extra weight.

Some of the best pep talks I've given have been before boxing matches. There's something about that setting that really brings out the motivator in me. One I remember specifically was when I was in the dressing room with Deontay Wilder before his rematch at the Barclays Center with Bermane Stiverne.

One of the keys to delivering an impactful pep talk is being able to read the energy in the room. And my read of the energy at that moment was that it was not where it needed to be. Deontay had his whole entourage with him, and there was no focus. Everyone was laughing and talking shit like they were at a party. Deontay had already beaten Stiverne once before, and it was clear to me that everyone thought the fight was over before it had even begun. But that's a very dangerous way to approach a fight. Yes, Deontay had beaten Stiverne, but the fight had gone the distance—the first time that had happened in Deontay's career. He needed to be locked in on the job in front of him. A lot of fighters have wound up knocked out because they didn't take their opponent seriously enough.

I waited until I got Deontay into a corner of the dressing room where there weren't as many people around. "You're not focused," I told him evenly. "I see you hitting the mitts and everything, but you're not in the zone, man." Deontay didn't have to say anything. He knew I was right. "Stop bullshitting. This man Stiverne is standing in the way of what you want. For the second time. Are you going to let him do that?"

"Naw, I'm not," Deontay replied.

"Good. So let's make him pay for his mistake, then," I told him, my voice rising. Suddenly, everyone around us realized the energy was changing. The room got quiet.

"Listen, man," I continued, my voice taking on a menacing quality. "You are going to make him pay for thinking he can step into the ring with you again. You are going to take this man into the deep waters. And then drown him."

Now I had Deontay locked in. He went back to hitting the mitts, this time with a purpose. Then I walked him out into the ring while performing "Many Men." The party was over. Now it was time for business.

It didn't take long. Deontay knocked Stiverne down three times in the first round, before the referee called it. The ref literally had to jump on Deontay's back to get him off Stiverne.

It all happened so fast that I didn't even have time to make it back from the ring to my seat in the skybox. Afterward Deontay said that he had felt "possessed" in the ring. "I was standing on the outside of my body just watching and observing myself beat this man," he told the *In the Corner* podcast. I know he was able to get to that state because I helped bring him there. Before I spoke to him, Deontay was going to walk into the ring in an unfocused state. After our talk, he went in there with a laser focus, which is what you need when your opponent is trying to smash your face in.

I gave a similar talk to Floyd Mayweather before his fight with Victor Ortiz. When I came into the dressing room before the fight, I immediately became uncomfortable with how comfortable Floyd was. It was clear to me that Floyd and his team thought this fight was going to be a walk in the park. Well, I wasn't going to let Floyd walk into the trap.

I wasn't the only one who noticed Floyd's energy was very nonchalant. "It certainly seems like this is his office," the TV announcer observed as Floyd slowly made his way to the ring. "He's not worried at all. He has no fear. Or butterflies."

Confidence is great, but too much of it can make a fighter vulnerable. Before a fight, a boxer *should* have butterflies. They *should* be a little nervous. They should feel like they're about to run into someone who's going to try to kill them, because that's exactly what's going to happen. Even someone like Floyd, arguably the greatest defensive fighter of all time, should never allow himself to believe that his opponent isn't capable of knocking his head off.

I needed to shake Floyd out of that state. If I couldn't make him scared, I figured I could at least make him angry. Ortiz hadn't demonstrated any animosity toward Floyd leading up to the fight—if anything, Ortiz's energy had said, "Thanks, Floyd, I really appreciate the opportunity." I was worried that Floyd was starting to feel friendly toward Ortiz. I had to get Floyd in a more appropriately aggressive mind state.

If you watch the video of the fight, as Floyd and I approach the ring, I whisper something in his ear. The cameras didn't pick it up, but this is what I told him:

"Fuck this bum. He's trying to make sure you can't feed your kids."

"What you say, Five?" Floyd responded.

"This motherfucker is trying to take food out of your children's mouth. Do . . . not . . . let . . . him."

When I told him that, it's like he went into a trance. First he started stomping his feet, then he ran into the ring, a man on a mission.

Floyd ended up knocking Ortiz out in the fourth round.

After the fight we all piled into a van to go back to Floyd's hotel. As soon as we pulled out, Floyd started yelling, "Yo, Five said some shit to me!" He was happy because he knew I'd put him in the right headspace. Before I got in his ear, he was probably feeling bad for Ortiz. Probably didn't want to go too hard on him. I corrected that mind-set. Knock him out and make sure the money is straight going forward. Which is exactly what Floyd did.

When I was first casting for *Power*, I had one person in mind to play the lead character, Ghost: Omari Hardwick. I had seen Omari in the movie *Next Day Air*, and I identified him as someone who could be the leading man in a hit TV show.

The network had some other actors in mind, but I was focused on Omari. To me he embodied the combination of intelligence, masculinity, unpredictability, and violence that was Ghost. I just needed to help Starz see it, too.

When it was time to begin casting, we first brought in Joe Sikora to read for the role of Tommy. As you're probably not shocked to learn, Joe absolutely killed it. From the very first page he was completely at home with the character. The energy in the room was vibrant as he went through his lines. As soon as he left, no one had to say a word. Joe had the role.

Next up was Omari. I was excited because I'd spent weeks hyping him up to the network executives. Now was his time to prove me right.

But, unlike Joe, Omari was very flat. He read the lines, but his energy was lacking. It was clear he wasn't connecting with the character. Something wasn't right. When Omari's read was over and he left the room, one of the executives looked at me and said, "Sorry, but we don't know if this is the right guy."

I understood why they felt that way, but I still believed in my vision of Omari playing Ghost. I just needed to help Omari see it, too. So that night I got on the phone with him.

"Yo, you all right?" I asked him. "You didn't seem like you was into it today."

"Yeah, I'm all right."

"Okay, but they're telling me they're not sure you're the guy. What are we going to do about that?"

"Well, if they feel that way, then they should probably just go with someone else."

That wasn't the reply I was looking for. It meant the conversation was going the wrong direction. I had to get Omari turned around and prepared to fight for the role, instead of feeling defeated.

I needed to take the gloves off and be real with him.

"You're talking about 'just give it to someone else,' but then what are *you* going to do next?" I asked him. "Do you feel good enough about your career to just walk away from a starring role without giving it your best? Do you have a strong plan B for what happens when someone else gets the role and all the glory? If so, fine. But if you don't, you better get back in there and read that role the way I know you can."

Omari kept telling me he didn't care if he lost the role, but I knew he didn't mean it. That was just his ego talking. He was disappointed that they didn't respond positively to his read. Omari knew he could act, he just was internalizing the information instead of performing it.

"Listen, there's a reason you're on the top of the call sheet," I told him. "I insisted that your name was first. And the reason I did was because I saw you in *Next Day Air*. I know you can kill this role. We wrote it with you in mind. You are going to be the star of a TV series playing Ghost. Do not let your ego trip you up here. If those execs don't think you're right for the role, go back in there and prove to them that you are."

Finally he began to see things my way. We started talking about Ghost's motivations and future storylines. His energy picked up. Omari began to see what I saw. "You're right, 50," he told me. "I can be this guy." By the end of the conversation, he was excited and ready to read again. I set it up for the next day, and this time he was completely locked in. He had swagger and was menacing, but there was deep intelligence in his eyes, too. He was in the pocket. He was Ghost.

Today, it's almost impossible to think of anyone *but* Omari playing that role. But there was absolutely a moment where Omari was prepared to let that opportunity pass without putting up a fight. What a mistake that would have been. Not only would it have negatively impacted *Power*, but it would have cost Omari so many opportunities that have come with being the star of a hit TV series. He's a household name now, with multiple movies about to come out. All because of what he's done as Ghost.

In order to get the best out of the people around you, sometimes you have to clearly and forcefully articulate the opportunities you see for them. Just because you see something for them, you can't assume they see it, too. If someone is not responding to, or taking advantage of, the opportunities you've created for them, you're going to have to take them to that place. That's literally what "leading" means.

You cannot construct a team and then expect everyone to instinctively know what position they're supposed to play. That's how confusion, and later frustration, sets in. If someone is not in a competitive mode, then it's on you as a leader to activate that mode for them. From your top lieutenant to the lowest person on the totem pole, you need to be able to articulate not only where you need that person to go, but also the steps they should follow to get there.

Most of the time, getting people on the right path will require bringing their competitiveness and cockiness down a few notches. Helping them, like in the case of Bang 'Em Smurf, be a little more realistic about what they're capable of and where they stand. But occasionally, like in the situation with Omari, you're going to have to take the opposite approach. You're going to have to lift them up a bit. Remind them of what they're capable of. Believe in them so openly that, eventually, they start believing in themselves.

The key is understanding that different people require different tactics. You can't coach everyone on your team the same way. If I had barked on Omari the way I barked on Bang 'Em, Omari would have never come out of his shell. Just like if I had gassed up Bang 'Em the way I gassed up Omari, Bang 'Em would have imploded on the spot. Accept that everyone on your team is going to have their own hang-ups, issues, and insecurities, and then address them with the appropriate energy. You can't have a one-size-fits-all mind-set when it comes to effective leadership. You need to tailor a specific approach to every single person on your team in order to get the most out of them.

LEARNING TO TRUST AGAIN

On August 30, 2012, I was at my office, working on promo plans for "New Day," a track I'd just done with Alicia Keys, when I received an urgent phone call from a friend. He had devastating news: Chris Lighty, my longtime friend and manager, was dead.

I had been standing in the middle of a bustling office, but when I heard the words "Chris is dead," it was like all the noise around me suddenly got turned off. "I can't really believe I just heard you say those words to me," I told my friend. "Say it again so I'm sure I'm hearing you right."

But there was no miscommunication, no mistake. Chris Lighty, the man who had helped guide my career both through the valleys and over the mountaintops, was gone.

Even more devastatingly, I was being told that he had shot himself. That Chris Lighty, one of the smartest, most self-assured, and most motivated people I'd ever met, had decided to take his own life.

To this day, it doesn't feel right to me.

C hris's death was a blow on many levels. The most devastating, of course, was knowing what his loss would mean to his children. Chris's daughter Tiffany and I in particular were close, and I knew she worshipped the ground he walked on. As soon as I learned he had passed, I made a vow that I would look out for Tiffany in his absence. I've tried to live up to that promise, re-writing my will to include her. I'm so supportive of Tiffany that I didn't even flip when she knocked the mirror off one of the Lambos I let her drive. That's how you know it's love!

Beyond its impact on Chris's family, I was also worried about what his death would mean for me. Out of all my business associates, Chris was easily the one I felt closest to. I had met Chris early in my career, when I was first out supporting my mixtapes. Even though he had grown up in the Bronx and was a little older than me, I felt like I had known him my entire life. We were very similar in our backgrounds and our energy.

Chris, going by the name Baby Chris, had come up with a Bronx crew called the Violators. From snatching people's chains in clubs he graduated to carrying records for the legendary DJ Red Alert. That relationship led to him becoming the tour manager for groups like A Tribe Called Quest and De La Soul. He later became a successful executive at Def Jam, before launching Violator, his management company, with Mona Scott.

Just like I was always seeking to find the balance between 50 Cent and Curtis Jackson, Chris had two distinct sides to him as well. Chris Lighty the executive could sit down in a boardroom and have no problem cutting a multimillion-dollar deal. But Baby Chris from the Bronx would still want to smack you in the face if you played too much around him. We were both constantly walking a tight rope between respecting our street roots and demonstrating our corporate character.

For that reason alone, we deeply understood each other.

With Chris, for the first time in my life I had someone outside of my immediate family who I trusted implicitly. With my money. With my visions. And with my future. A trust, as I've said, that is very hard for me to build.

I didn't realize how much I trusted Chris till not long after he died and I had to appear at a deposition about one of my businesses. As a lawyer quizzed me about how the operation was run, I began to realize that my answer to almost every question was, "That was something that Chris handled." It really brought home to me what a huge role Chris had played in my career.

I've really struggled to fill that void since Chris passed. I know I'll never find another manager like him, but there is someone out there with similar qualities who could help me. Who could take some of the burden off me and allow me to focus on the bigger picture. Who could advise me. Push me toward even greater achievement. Who could understand both 50 Cent and Curtis Jackson.

I started this chapter by saying that the greatest attribute of most successful entrepreneurs is being an astute judge of character. So the question I have to ask myself is, have I lost faith in my ability to judge people astutely? Or have I been uneasy about opening up my life and career to someone the way I did with Chris? Because to really let a manager do their best work, you've got to let them into almost all aspects of your life.

I believe the answer is that I've been too guarded in trying to find another Chris. One of the goals I've got to set for myself is reestablishing my confidence in my ability to evaluate and read people. I've always been confident in that regard, so I need to embrace that skill set and start the process of establishing that trust with someone again. It can be scary to open up your life to someone new, but when you pick the right person, it can also be incredibly beneficial.

CHAPTER 4

KNOWING YOUR VALUE

Know your worth. Then add tax.

— UNKNOWN

Wouldn't it be great if you always got paid your worth? Without having to fight for it?

If every time you went for a new position, tried to negotiate a raise, or asked for a bonus, you were compensated fairly?

Of course, life doesn't usually work that way. If anything, the opposite is true.

Whenever you work for someone else, they're going to try to pay you less than what you're worth. Doesn't matter if they're a "good guy," a friend, or even family. If they can save a couple of bucks, they're going to try to at your expense. You can't even be mad—it's just business.

But what you *can* do is be strategic. Ensure that, instead of getting overlooked, swept to the side, or hustled, you always receive maximum value for your efforts.

It's not as hard as it might seem. Even more surprising: oftentimes, the best way to extract that maximum value is by choosing *not* to drive the hardest bargain.

"Gimme the loot"

"I got my mind on my money, and my money on my mind"

"Fuck you, pay me!"

Those classic hip-hop lyrics and many others like them helped re-shape people's attitudes about demanding their full worth. That energy is one of hip-hop's greatest cultural contributions. The Isley Brothers are funky as hell, but they aren't putting out "fuck you, pay me" energy. I love Earth, Wind & Fire as much as the next man, but they don't have folks ready to demand a raise.

Hip-hop gave you that energy—on steroids and washed down with a Red Bull. We made getting paid in full a cornerstone of the culture. The critics don't want to admit it, but hip-hop absolutely empowered people to stand up for themselves in a way no other art form has.

As 50 Cent, I've definitely promoted that mind-set as much as anyone. From the moment I picked up a mic, I've been rapping about getting money. Do a GIF search for "pay me" and my face is literally one of the first images that comes up. I'm proud to have helped spread that energy.

Curtis Jackson, however? He's become a little more nuanced.

I've learned over the years that, though the "pay me" energy is incredibly powerful, I have to apply it judiciously. If I walk into a situation with my aura screaming "Gimme the loot, gimme the loot," it may match the 50 Cent persona, but it will also grind a lot of situations to a halt before they really get moving to the right destination.

Today, I'm extremely strategic when approaching a new opportunity. Instead of focusing on just how big my initial payday is going to be, I try to evaluate all the ways the situation could benefit me—even those that don't include a check.

If there's been a single hallmark of my career outside of rapping, it's been my ability to identify value in unexpected situations. If I had just followed the normal "rapper's playbook," I wouldn't have had much of a career outside of music. A couple of endorsements and then off to the hip-hop retirement home.

I've always had other plans, though. I was going to get all the money my talents deserved, even if it meant taking some unorthodox steps.

THE RIGHT DEAL IS OUT THERE—WAIT FOR IT

Because I'm known as a pretty aggressive guy who moves quickly toward the action, it might surprise you to learn that one of my greatest negotiating strengths is actually patience.

No matter how much money is on the table, how much pressure I'm under, or however good or bad my last venture performed, I will always wait for the best deal before I commit.

The best example of this is my decision to sign with Eminem's Shady Records and Interscope. It's a decision that, in retrospect, seems like a no-brainer—a layup that anyone could have made. Maybe, but I promise you that the decision wasn't so obvious at the time. A lot of people (including some very respected names in the music business) thought I was crazy for turning down some of the other deals I'd been offered first.

To understand why they felt that way, let's consider the context.

My first record deal was with Jam Master Jay's JMJ Records, which I signed when I was around twenty-one years old. Jay is the guy who taught me how to actually put together a song. Before I met him, I was just spittin' over beats without any direction. Jay groomed me. He slowed me down and showed me how to incorporate melody and structure into a fully fleshed-out hit song.

Those were critical skills for me to develop, but, at the end of the day, JMJ wasn't a *real* label. It was more of a production company. Jay had a studio where he recorded artists (and, sadly, where he would later be murdered). Once he thought an artist was polished enough, he would bring their music to an "actual" label like Atlantic or Def Jam to pitch their A&R department. If the label was into the music, Jay would sign a deal for JMJ. Then, in theory, the artist would get paid out of Jay's deal.

I wasn't aware at first that that's how it worked—I thought once I'd signed to JMJ, I'd officially "made it." I won't ever claim to be the smartest guy in the room, but I do catch on to things pretty quickly. Once I realized JMJ wasn't going to put my records out directly, I said, "Nah, this ain't it," and asked for an exit. Jay didn't want to let me go scot-free, and in the end I had to pay him $50,000 to get out of my contract.

After that I hooked up with the production duo the Trackmasters and through them was able to land a "real" deal with Columbia Re-cords. I recorded a bunch of songs for my debut album, but then things stalled (more on that shortly). Before the album could come out, I got shot. As the rumors began to spread about what was behind the shoot-ing, Columbia panicked and dropped me.

At that point I was almost twenty-five years old. Very young for a teacher, doctor, or lawyer, but not so young in a youth-oriented cul-ture like hip-hop. Worse, I was perceived as damaged goods. On top of being shot, I'd already forced my way out of one deal and been dropped by a major label. Most people in the industry didn't think I was worth the headache.

A lot of rappers in my situation would have felt very uneasy. They would have worried that their dream was about to slip out of their reach. Racked by anxiety and confusion, if a label—any label—offered them a deal, they probably would have signed it that day.

And yet, that wasn't my mentality. I didn't care about what had already happened to me. I wasn't signing anything unless I was sure it was the best deal for me—in that moment *and* going forward. My past wasn't going to cloud my vision for the future.

The first deal I got offered was from Universal. They said they wanted me, but when I had a lawyer review their contract, I learned the actual deal they were offering was a joint venture with $1.3 million for a solo album and a G-Unit project. I saw it for what it was: a way for them to work with me while hedging their bets.

I wasn't looking to partner with anyone who wasn't prepared to go all in with me. I passed on Def Jam.

Then a guy named 3H from Capitol Records reached out. He flew me out to LA, my first trip to the West Coast. When I got there, I was surprised to see that he was this little white kid. It seemed crazy to me that he already had so much juice, but I thought it was ill that he'd already maneuvered himself into a position of power. He was hungry and cocky, not unlike myself. I was very tempted to work with him.

Then his boss at Capitol got cold feet. He told 3H I was "too scary" and that he "didn't want bodyguards" at his house. He wasn't incorrect—there was a menacing aura around me at the time, and bodyguards followed along everywhere I went. Still, I wasn't going to try to convince someone who couldn't see my value. As much as I liked 3H, I knew that Capitol wasn't the right situation either.

At the time I was represented by Violator. Chris was my manager and someone I leaned on for advice. He supported me when I didn't take those deals, but I could tell it wasn't easy for him.

Chris had to worry if I was ever going to give him a return on his investment in me. Yes, I had the streets buzzing through my mixtapes, but I had a lot of baggage, too. The safe move would have been to take one of those deals and finally get my debut album out.

Things got even more complicated when Todd Moscowitz, who was working with Chris at Violator, lined up a deal for me with J Records. Todd said it was the perfect situation. I'd be working with the industry legend Clive Davis, which would calm a lot of folks' fears about me. Todd pushed hard for me to sign with J Records.

At almost the same time Todd was making his push, I got word that Eminem was interested in signing me to Shady Records, his imprint on Interscope. I knew right away that *that* was the right situation. *The Marshall Mathers LP* had just sold 22 million. Em was the reason so many white fans were embracing hip-hop culture. It was the type of association you might get access to only once in a lifetime, if you're fortunate.

I was faced with a difficult decision. Today, people believe I would have succeeded no matter what label I signed with. Go into chat rooms and message boards, and you'll even see fans claiming things like "50 was so hot back then. He coulda signed with Koch and still sold all them records."

Yeah, I was hot, but even if my ego would like to believe otherwise, my career wouldn't have had anywhere near the same trajectory had I signed anywhere other than Interscope. Not Koch, not Def Jam, not J Records. It wasn't just Eminem's presence, either; Interscope gave me access to Dr. Dre, one of the greatest producers of all time. There was no other deal out there that could have matched the power of that tag team.

I knew I had been groomed for the moment by all my other failures and misses. When that door opened, even just a crack, no one had to tell me twice to walk through it.

Before I could take the step, though, Todd Moscowitz had to get out of the way. The J Records deal would mean money for Violator. The Eminem deal wouldn't. Todd refused to let it go. So some of my crew and I had to go to Violator to discuss the situation.

Todd came on very aggressively, explaining that we were contractually obligated to sign his deal. I looked to Chris for help, but he shrugged his shoulders like there was nothing he could do. He was caught between what was best for his artist and what Todd thought was best for the company. It was a surreal situation—listening to this guy in a sports jacket and dress shoes trying to convince me I should pass up the opportunity of a lifetime to sign what I knew was a lesser deal.

What Todd was saying didn't sit right with me or my people. We expressed our concerns. We might even have been a little aggressive in articulating them. At one point I remember Todd running out of his office and down the stairs toward the street, his dress shoes clicking and clacking on the steps the whole way down. Suffice it to say that was the last of any talk about my signing to J Records. Interscope would be my new home.

We all know how the deal turned out. It made me one of the biggest stars in the history of hip-hop. But I have to stress this again: at the time, it was not a clear-cut decision.

It was harder to tell Violator no. I didn't give a rat's ass about what Todd Moscowitz wanted, but Chris was a good friend. Passing on J Records put him in a tough spot. He'd stuck with me when a lot of other folks had abandoned me. He'd kept it real when others had blown smoke up my ass. It would have been a lot easier to just sign the J Records deal, get a good check, and make everyone happy. It would have been a compromise, but one a lot of people could have lived with.

Not me.

You cannot, under any circumstances, compromise when it's *your* vision on the line. You have to be prepared to go against popular opinion and turn down money—even if it jeopardizes your relationships—until you're confident you've found the right opportunity.

Would you marry a man just because he proposed? Or a woman because your friends think she's great? I hope not. You don't make a commitment like that just because someone else wants you to. I don't care if you're single, thirty-seven years old, and every time you talk to your mother the first thing out of her mouth is, "When you giving me a grandchild?" You wait until you're 100 percent sure he's Mr. Right before you even think about saying yes.

Would you put an offer on a house because the agent you're working with is getting tired of showing you around and just wants his commission? Hell, no! You'd get another agent and go to open house after open house until you finally find the home you can afford and that you're excited to spend the rest of your life in.

When you settle, you're demonstrating a lack of confidence. If your journey hasn't been easy, you might start to question the value of what you're doing. Maybe you'd better grab the next thing that gets offered before you never get offered anything again. When you begin thinking like that, you've lost the hustler's spirit.

I was recently talking to a friend who was struggling to find that confidence. He'd started a business from the ground up and poured his heart and soul into it. After years of hard work, he found success, and bigger companies started making offers. He looked at where his industry was heading and decided it was the right time to sell. He entered negotiations with one company and spent months and months going over the terms of the deal. He spent tens of thousands of dollars on lawyers. Then, just before he was about to sign on the dotted line, the other company pulled out. The deal was dead.

My friend was stunned. It seriously messed him up. He'd already started thinking about that dream house he would buy with the proceeds. Vacations he'd take his kids on. He'd seen all those zeros in his bank account, and now they were gone.

He was depressed. He felt like he'd spent so much time and money for nothing. The idea of starting new negotiations gave him anxiety. He told his lawyers to find the quickest deal they could. He wasn't worried about fit. He wasn't worried about long-term potential. He just wanted to get something done. He'd lost confidence in his value.

It was time for a pep talk. He needed to reconnect with the hustler's spirit that had led him to start the business in the first place. "Remember, if just one person was interested, that means your idea has value," I reassured him. "Don't panic. Don't settle for something else unless it's right. There are companies out there who prey on people in your exact situation. Don't walk into their trap. Get back to work and wait for the right partner to emerge."

I could address his uncertainty directly because I could relate to what he was feeling. When you pour everything you have into something and it doesn't work out, insecurity sets in. That's when you're vulnerable. The predators will sense that self-doubt and try to take advantage of it.

I felt the same kind of vulnerability after I got dropped from Columbia. The self-doubt started to sabotage my energy. My fans probably didn't sense it, but it was there. Thankfully, my hustler's spirit was stronger than any pessimism that might have infiltrated my spirit.

I had the confidence and patience to wait until the right deal was in front of me. I believed in my value, and eventually I was rewarded for it.

In just a couple of years I went from being dropped to releasing one of the bestselling hip-hop albums of all time. Now, the guys I used to sit next to that I hustled with? They would say I was lucky that Interscope came after me. But, as my grandmother would say, "You were truly blessed."

It might seem obvious, but people don't always see the value of a strong association. Sometimes—and this is especially true with artists—they get so caught up in their own hype that they don't think they need anyone to cosign them. They believe their heat alone is more than enough to get the job done. It's great to have confidence, but never let your ego blind you to an association that can take you further than you'll go on your own.

I saw this happen firsthand with a Philadelphia rapper named Gillie Da Kid. He was brought to my attention by the legendary Philly disc jockey Cosmic Kev. At the time, I was riding sky-high off my first couple of albums and constantly had people pitching me their artists. Kev was seasoned, so he knew the best way to get my attention was to approach me humbly. "Yo, I've never asked you for anything," he told me, which was true. "But I need one favor: I need you to listen to Gillie's joint, 'cause this is gonna pop."

I had a lot of respect for Kev, so I gave it a listen. He was right—it felt like a hit. I liked the song so much I decided I would "walk" Gillie into Interscope. If you're not familiar with that term, it means that instead of making him pitch his music to an A&R person, I would personally take his music to the executives in charge.

Having someone "walk you in" is what you want as an artist. It allows you to bypass all the lower-level people and talk directly with the top brass. It's especially valuable if the person walking you in just sold 25 million records for the label. Then you've really got everyone's attention.

I played Gillie's song for one of the top executives. At first they weren't as sold as I was. Then I told them my plan. "Listen, I don't think it makes sense to put Gillie on G-Unit," I explained. I didn't know if his sound would mesh with what we were doing at the time. "But if you guys sign him, I'll give the project my full support. I'll put the battery in his pack." The executive said, "Okay, that changes things. Let's do it." If I cosigned it, they knew it was going to sell.

We sent word back to Gillie that there was a deal on the table at Interscope. I forgot exactly how much they were offering, but I remember it being fair. Evidently, Gillie didn't see it the same way. "Nah, fuck that," he replied when Kev told him the number. "They gotta give me a million to sign."

I was surprised at his response, but out of respect for Kev, I went back and told the execs what he wanted. They felt it was way out of line for someone without much of a track record. They were willing to bring him on, but not for a million bucks outright.

Gillie wouldn't budge. People tried to talk to him, telling him that there was momentum he needed to harness, but he had his mind set on that million dollars. And when Interscope wouldn't give it to him, he passed on the deal. It was an ill mistake.

His error was he allowed himself to get in a zone where it was all about the money. His vision was too limited. Another factor was his environment. Philly is a big enough city, but its rapper community is pretty small. Everyone knows what the other guy is doing. Gillie probably heard about what Beanie Sigel had signed for, or what Philly's Most Wanted had gotten, and figured he had to hold out to be in the same league.

It was the wrong way to assess a deal. Instead of focusing on what the next man got, he should have focused on the larger opportunity, which was having me get behind his project. With all my momentum, I could have given him the heat he needed and then some. I have zero doubt that with my cosign, Gillie would have ended up making way more than a million dollars from Interscope.

Instead, he signed somewhere else, and several years later released an album that didn't get the proper support or attention. That was pretty much it. He never had his moment, despite his proven skills. Today, Gillie's a respected OG on the Philly scene and has a popular podcast, but he never experienced the level of success he should have as a rapper.

FOCUS ON THE POTENTIAL—NOT THE PAYDAY

When we look back at how I evaluated the Eminem deal, notice all the positives I focused on: elite talent to work with, a lack of internal competition, and access to a new fan base.

Now notice what I didn't mention: money.

I knew whatever number we agreed on would ultimately be irrelevant compared to what I would earn long term with the proper plan in place. My signing bonus with Shady Records was "only" one million dollars. But I ended up earning so much money off that deal, the signing bonus is almost irrelevant.

It might sound counterintuitive, especially in a chapter titled "Know Your Value," but the first check you receive should never be your biggest concern. Always focus on the long-term potential instead.

That was the principle behind one of the best business decisions I ever made, which was my deal with Vitamin Water back in 2004. Today I'm celebrated for that decision, but like when I signed with Eminem, at the time it had a lot of people scratching their heads.

That includes Chris Lighty, who was skeptical when I first told him I wanted to invest in a water company. "Sell water? To who?" he asked. At the time, a lot of rappers were making good money by promoting liquor like Hennessy and Courvoisier. In Chris's mind, booze was the smarter space to invest in.

There was a method to my madness, though. I knew, through personal experience, people don't always drink alcohol at live events. Maybe they're under twenty-one or don't want to shell out $20 for a stale beer. One thing that is always available and popular at any concert, however, is water. It's always going to be the top-selling beverage at events.

One day I was walking through the water aisle in the supermarket and noticed a "premier" brand selling for $3. Then I saw the no-name brands were going for closer to 75 cents. I thought to myself, *If you blindfolded me, there's no way I could tell which is which.* The premium brands had just done a better job at marketing and promoting. That was another breakthrough. It had never occurred to me before, but just like booze, you could mark up water.

Not to mention, water was a more authentic representation of my lifestyle. I don't really drink alcohol, but I definitely consume lots of water. And because I consume so much of it, I know drinking pure water alone got boring. To switch things up a bit, I started drinking flavored water. One day I was working out in a gym in LA and my trainer gave me a bottle of something called Vitamin Water. I took a swig and liked it so much that I made a mental note that it was a company I should invest in. Just to make sure I didn't forget, I actually threw my empty bottle in my gym bag.

When I got back to my hotel, I called Chris and told him about the flavored water I liked so much. He did some research and found out it was distributed by a company called Glacéau that was based in Queens, of all places. With my insistence, we decided that this was the brand I should be working with.

Once I'd sold Chris on my vision, we hatched a plan. During a commercial for my Adidas sneakers that showed me working out in a boxing gym, we snuck in a shot of me taking a sip of Vitamin Water. It was barely half a second, but it was enough. A friend of Chris's who worked at Glacéau saw the spot and reached out to see if I'd be interested in an endorsement deal. They had just developed a new product called Formula 50 (because it contained 50 percent of the RDA of seven vitamins and minerals). Who better to sell Formula 50 than me?

I agreed, but I countered with something different than the standard endorsement deal. Instead of taking a five- or low-six-figure deal to appear in the ads, I wanted to invest in the entire company. Instead of taking cash from them, I actually wanted equity in the company.

It was a very aggressive ask, and it caught Glacéau off guard. They weren't opposed to the idea, but they were nervous about getting into business with me on that level. They only knew me as the rapper who had been shot nine times, and they weren't sure they wanted to be associated with that sort of energy.

I needed to put their minds at ease, so I took a meeting with the company's CEO. I didn't show up with an entourage, just Chris and me. I expressed how much respect I had for their brand—I was already a loyal consumer—and how hard I planned to work at spreading the word. I didn't give off the arrogant attitude or aggressive energy they were probably expecting. I presented myself as someone who saw a special business opportunity and was prepared to work his ass off to make it happen. And that was the truth.

My approach helped them get over their apprehension, and we were able to strike an equity deal. The next order of business was to reimagine Formula 50. To me, Vitamin Water was just a more upscale version of "quarter water," the flavored drinks you would get in bodegas for 25 cents a pop. As anyone from the hood can tell you, the most popular flavor of quarter water has always been grape. No one from the hood was trying to mess with lychee- or passion-fruit-flavored water, which was what they had been thinking about. Formula 50 had to be grape to resonate with my base. Glacéau respected my vision and changed the flavor to grape.

Once everything was settled, I promoted the hell out of Vitamin Water. I was on billboards and bus stop ads across the country. I filmed an iconic commercial where I conducted a symphony orchestra playing "In Da Club" while taking sips of Formula 50. It seemed everywhere you looked, I was extolling the virtues of Vitamin Water.

Glacéau's market share began to rise, and the beverage industry took notice. So much so that, in 2007, Coca-Cola purchased Glacéau for $4.1 billion. Of course I got piece of that. I'd like to give you the number, but I signed a nondisclosure agreement to never name the actual price. Let's just say I did very, very well.

It was the biggest come-up of my life, which I later celebrated in my song "I Get Money":

I took quarter water sold it in bottles for 2 bucks
Coca-Cola came and bought it for billions, what the fuck?

"What the fuck?" was definitely what the rest of hip-hop was asking once they heard about how much I'd made. There had been groundbreaking hip-hop deals before—Run-DMC and Adidas, LL Cool J and FUBU—but nothing even remotely on this level. In an environment where everyone was looking for the next deal, I had identified something that was sitting in plain sight but that no one else had been able to see.

I was confident enough in my vision not to get caught up in worrying about the up-front money. To be fair, I was still riding high off of the success of my recording career and wasn't pressed for another $100K. I understand that not many people may find themselves in that position. Still, no matter what your situation is financially, if you really believe in something, I'd always recommend you go for the piece of equity over an up-front payday.

When you ask for equity, you're essentially betting on yourself. When I did that with Vitamin Water, it was a fairly unique bet to make. Now, with the rise of start-ups, it's a form of compensation that a lot of people are looking for, especially in the tech and media fields. It's always smart to negotiate for equity, but you also have to be savvy about what sort of equity you're getting. Because all slices of the corporate pie are not always equal.

If you're about to negotiate a deal with a company that might include equity, the first thing you must do is hire a lawyer. I don't care if you're broke, this is something you must do. Borrow the money if you have to. Then make sure it's someone who is familiar with corporate governance. Don't hire your cousin who does real estate work or the guy who handled your divorce because they're a little cheaper. Get someone who specializes in these sorts of contracts. Spending a few extra dollars at this stage, even if it hurts for a minute, can save you a ton of money down the road.

You should also familiarize yourself with some basic issues so that you're educated when you do speak with someone. Most people aren't going to be in the same position I was in with Vitamin Water, where I could actually get a piece of the company.

Instead, you're probably going be in a situation where a company is offering you a lower salary offset by stock options. Before you can determine whether that's a good deal, you need to know the overall valuation of the company. If the company already put out an IPO (an initial stock offering), you can calculate its market value by multiplying the company's stock price by the number of shares outstanding. If it hasn't issued any stock yet, it's going to be harder to figure out. You're probably going to have to ask the founders what their method of determining the valuation of the company was. If they don't want to tell you, or give you a vague answer that doesn't make sense, then it's probably not a deal that you want to pursue anyway.

If you're being offered stock, you need to know whether it is vested or not. Most stock options are vested, which means you have to stay with the company a certain amount of time before you can cash them in. If your option doesn't vest for four years, you need to ask yourself if you're comfortable staying with the company that long. If not, the equity might not be worth it.

A lot of times people hear the terms "equity" or "stock options" and think they've hit the lottery. It is true that equity and stocks are one of the quickest ways to get a lot of money, but you just can't walk into a start-up situation blindly. You have to educate yourself and ask a lot of difficult questions early in the process. That way, if the start-up you're working for does become one of the rare ones that sees its value skyrocket, you're going to be perfectly positioned to reap the rewards.

I've seen a lot of people miss out on golden opportunities by chasing a check instead of maneuvering for a piece of equity. Probably the most egregious example is my former associate Sha Money XL.

I met Sha when I was first getting into music. Before signing to Interscope, I recorded a lot of the songs for my mixtapes in a studio Sha operated in the basement of his house on Long Island. It wasn't a professional setup—not by a long shot—but it got the job done. More important, Sha provided a safe and secure space to record when a lot of bigger studios didn't want to fuck with me.

Because of his loyalty and consistency during a difficult time, I considered Sha my partner. We never formalized the relationship, but in my head it was a foregone conclusion that when I signed my next major label deal, Sha would eat off of the situation, too.

So imagine my surprise when one of the first things Sha did after I signed the Interscope deal was present the label with a $50,000 invoice. He wanted to be reimbursed for the recording sessions we'd done at his house. That blew me away on several levels. First off, we'd never discussed Sha charging me for the time at his place. And, if that was something he felt he was owed, why would he submit something so overinflated? Fifty thousand dollars to record in a basement? It was disrespectful.

I decided to try to talk some sense into Sha. "Look, I didn't think you were going to hand me a bill for what we did at your crib," I told him. "But if you feel like you need to get paid for those sessions, just take $30,000 and a point of the album."

I was offering less cash than he wanted, but it was actually a very generous deal. A "point" was an industry term that meant for every album I sold, Sha would receive 1 percent of the royalties earned. In the record business, points are what everyone is looking for. If an album really takes off, there's no limit to the amount you might make. Judging from the buzz around me, we were talking about an album that was definitely going to take off.

Sha wasn't interested in the point. Even his lawyer told him he was crazy. "Take the fucking point," the guy told him. "I'll give you $20,000 right now for it. What the fuck is wrong with you?"

He wouldn't even listen to his own attorney. Sha wanted his $50K from me and wasn't going to budge. He ended up getting it, but it would be a decision that cost him dearly. That single point on *Get Rich or Die Tryin'* ended up being worth $1.3 million.

He didn't just lose over a million dollars either. After *Get Rich or Die Tryin'* started flying off the shelves, Interscope offered me a $15 million deal for G-Unit Records. Once that deal was signed, I noticed Sha started hanging around my offices a lot; I guess he thought he was going to get some of that budget, too. Nope. "You ain't getting none of this money," I was quick to tell him. "You took your equity out of the situation when you demanded that fifty thousand. Now you've been paid for everything you've done."

Our relationship was never the same. In just a few months I'd gone from seeing Sha as a partner I was prepared to share millions with to just another contractor.

Sha undercut his own position by not understanding how to negotiate. He got fixated on that $50,000 and couldn't get himself unstuck.

This is one of the biggest mistakes you can make when entering a negotiation: Never get fixated on a number. You want the person you're negotiating with to *think* you're stuck, but when the right moment comes, you have to be prepared to move off it. That's not undervaluing yourself. It's just a matter of understanding that successful negotiations are built on give-and-take. If you refuse to concede anything, the conversation isn't going anywhere.

If Sha had understood that basic principle, he would have seen that there was a very easy path toward getting what he wanted—and then some. Let me show you how he should have handled it.

When I offered him $30K and a point, he shouldn't have dismissed it out of hand. Instead, he should have come back to me with some humility. "You know what, Fif? I was trippin' by submitting that bill. Don't worry about the $50K." Even if he didn't believe it in his heart, he should have sensed I was pissed and softened his position a bit.

Once he had gotten me to let down my guard just a bit, he could have come back with a stronger ask: "I know I was thirsty with the bill. But I did put a lot of time into this album. We were really in the trenches together on it. And I really appreciate you offering the point. But instead of one, could we do two points?"

If he had said that, I wouldn't have been upset. He *was* in the trenches with me, after all. He had proved his worth and loyalty. I would have probably said, "Lemme think about it," and then countered with one and a half points.

In all likelihood, that's where we would have settled. Sha would have walked away with close to $2 million from that deal alone. Plus, our relationship would have remained on strong terms, and he would have likely gotten points on subsequent albums as well.

Instead, he got only a fraction of that. I was offering him a chance to enter a new tax bracket, and he negotiated himself into nickels and dimes due to ego, insecurity, and, possibly, lack of faith. That's not hustling stronger. It's hustling weaker.

I believe one of the reasons Sha failed to negotiate his proper value is because he took the process personally. Maybe his pride told him he shouldn't have to ask me for anything. Maybe he didn't trust me. Or maybe it was just plain old greed.

Whatever his reasons, Sha clearly let things get personal. This is the other huge mistake people make when they start negotiating. They take offense at what's being offered because they feel it's an unfair representation of what they've put in.

Please understand this: negotiations are not personal. Again, I don't care if you're dealing with a longtime business partner, a friend, or a family member: the other person is *never* going to start at a number you think is fair. It's just not how the process works. They're always going to start at a lower number and then come up if you push back. Just how high they come up depends on how good a negotiator you are. But they're never going to *start* at that number.

Trust me. I've been part of thousands of negotiations, and none of them have started exactly where I wanted them. Even with all the leverage I have as a proven entrepreneur and entertainer, to this day I still have to work to get to the number I'm looking for.

The key is I never react emotionally. Even if the energy I'm projecting is of someone who is pissed off and about to walk away, internally I'm cool. I'm just waiting to see how my energy is received. If I push and push, and the other side still won't move, then I will walk away. But more often than not, a few pushes get me to where I want to be. And then we seal the deal. Once it's done, it's like all the posturing and threatening never even happened. Everyone hugs, raises a toast, and talks about how excited they are to be in business together.

When I first started operating in corporate America, I can't lie, this threw me off a bit. In the streets, there are certain words that you can't come back from. In the boardroom, it's different. People will call you "outrageous," "liar," "motherfucker," and "cocksucker" but then act like it never happened once the deal is reached. In the streets those might be the last words you ever say if you say them to the wrong person. But in the corporate world, it's different. Those words never really carry any weight to them. It is all part of the process, something that has to be tolerated to reach a common ground.

You should always fight for your worth, but never take offense that you have to fight in the first place. When you do that, you're moving off of emotion. It might not be *fair*, but to get what you want, you can only move off of strategy. Anything less will leave you hustling backward.

CREATING REAL *POWER*

One of the best deals I ever negotiated was with Starz for my TV show *Power*. It was also, at least initially, one of my *least* lucrative deals. But that didn't faze me at all. My strategy when I started talking with Starz was not to get the biggest check possible — it was to create the biggest opportunity possible.

From the moment I came up with the idea for *Power*, I knew I was sitting on something special. My goal wasn't just to launch a single TV show. I was looking to create a franchise where the characters were so compelling that eventually they could support their own spin-offs. What Marvel had done in movies, I wanted *Power* to do for TV. I wasn't trying to create a planet. I wanted to create a universe.

To bring that universe into existence, I had to be very humble with my initial demands. Despite my success in music and movies, my track record in television wasn't as strong. My only other foray into TV, an *Apprentice*-esque reality show for MTV called *The Money and the Power*, had been canceled after one season. I had to accept that I didn't have the leverage to demand a superstar-size check. Yes, Starz believed in my vision, but they weren't ready to break open the bank. The budget they were offering was limited. If I wanted the show to be a hit, I'd have to spread that money around.

That's why I agreed to do the first season for just $17,000 an episode. Over eight episodes, that came out to $136,000. Mind you, it wasn't just $17,000 for acting in the show. I was also the executive producer. That meant I spent months in the writers' room and working with showrunner Courtney Kemp. When it was time to promote, I had to be front and center on *Good Morning America*, calling in to radio stations, and shaking sponsors' hands. I was making a total commitment to the show. For 136 grand.

From a strictly financial perspective, it looked like a terrible deal for me. I could have made three times the amount just by doing a few club appearances or a ten-minute show. Forget about getting paid "fairly." Given how much time I invested, I basically paid myself to make that first season of *Power*.

When some people found out how much I'd agreed to do the season for, they were shocked. They figured I would have told Starz, "Man, I'm 50 Cent. I can walk into a club, pretend to drink a glass of champagne for five minutes, and get paid fifty thousand dollars. No way I'm signing this." That response might have seemed in character for 50 Cent, but it would have been a very shortsighted strategy. That's how Sha Money or Gillie Da Kid might evaluate a situation. But not Curtis Jackson.

By doing *Power* for well below my normal rate, I was betting on myself again. And this bet paid off spectacularly. *Power* quickly became Starz's highest-rated show by a wide margin. Over the past five years, it's singlehandedly driven the network's success. That metric has given me a lot of leverage in negotiations. When I first started talking to them, I had to be a little down-to-earth. After the show blew up, I could afford to be more aggressive.

I built so much leverage that I just re-signed with Starz for $150 million. The deal includes a three-series commitment and a fund to help develop other G-Unit projects. When it's all said and done, it will probably be worth a lot more than even that.

Even as I was hustlin' on the set, in the writers' room, and on the promo runs, I never for a second thought my true value was only $17,000 an episode. That was just the number I had to agree on to jump-start the process. My true value was going to lie in executive-producing and starring in a hit TV show that would birth multiple spin-offs — and multiple revenue streams. Everything I was doing in Season 1 was meant to put me in a better position to make that happen.

To be fair, I could afford to work for cheap that first season. I understand most people aren't in such a fortunate position. For you, taking less money up front might mean encountering real hardship. It might mean having to work a second job on top of whatever venture you're pursuing. It might mean taking out loans or giving up your apartment and moving in with a roommate. I realize steps like that can be demoralizing, but I promise that these choices will be worth it in the long run. Securing the best long-term potential is always worth making sacrifices in the moment.

JUST DO SHIT

Not long after *Power* launched, I was at a party at Jamie Foxx's house in LA. At one point I was telling Jamie and a bunch of guys on his team a version of the same story I just shared with you—how I went to Starz with a vision, didn't get caught up on how much I was getting paid, and used that financial flexibility to fully execute my vision.

"You see that? You see how 50 just did that?" Jamie told his friends when I was done. "He just be doing shit. We gotta stop asking and just start doing shit, too! Let's go!"

Jamie was just trying to motivate his team—in reality, he makes as many things happen as anyone—but in that moment he managed to capture one of my fundamental principles in creating success: just do shit!

It seems like an obvious enough approach, but we spend a lot of time waiting for permission to do shit instead of just making it happen. We fall into the trap of thinking the so-called gatekeepers—a boss, an executive, an agent, a critic—have to unlock that door ahead for us when, more often than not, it's already wide open, just waiting for us to walk through.

One of the best ways to bypass those gatekeepers is to go directly to the people with your ideas. The more time I spend with corporate executives, the more I've noticed how clueless they are about how to connect with the public. They'll form focus groups, commission studies, hire influencers—everything *but* go directly to the people.

My strategy has always been the opposite. I always try to connect with people on the most basic level. Take my involvement in the spirits industry. When I first got involved with Effen Vodka back in 2015, the conventional wisdom said that the best way to sell vodka was to make it appear aspirational. Premium liquor had to represent a lifestyle that was slightly out of reach.

That might have been what the marketing departments thought would work, but that's not how I was going to approach things. I decided the best way for Effen to increase its market share was for me to be literally within reach of my fans. The way I would do it was by hosting as many promotional events as possible.

When I first got into the music business, meet and greets were an incredibly effective way to sell CDs. If I did an event at Tower Records, Best Buy, or Virgin Megastore, there would be lines out the door and around the corner. People wanted to shake my hand and get a picture— to have a connection with me, even if it only lasted five seconds.

Then MP3s replaced CDs, and there wasn't anything to sell in person anymore. Meet and greets largely went out of style.

I could understand the music business moving away from them, but why couldn't they be relevant for spirits? CD sales dried up, but last time I checked, no one had managed to figure out how to stream a bottle of vodka. I didn't see any reason why meet and greets couldn't be extremely effective to sell liquor. That desire for a connection was still there.

To test my theory, I decided to do a series of meet and greets in liquor stores around the country. Specifically, I focused on smaller cities—places like Milwaukee, Pittsburgh, and Jacksonville—where I knew my presence would be a big deal.

The meet and greets were extremely successful. People would hear I was going to be at a liquor store in their town, and they'd line up just like they used to for CDs. Even better, when people waited in line for a CD, they usually bought just one, but if you wait for two hours to see me at a liquor store, you're probably not going to buy just one bottle. Instead, you might say, "I'm gonna get one bottle for tonight. But I might as well get another couple bottles, since Christmas is coming and a lotta people are going to be over." Just like that, I've sold three bottles to one person. And the line is around the corner.

My in-store appearances were so successful that Puffy tried to copy them by having one in the Bronx with French Montana for Cîroc. It didn't work for him, though. The problem was that French is always in the Bronx. You might see him pull up to the liquor mart on a regular day, so why wait in line to see him? What Puffy should have done was follow my lead and hold the event in a smaller market. Then he would have sold some bottles.

In addition to meet and greets, I used social media to connect directly with the public. If someone posted a picture of themselves on IG holding a bottle of Effen, I might repost it to my page. That person would see their followers increase dramatically, and they'd become loyal to the brand. Other people would see what was happening and be encouraged to post their own pictures with Effen bottles. I was training my fan base to see the incentive in supporting Effen. It became a cool thing to do. I had created an online movement without spending a single marketing dollar.

I see a lot of parallels between how we moved in the crack game back then and how savvy people are moving on social media today. People move based on direct interaction. Not on what a suit tells them.

The internet is making the gatekeepers much less relevant. For instance, back in the day, if you had a great idea for a film, you had to pitch it to a studio. Because you needed access to their money and promotional potential, the studio was the gatekeeper that confirmed whether your idea had any value.

Today, if you have a film idea you're passionate about, you don't need that studio to get it off the ground. You can literally shoot that movie with a smartphone, edit it on your laptop, and distribute it yourself on YouTube. If your work is good enough and speaks to your audience, people will watch it. It might take time, but eventually the word will spread that you've made something of value.

Then the studios will reach out to you. You've proved that you have an audience. But even more important, you've shown that you actually know how to make something. That's critical.

All sorts of people have ideas. Some people even have scripts. But very few people have proved that they actually know how to make something. To build it from scratch. That's actually the most important thing to a studio. They want to know that if they sign you to a deal, you're not going to waste their money and never deliver anything. Sure, they'd prefer it not suck, but the most important thing to them is that it actually gets made. Do you ever wonder why in Hollywood some directors keep getting rehired even though they haven't had a hit in years? Because at least the studio knows they're going to deliver.

By creating your movie on your own, you've already passed that test. You've shown that you can make something, that if a studio gives you a check, you're actually going to give them something back in return. Combine that with a built-in audience and *bam*! Now you've got leverage! You're not a dreamer with an idea hoping that someone takes a chance on you. You're a proven asset who can sit back and wait for the best deal.

I'm using film as an example, but adopting a "just do shit" mentality will help you in every field. Don't sit around hoping someone will invest hundreds of thousands of dollars in your restaurant idea. Start a food truck for a lot less and make sure what you're serving is so delicious that the lines are around the block. If you do that, it's only a matter of time before an investor shows up with a check.

Another example that I'm inspired by is travel bloggers. Those kids aren't waiting for a big travel agency or a TV network to write them a check. They bought a plane ticket and a decent camera, traveled to some cool places, and started creating their own content. No gatekeepers told them they could do it, they just did it. In fact, a lot of older folks hated on the concept. "These kids want to get paid for posting videos on vacation?" skeptics would say. "They need to get a real job." But those kids had a vision. They stuck with it and basically created their own industry. Today, over 30 percent of travelers say they consult travel blogs when picking their next vacation. Because of that, tourism boards pay travel bloggers hundreds of millions of dollars to promote different locales. Resorts give them free rooms. Airlines give them free flights. There's a reason it's become one of the most desired jobs for millennials. But it never would have happened if some young kids with a connecting flight and a camera hadn't said, "Let's just do this shit!"

THE GREATEST EXPENSE

I've bought a lot of luxury items over the years: more watches and chains than I can count, enough Lamborghinis, Rolls Royces, Maseratis, and Ferraris to fill up a parking garage, and one of the most opulent mansions in America.

But easily the most expensive thing I spend is time.

I've taken chains back to my jeweler (most of them, actually). I once even returned a Ferrari because I couldn't figure out how to start it. And yes, I did sell that mansion.

But I don't have a receipt that can get me back the time I've put into something. That's why you have to place a premium value on how you spend the limited time you have.

The person who really drove that lesson home for me was Eminem. Many years ago I was hanging out with Em in the studio, and I started thinking about putting together a massive world tour. "It could be me, you, Dr. Dre, and Snoop," I told him. "That show would sell out stadiums all over the world. There's nobody who wouldn't want to see that show."

Even as I was pitching it to Em, I could see the stadiums filled with excited fans. I could see millions of dollars going into each of our bank accounts. It was like a dream sequence in my mind.

"Em, we need to do this!" I shouted, almost jumping out of my seat. Em heard me out and then said, "Man, this sounds great. It sounds really amazing . . . but I don't want to do it."

His answer didn't register with me. Did he just say we're not going to go and get that money? That couldn't be right. "Why not?" I asked incredulously.

"Because I don't want to go on tour for months and then I come home and Hailie's grown," he explained, referring to his daughter.

In that moment, I didn't understand where Em was coming from. I couldn't get past what I viewed as a missed opportunity. But, over time, I came to understand Em's perspective better.

Yes, it's always nice to pick up a check. But a check is never more important than an experience you value. Granted, Em had the luxury of already having made tens of millions of dollars. He didn't have to worry about financially supporting Hailie. He was good on that count. He just needed to focus on emotional support.

But I believe Em would have made the same decision even if he was still broke and living on Eight Mile Road in Detroit. One of the reasons Em has been so successful is that he's never chased things. He's never let external forces tell him what to care about. He's cognizant of what matters to him, and that's what he focuses on. And I would argue that *not* chasing dollars is one of the main reasons he's made so many of them. If Em had chased the "easy" money, he would have come out of the gate presenting himself as a Vanilla Ice knockoff. Or he would have made rock 'n' roll records, which is what a lot of folks told him to do. But he had too much talent and respected hip-hop too much to ever do that. He was going to pay his dues and establish himself as a real MC, even if it meant putting off getting paid at first.

Money is the goal, but oftentimes in order to get it, you have to retrain your brain to value experience. Especially if you weren't born with a silver spoon in your mouth. Maybe you weren't able to go to a college where your friends could "walk" you into their parents' company and get you a good job. If you weren't blessed with any of those advantages, you have to figure out how to get access to whatever world you're trying to get a start in. And a lot of times the easiest way to break in is by working for free—as an intern.

I did that a couple of times when I was trying to get into the music business. The first time was when I was working with Jam Master Jay. I was getting frustrated that I was stuck out at Jay's studios in Queens most of the time and wasn't really getting a taste of the larger scene. So Jay did me a solid. He was friendly with a guy named Jesse Itzler, who was active in the music industry. Jesse had written a bunch of songs for artists like Tone Loc, as well as the New York Knicks theme song "Go New York Go." Through that, he'd gotten a job to run the Knicks street team. After Jay introduced us, Jesse made me an offer: if I'd help him with the Knicks street team, he'd show me the ropes in the music business. Sounded like a good deal, so every day I'd link up with Jesse and spend a few hours driving around New York in a Knicks van handing out team wristbands and keychains. Then we'd head back to Jesse's studio, and I'd help with whatever song he was working on. Maybe help him find a sample, or figure out how to voice a chorus. My only payment was free Knicks gear, but it was a great education for a kid who was trying to figure out how songwriting and the music business worked.

My most valuable internship came a few years later, after I'd signed to Columbia. Once I realized they were stalling the release of my album, I was left with a choice. Was I going to just head back to the hood and bitch about how this label was fucking me over? Or was I going to do something constructive while I waited? I chose the constructive path. The way I saw it, Columbia might have been stalling, but I was still signed to them. I still had access to their office. I was going to make the most of that access.

Nobody invited me—*just do shit*—but I decided I was going to be an unofficial intern at Columbia Records. I'd been an unofficial intern for Jesse Itzler, who was just hustling for himself, and I'd learned some valuable information, so why not a major company like Columbia? What were they going to do, tell me no? I knew they would let me intern because it was easier than having another conversation about why my album didn't have a release date yet.

Every morning I would take the subway from South Jamaica to the Sony Building in Midtown Manhattan. When I got there, I wasn't messing around, trying to flirt with assistants or smoking weed in the stairwells like most of the visiting rappers. Nope, I got to work. I would pop in on every department and try to soak up as much information as possible.

I'd visit OJ, who oversaw street radio promotion. I'd pick his brain and try to understand how he approached getting a single out to the right people. Then I'd go and sit with Gail, who was my publicist. I'd watch her work the phones with editors and journalists, trying to get stories placed in magazines. She was dealing with other people's projects, but I wanted to learn how the publicity machine worked.

Then I'd go and shadow Julian, who was in charge of artwork. I'd ask him about his thought process when he was designing an album. What sort of visuals were effective at selling albums, and what sort of images didn't work as well?

I basically did that with every department. I kept asking questions and soaking up information until I finally came to a realization: the label couldn't do everything for me.

This might seem like an obvious statement, but back then most rappers didn't truly appreciate the limitations of a label. They thought once they got signed to a major, they could just put things on cruise control and the folks in the offices would do the rest. Those artists thought the record companies were God, but after poking around, I learned that they were very human. Labels could do some things well, but there were other elements that were pretty much out of their hands.

Through "interning," I was able to see that I was going to have to make myself hot before OJ could get my songs played, or Gail would be able to get me magazine articles. I realized that the labels could build on momentum, but they were limited when it came to creating it.

That's why I ended up releasing "How to Rob." I identified that I needed to create a buzz that was going to jolt the label into action. I needed to create my own energy, not hope that someone was going to flip a switch for me.

I would have never come to that realization if I hadn't first decided to create my own internship. They weren't paying me to come in every morning, but the information I absorbed was invaluable. Having a realistic understanding of what a record company *wasn't* going to do for me probably saved my career.

Today, internships seem to get a bad rap. A lot of young people have complained that they're exploitative. Some folks even want to make unpaid internships illegal.

That's shortsighted. If you're interning in an industry that you're passionate about, you're not being exploited. It's just up to you to get the most out of the experience. An internship is an open door. Once you're in, you must take it upon yourself to check out every room in the house.

Let's say you want to be a sneaker designer. Through a lot of hustle, you manage to land an internship at Adidas, but in the marketing department. You don't care about marketing, but you take the position anyway. Smart move, because now you have access.

You must attack working for marketing like it was actually a design position and win the respect of your bosses. Then you parlay being in the building into making other connections. Figure out who works in design and approach them in the cafeteria. Compliment their kicks.

Strike up a conversation. Keep making a point to bump into them until a little bit of a relationship has formed. Then let them know that your true passion is design. Ask if it's cool to come by their department one day and just be a fly on the wall.

If that person senses that you're sincere in your hunger, they'll probably say, "Sure, come through." Now you have an in. You're around people who are doing what you want to do. Capitalize on that opportunity. Ask questions, make observations, and soak up game. Even if it doesn't lead to an actual job down the road—though it might—you'll leave the situation with a tremendous leg up on your competition. You'll have real information on how your passion gets put into practice.

S omeone who really capitalized on the intern experience was Corentin Villemeur, the photographer I mentioned earlier. Corentin grew up in France, where he was a huge hip-hop fan. In 2006 he decided to move to New York City so he could be closer to the culture.

When he got to NYC, one of the first things he did was look up the number for the G-Unit offices, since he was a big fan of our music and lifestyle. He called up, asked if we were hiring, and was told, "Nope, no jobs are available." Corentin didn't accept no for an answer, though. Instead, a few days later, he physically showed up at the office and knocked on the door, hoping to make a case for himself in person. He explained that he had just moved to New York from France, was a huge G-Unit fan, and was willing to do whatever it took to work with us. He met Nikki Martin, who was intrigued by his story, but since there really weren't any jobs available, Nikki told him, "We'll be in touch if anything opens up."

Usually that phrase marks the end of the story, but Corentin still wasn't ready to give up. In addition to being a hip-hop fan, Corentin was also a skilled computer coder. At the time, we had just launched

ThisIs50.com, which was running on Flash. Corentin knew the site would run much better on HTML, which, at the time, very few people were knowledgeable about.

So he called the office back and explained he knew a way to improve our website. Now he really had our attention. When it was clear he knew what he was talking about, we offered him an internship working on the site. Corentin jumped at it and, true to his word, almost immediately made the site better.

That established his value within the organization. I promoted him from an intern to the person in charge of all of my internet platforms. Since he was also a very skilled photographer, he became my in-house photographer. In that role, he's gotten to travel the globe with me, from Africa to Australia, taking pictures and experiencing hip-hop on a global scale.

Corentin was able to make his dream back in France a reality because he understood two key concepts. The first was persistence. He didn't wait for us to post a job listing somewhere. He took the initiative to cold-call our offices. When that didn't lead anywhere, he showed up at the office. That visit didn't directly lead to a job, but it helped him establish a connection with Nikki. It allowed him to go from a name on an email to someone with a story, someone who made a positive impression.

The second smart thing Corentin did was he didn't call us back *asking* for an internship. Instead, he *offered* us something. He studied our organization, saw where we could use improvement, and then saw how he could add value. I don't care if it's hip-hop, film, or the financial sector—if you can make a convincing case that you can add value to an organization, they're going to find a spot for you. Once you've got that spot, now you can build up *your* value. Either within that organization or in another one once you get some experience and titles under your belt.

GET IT ON PAPER

A final word on making sure you always get your fair value. While it's critical to establish your worth, once you do, the most important thing you can do is get it down on paper.

Getting all your agreements, promises, and plans down on paper in the form of a contract is absolutely essential. Never let your value rest on someone's "word."

So many deals in hip-hop have been cemented with a handshake or a pound, instead of a signature on the dotted line.

I've heard so many big promises that never get delivered on. It's easy to promise someone half of nothing. It's easy to promise someone you're going to take care of them "once we get on."

But as soon as someone starts getting paid, those promises get forgotten. Handshake agreements aren't worth shit. When the money starts coming in, the knives start coming out.

In hip-hop, in particular, words like "family" and "forever" get thrown around freely. But they aren't worth a thing. Ask Freeway, Beanie Sigel, or hell, Dame Dash, how tight Roc-La-Familia really was. Not very.

Puffy loved to talk about "Bad Boy for Life." Ask Shyne or Loon how long that life lasted.

Hell, to hear Young Buck or Lloyd Banks tell it, I probably let them down, too. I see it a different way, as I'll explain later, but that's been their perspective at times.

But the bottom line is this: promises aren't worth shit. You have to get papered up.

Whether you're collaborating on an album, a TV script, a landscaping business, or a brewery, you need to get the terms and expectations on paper before you sink too much of your time and equity into it.

Trust me, everyone loves each other at the start. That handshake agreement feels firm when you're starting out. But jealousy and envy are real. They might be buried so deep in a person's nature that it could take years for them to come out, but they'll find a way if there's money involved.

Protect yourself. Put it on paper.

CHAPTER 5

EVOLVE OR DIE

*Look around you. Everything changes. Everything on
this earth is in a continuous state of evolving. . . . You were
not put on this earth to remain stagnant.*

—STEVE MARABOLI

n 1974 David Falk was a student at George Washington University
Law School. He got it in his mind that he wanted to work at Pro-
Serv, a small sports agency in Washington, DC, that specialized in
representing pro tennis players. For months and months he called the
ProServ offices trying to get a meeting with the company's founder,
Donald Dell. He never got a reply. One day he even called seventeen
times during a three-hour period. Dell, either impressed or just an-
noyed by Falk's tenacity, finally took the call. At the end of the convo,
Falk had talked his way into an unpaid internship.

Falk excelled as an intern and landed a full-time job at ProServ
when he graduated law school. Falk wasn't much of a tennis fan,
though. Basketball was his favorite sport. While the rest of the agents
were focused on signing tennis stars, Falk started targeting college basketball players. He built a relationship with Dean Smith, the legendary
coach of North Carolina, and signed several players from the program
when they went to the NBA.

That relationship really paid off when Falk was able to sign a young star from North Carolina named Michael Jordan. In the summer before Jordan's rookie season, Falk set out to get Jordan a sneaker deal.

At the time, the sneaker deals for NBA players were pretty straightforward: you picked a brand (Jordan himself preferred Adidas) and negotiated a contract, and maybe got a supply of sneakers to wear during the season. If you were a superstar, you might also appear on a promotional poster or a TV ad. That was it.

The sneaker companies didn't want to commit too much to NBA players, because there was an unspoken belief that it would be difficult to market an African American athlete to mainstream America.

Falk didn't have any use for the same blueprint everyone else was using. He'd noticed that when the tennis agents in his office struck a deal with a brand, it wasn't just for sneakers. If a tennis player signed with Nike, in addition to sneakers, they'd also rep Nike tennis rackets, sweat suits, shirts, pants, and socks. The tennis players were promoting a complete lifestyle, and Falk didn't see why an NBA player—especially one as spectacular as Michael Jordan—couldn't do the same thing. The agents and brands may have been stuck in their old way of thinking, but Falk sensed that the public was ready to embrace and support black athletes the way they'd supported white icons like Mickey Mantle and Joe Namath.

Falk pitched Nike on a deal that centered on Jordan being the face of his own Nike lifestyle brand, which Falk later dubbed "Air Jordan." Then he added a twist: at the time, players typically only got a flat endorsement fee, but Falk demanded that Jordan receive royalties on all Air Jordan sneakers sold. Nike agreed to Falk's terms on a five-year deal, but with a caveat: if Nike didn't sell $4 million worth of Air Jordans in the first three years, they could walk away from the contract. They were still skeptical that a black athlete could connect with the American public.

They couldn't have been more wrong, and Falk couldn't have been more right. Forget about three years—Nike ended up selling $70 million worth of Air Jordans in the first *two months* after the line launched in 1985.

Turned out black NBA players *could* support a lifestyle brand after all.

Falk would go on to become one of the most successful and powerful agents in NBA history, negotiating over $800 million in salaries. And, of course, Air Jordan would become one of the most iconic sports brands of all time. In 2020, it's expected to generate $4.5 billion in sales.

Falk's deal for Air Jordan is the type that almost every entrepreneur dreams of. So what enabled him to execute such a winning vision?

More than anything, it was his ability to evolve beyond whatever sorts of roles and expectations had been assigned to him and create a new model to support his client.

Falk didn't talk his way into ProServ and then settle into the routine of repping tennis stars. Sure, tennis was extremely popular at the time, but he could sense that the NBA was about to blow. Once he got in the door, he started pushing the company to evolve. By pushing for change, Falk managed not only to change his own career but also to revolutionize the entire sports marketing landscape.

In every profession or field, the most successful people are always the ones who refuse to settle into the status quo, who don't get satisfied and complacent once they achieve something, but always push toward the next goal or challenge.

Conversely, people who get too comfortable or are unwilling to adapt are usually the ones who get left behind.

KNOW WHEN TO SHIFT

In 2009 I appeared on the single "Crack a Bottle" alongside Eminem and Dr. Dre. It was a big track. It went to number one in the US, the UK, and Canada, and would later win a Grammy for Best Rap Performance by a Duo or Group.

To capitalize on its success, I went on a quick world tour, hitting places like Croatia, Switzerland, and India. Everywhere I performed, people went crazy for the song. There's nothing like standing onstage in a foreign country in front of 50,000 people and hearing them singing your lyrics. It's an electric energy you can feel running through your body.

When I got back to the States, I decided to hit the road for some spot dates. When I performed the same song for American audiences, however, the response was totally different. Where the international audiences had been alive and pulsing, the US audiences were lethargic. It was a number one song, but people weren't reacting to it.

It would have been easy to come up with a rationale for the crowd's reaction. Eminem and Dre weren't performing it with me. It hadn't been properly promoted in the urban market. Or we were playing the wrong kinds of venues.

Those would have just been excuses. I'd performed songs without featured artists before. Just like I'd performed songs that hadn't been promoted properly before in venues that were the wrong size. None of that had mattered before. I'd *always* rocked the crowd.

I'm not interested in excuses. What I'm interested in is analyzing information and coming to conclusions.

When I took a hard look at my situation, the answer was clear: hip-hop culture had decided to give me resistance. I had come into the game as the underdog, but now that I was an international success, they couldn't see me the same way anymore. I knew I was still the same guy, but hip-hop had moved on. It was imperative that I diversify if I wanted to keep growing financially and professionally.

It wasn't an easy conclusion to accept, but I understood it. I am a close observer of our culture, and I recognized that my own career had fit into an unmistakable pattern.

Hip-hop loves things that are damaged. It's been the defining trait of the culture. That's how it's been since dudes were rhyming at park jams in the Bronx in the seventies, and it looks like that's how it's going to be until they turn off the damn lights on this thing of ours.

Think about it: every few years, a new "dangerous" and "damaged" rapper appears on the scene and captivates the culture. It started in the Bronx in the early eighties with groups like Grandmaster Flash and the Furious Five. They might look funny today with their skin-tight jeans, knee-high leather boots and studded bracelets, but when they broke on the scene, they were dangerous. America had never seen anything like them before. And, most important, they were damaged. "Don't push me, 'cause I'm close to the edge. I'm tryin' not to lose my head." They set the tone for what the culture wanted from its heroes.

By the late eighties, acts like the Furious Five had been phased out by newcomers like N.W.A. No one had seen a group that damaged and dangerous before, and N.W.A. made those OGs seem safe and cuddly by comparison.

For several years, N.W.A. was the illest thing in sight, until Wu-Tang stormed onto the scene and grabbed that mantle. They were young, wild, and out of control. The culture couldn't get enough. Then 'Pac brought the West Coast back. No one was more thrillingly damaged than 'Pac after he signed with Death Row. He was taking shots at undercover cops, strutting in courtrooms, and surviving assassination attempts. There's no telling how long his reign could have lasted if he hadn't been killed.

After 'Pac, it was my turn. I raised the damaged bar as high as it could possibly go—"He got shot nine times and didn't die"—but eventually the culture didn't see me the same way anymore, either.

I might have been phased out, but the pattern kept going and going. The most recent rapper to harness that energy was Tekashi, but he wasn't able to control it. By the time this book comes out, there will probably be another young boy who has filled Tekashi's shoes. Or maybe even a young girl because nowadays female rappers like Nicki Minaj and Cardi B are going out of their way to let you know that they're just as damaged as the guys.

The fatal mistake a lot of rappers make is refusing to accept the pattern. In their minds they're still damaged, still the same person who broke into the game. But, as I wrote earlier, people tend to stop viewing you as human once you taste success. In the public's mind, once you make it, you're fixed. Time to move on to the next one.

The perceptive artists accept this reality and evolve. The non-observant keep fighting the inevitable, all the way into obscurity. If you look at the rappers of the past, which ones are still relevant today? Outside of myself, it's Ice Cube, Dr. Dre, Method Man, and Snoop. And it's not because of their music. Times change, and no one's checking for that anymore. It's because those first three recognized that their time as a rapper wouldn't last forever, and they transitioned into other pursuits: Method Man into acting, Cube into acting and the Big Three basketball league, and Dre hit the jackpot with headphones and Apple.

Those guys were smart enough and humble enough to understand that the public can never be wrong. When people don't respond to what you give them, they're telling you they've moved on, loud and clear. If you don't hear them, then you're just not listening.

I'm still passionate about making music, but it's not my defining identity anymore. Let's say I went into the studio one night and was able to capture the magic that's behind every great song. The energy was right, the beats were slapping, and I laid down some of my best verses. When the sun rose in the morning, I was sitting on hits.

I might have just created great content, but I still probably wouldn't release those songs myself. Instead, I'd give all those songs to a solid youngblood. Someone with tats all over their face. Who is on Molly *and* lean. Who always looks like he's in zombie mode. Someone who seems like they're *really* damaged.

Why? Because I'm realistic enough to concede that the public is going to be more receptive to it coming from their voice than from my own. Why not give that talented young artist something that can take him to the next level? I can have a piece of the song, and he can get a taste of success. Sounds like a good deal for everyone.

I've accepted that my role in the culture has changed. That doesn't mean I can't still impact it. I just have to utilize different methods.

No matter what you do, you have to be able to accept that your role is going to change. When you first break into a space or industry, you view that inevitability as a positive. If a company's or organization's staff didn't evolve, you'd never get a chance in the first place. That endless evolution is the key that opens the door for you.

Then you work a few years and start to get comfortable. You start to develop habits. If you're good, you might make your company some money. Maybe even a lot of it. Then you'll start to think that the company owes you. Not only for what they're paying you in the moment, but for all you've done for them in the past, too. Maybe you start to take your foot off the gas a bit and begin to believe that your track record will secure your spot forever.

Sorry, but the world doesn't work like that. The same change that brought you in the door can sweep you right back out if you don't keep pushing yourself forward. No matter how many promotions you've received, how many corner offices you've moved into, or even how many times you've seen your name in the headlines, you can *never* settle. You have to keep finding new ways to challenge yourself.

A guy named Ray Dalio runs Bridgewater Associates, one of the largest hedge funds in the world. His personal worth is around $18 billion. He knows a thing or two about what motivates continued success. Here are his thoughts on the importance of personal evolution:

> Once we get the things we are striving for, we rarely remain satisfied with them. The things are just the bait. Chasing after them forces us to evolve, and it is the evolution and not the rewards themselves that matters to us and to those around us. This means that for most people success is struggling and evolving as effectively as possible.

I can promise you that Ray understands what it takes. I've gotten all the things I've ever strived for, and then some. And I'm still not satisfied with my situation.

I've sold almost 30 million records. Evidently, a few people like me as a rapper. But every time I step into the booth, I'm still trying to come up with that killer line. I still want to prove that I've got the best verse.

Just like I want to create more great TV, sell more books, and launch more liquor brands. And a couple of years from now, I suspect I'll have some new project I'm about to launch that I'll be just as excited about as when I was signing my first deal with Interscope.

The moment I close the door on my personal evolution is the moment I need to hang it up. I don't see that door closing anytime soon.

CHANGE WITH THE CULTURE

Being willing to evolve in your own job or position is just part of the battle. You also have to be willing to change with your culture too.

There are a lot of reasons why *Power* has become a bona fide hit. I've received a lot of support from Starz. My showrunner, Courtney

Kemp, has blessed us with fantastic scripts. Cast members like Omari Hardwick, Joseph Sikora, Naturi Naughton, La La Anthony, and Lela Loren all did an incredible job breathing life into our vision.

But one of the biggest factors behind the show's success is that I constructed it to reflect my audience's evolution.

I conceived *Power* for my audience and my audience only. I wasn't trying to tap into a new demographic or attract a wider viewership. I understood I was going to get one chance to get it right with *Power*, and in order to do that, I had to speak directly to *my* people.

I was very confident in my ability to do that. I am nothing if not observant, and I'd spent a lot of time paying attention to my fans over the years. When I first came out, my core audience was young: college-aged kids, or twenty-somethings who were going out to the clubs for the first time.

So what did I do? I made music that I knew would connect with their lifestyle. Take the famous line, "Go shorty, it's your birthday / We're gonna party like it's your birthday!" That *had* to connect. My audience was in the clubs, and every night it was going to be *somebody's* birthday! That line reflected how they were living, and it could never lose its relevancy.

By 2014, my audience wasn't in the clubs every night anymore. If it was their birthday, they might be having a quiet celebration at home with their spouse and young kids. They were maturing.

This is why I built the show around themes that would speak to an older audience. What happens when a love from someone's youth unexpectedly reappears on the scene? What is the fallout when a husband and wife don't have the same vision for their future, or when a son betrays his father? Those are themes that resonate with adults.

At the same time, I needed to capture the energy and excitement my audience felt back when they were still out living the life, still partying and getting into drama every night. That's why I insisted on *Power* being very graphic, especially sexually. It needed that spark.

When I came into the game, rapping about "I'll take you to the candy shop, let you lick the lollipop," it was still considered risqué. Now you have women singing, "Eat the booty like groceries." The ante has been upped, and *Power* needed to match it.

It was no easy task. Saturday night has traditionally been a TV ratings graveyard. Outside of *Saturday Night Live*, there have been very few hits during that time slot over the last forty years. It's the night when the least number of people are sitting at home in front of their TV sets. By putting *Power* on Saturday nights, Starz was basically setting the show up to fail.

Instead, we shocked the network, and the entire industry, by pulling in very strong ratings on a Saturday night. The executives couldn't figure it out at first, but I knew exactly what was happening: my audience was staying home on Saturday nights. I was giving them that old energy, but from the comfort and safety of their couch. Then younger people heard the buzz and started DVRing the show like crazy so they could watch it the next morning. Or they were watching it on their phone via the Starz app. We were killing it across all platforms.

It's been a winning transformation for Starz, too. I allowed them to tap into an audience that they didn't have before. Before *Power*, the network lacked identity, but now they're realigning themselves to be a younger and more diverse version of HBO. It all started with *Power*.

Power's not done evolving yet, either. We're going to roll out four spin-offs on Starz, including one starring Mary J. Blige and Method Man that I'm very excited about.

We've also got a drama about the Black Mafia Family coming next. It's such an organic project, combining the rap and music elements that are so fundamental to hip-hop. I'm confident it's going to be a smash, maybe even bigger than *Power*.

If one generation knew me as a rapper, there's going to be another that knows me as a TV mogul. But only because I was willing to change with the times and my audience.

REFUSING TO EVOLVE

If the success of *Power* was one of my greatest accomplishments, then one of my biggest disappointments is the unfulfilled potential of Lloyd Banks and Tony Yayo of G-Unit.

Both *Power*'s rise and G-Unit's fall are testaments to how growth is often the key element in any successful journey. I always felt that if I had maybe done a better job teaching Banks and Yayo how to evolve and change their habits, they each would be in better places right now. Instead, they both stayed stuck in their mind-sets, and as a result, the success they desired has eluded them.

In Banks's case, a lot of his failure to grow as an artist is connected to his emotional composition. Banks grew up in the same neighborhood as me but was never a part of it in the same way. While I was out hustling (I actually hustled with his father), Banks was more content staying on his porch and watching the world from there.

There's nothing wrong with that, but it underscored a particular aspect of his personality—Banks wanted things to come to him, as opposed to going out and getting them for himself. That's not me trying to assassinate his character—the guy has "Lazy Lloyd" tattooed on his arm. He literally wears his laziness on his sleeve.

He's always projected an unhelpful mixture of being both introverted and cocky at the same time. The kind of person most comfortable being a big fish in a small pond. If Banks was hanging out in the studio with a bunch of unknown MCs, he'd be very confident. He'd enjoy being the center of attention. But if I suddenly showed up, then he'd feel like he got demoted. He'd be bitter he didn't feel like the center of attention anymore.

I get it. I can take up a lot of the air in a room. The problem is that he'd never fight to get some of that oxygen back, which is exactly what a star is supposed to do.

I believe a true star must possess four fundamental abilities: create great material, be a high-energy live performer, have a unique appearance, and possess a strong personality.

Tupac had all four. So does Mary J. Blige. Chris Brown too.

Biggie didn't have all of them, but he was able to compensate in the areas where he was weaker. His appearance wasn't strong initially, so Bad Boy got him new sweaters and put sunglasses over his eye that kept moving all over the place. He couldn't move around the stage so much as a performer, so the head of his label became his dancer. It was a great distraction. The overhaul worked for Biggie. He came into the game with transcendent material, and then they picked up the slack in the areas he wasn't as strong in. He transformed himself into a star with a little management.

If I'm being honest in evaluating Banks, he possesses maybe one of those qualities: he is a very good lyricist. Among what are known as the "punch line rappers" (rappers who will end their bars with a funny or tongue-in-cheek line), Banks likes to call himself the PLK, or Punch Line King. I don't know if he's the king, but I'll give it to him that he's in the conversation.

He is not, however, a great live performer, stylish dresser, or domineering personality. So if he doesn't check those three boxes, how is he going to get bigger and become the star in real life that he is in his head?

To me, one answer was to change how he interacted with the culture. That's why years ago I told Banks to film a video of his life and post it on YouTube. Introduce people to his lifestyle. Let the camera follow him around for a while and see how he moves. Maybe something he says or does will create a spark, go viral, and then he'll have some heat around him again.

What I didn't want him to do was sit there writing punch line after punch line and then grow resentful when no one seemed to care about his mixtapes anymore. They say insanity is doing the same thing over and over again but expecting a different result. If that's so, Banks's temperament was definitely a little crazy.

I'm not saying anything here I haven't said to Banks directly. Another time I sat down with him, just when IG was starting to pop off, and tried to drop this gem on him.

"You gotta get on Instagram," I encouraged him. "You can be a little awkward in person, so this is actually a better way for you to communicate with people. You just put pictures of what you think is cool on your page. That way you can control the conversation without having to feel uncomfortable. It's perfect for you."

"Nah, I don't want to do it," he said.

"Why not? You just put up the pictures and then write some witty shit around it. You can literally put punch lines under your pictures. You can utilize what you're good at to make some new fans!"

"Nah, that's corny," he told me, before adding, "Biggie and 'Pac didn't do that shit."

"They're dead, my man," I told him. "They died before this stuff was even invented. And how do you know they wouldn't be posting on IG if they were alive?" But Banks was adamant. Biggie and 'Pac didn't do social media, so he wasn't going to do it either.

It was a line of thinking that really blew my mind. It suggested that if Tupac were alive, he'd still be wearing leather vests and red bandannas tied around his head, sending girls his beeper number. Or that Biggie would still be wearing Coogi sweaters and playing Mortal Kombat II every night. It's ridiculous. Those guys would have evolved with their music, style, and personality, too.

Biggie was hysterical. His IG probably would have been one of the most popular pages in the entire world. I believe 'Pac would have eventually returned to his revolutionary roots. He would have had an impact on society way beyond music.

Hell, even *I* had evolved in my attitude toward Instagram. When it first came out, I also thought it was corny. In 2014 I told the UK *Guardian*, "I think it's messing up everything. It's giving us all really weird habits. Taking pictures of things you don't even like."

I felt that way at the time, but I didn't close off my mind to it, either. Over time, I started to realize that I just didn't know the platform well enough. I didn't intuit the rhythm of how to post or understand what sort of content resonated. Most important, I didn't appreciate how effective it was in directly reaching people. So I jumped all the way in and embraced it fully. Today, it's one of the most important public-facing tools at my disposal.

Banks was resistant to that sort of evolution. His mind was stuck in the mid-nineties, and he was in no hurry to release it from that trap. To be fair to Banks, it's actually a natural instinct. Scientists are starting to learn that the music we listen to as teenagers has a greater impact on us than music we might hear at any other point in our lives. Our brains are developing at their fastest pace between twelve and twenty-two, and it seems that whatever we listen to during that period tends to get embedded in our minds forever.

Banks was around fourteen years old when Biggie and 'Pac were both popping, so that makes sense that they still resonate with him so deeply. I can relate—I still love the music from when I was that age, too. The difference is that I haven't patterned my career after KRS-One and Kool G Rap. What would be the point of that? They were both incredible in their moment, but I've always been more concerned about creating my own moments rather than copying theirs. When Banks made that comment to me, I realized he'd gone as far as he could go. In fact, my exact thought was "This is someone I can't invest another minute or dollar in."

Everyone knows someone like Banks. The person who only respects a certain era and thinks everything else is trash. It could be music, but it could also be TV, film, sports, or fashion. At first it seems kind of cool that they're so passionate about protecting a legacy, but after a while it gets tired. Most people don't want to keep being lectured about why whatever they're enjoying in the present isn't as good as what came before it. It's great to respect the past, but never to the point that it stops you from moving into the future, or even making the most out of the present.

People who are stuck in the past age prematurely. Their driver's license might say that they're thirty, but their mentality is older than a lot of folks in their fifties and sixties. Age isn't about what year you were born—it's about how you approach the year you're in right now. If you're open to new experiences, willing to take chances, and curious about new topics, you're young. Period.

On the other hand, if you're set in your ways and aren't interested in trying new things, or think you've already learned all there is to know, then you're old. In fact, you're dying.

My beard has a couple of gray hairs in there, but I'm young. I feel and look fresh. Not because I still got a six-pack or wear cool sneakers, but because my spirit is youthful. I'm as excited about what's going to happen this year as I was in 2002 or 2012.

Someone could put me on to a new rapper tomorrow, and I'd be as pumped up as the first time I heard Nas. Just like I could watch a new sitcom and laugh as hard as the first time I watched *Sanford and Son*. I'm never going to cut myself off from new experiences.

I really did try to help Banks, but you can't help anyone who is stuck in either a time or a mind frame. If you feel stuck yourself, then you have to have the courage to come out of whatever little cocoon you've wrapped around yourself and experience all the excitement the world still has to offer.

Tony Yayo's issues were a little different. Like Banks, Yayo was from my neighborhood, but unlike Banks, he didn't stay on his stoop. He was very much out in the streets and running straight into as much action as he could find.

Yayo was wild from the day I met him. In our world, it was a temperament that served him well. He was liable to do anything at any time, and people gave him a wide berth because of it. At the time, I aided Yayo in being so wild. As a crew, we needed that aggressive and unpredictable energy.

Even after we first started experiencing success, we were still living that lifestyle. We didn't see any reason to change. That meant we were going to be very aggressive in taking what we felt was ours. If someone disrespected us or got in our way, our response was to get them out of our way. Whatever it took.

One of my skills is that I absorb information and process it faster than most people. So even as we were running wild through America's stadiums, nightclubs, and hotels, I was beginning to pick up signals that we were going to have to change how we approached things.

The most obvious sign was that there were police everywhere we went. Stadium concourses, hotel lobbies, out in front of clubs—the cops were always there. You'd think there was no other crime happening in whatever city we were in, considering the way they followed us around.

Some of the other signs were less observable. There was a lot of nervous energy around us. It's an easy thing to miss when everything is moving so fast, but if you look past people's acquiescence, the fear is evident. I could read it in the radio jocks, studio engineers, TV hosts, club managers, booking agents, and program managers. They wanted to do business with us, but not if they thought a gunfight might break out any second.

Realizing this, I accepted that I'd have to change how I approached disagreements and confrontations. I was going to express my dissatisfaction differently. I would have to press for what I wanted using managers and agents. I was going to have to fight with lawyers. I was going to have to diversify my strategies if I wanted to capitalize on the opportunities that success was presenting to us.

I also recognized that we'd have to change how we approached time commitments. In the streets, if you want to start selling crack at 1 p.m., then that's when you started. If you want to take a break at 5 p.m., you took it. Want to skip two days outright? That's on you. Just make sure you get it sold. It's a lifestyle that conditions you to do what you want, when you want, so long as you got the product moved.

It's not a lifestyle, however, that's conducive to interacting with corporations. If a radio station expects you at 8 a.m., you shouldn't wander in at 1 p.m. and still expect them to play your song. Just like if a record label books you to record in a studio for two weeks, you shouldn't wait till the tenth day to finally show up and start recording.

Transitioning from the street lifestyle to a more public persona was going to require a new mind-set. Yayo didn't seem to register that. If I got into a disagreement with another artist, Yayo's reaction was "Let's just bang 'em," because that would have been his response back in the neighborhood.

If we got $100,000 for a series of club appearances, Yayo wasn't thinking about putting it in the bank. His first thought would be "Hey, this could get us three and a half kilos of cocaine. Let's flip those, and we'll be sitting on some real money."

Time and time again I'd have to tell him, "Yayo, we can't do that. Nothing else is gonna work if we're just running around doing that dumb shit. We're gonna be outta here just as fast as we got in here."

In Yayo's mind, I was being too uptight. We had always done what we wanted, how we wanted, when we wanted. That's the attitude that had made us hot. Why did that have to change?

In retrospect, a large part of the problem was that success initially came very easily to Yayo. He was locked up when *Get Rich or Die Tryin'* first broke. As soon as he got out of jail I put him onstage. There was no transition period. He didn't have to spend time as an unknown MC slowly getting his feet wet, learning how to interact with industry folks and getting a feel of what it was like to be around corporate people.

Instead, I dropped him directly into the national spotlight and put a lot of money in his hands at the same time. I should have realized that it was not the ideal circumstance in which to suddenly ask him to change habits that had been developed over a lifetime. If anything, I should have known those habits would establish an even tighter grip on him.

I learned that when things are moving very fast and you're constantly being put in new situations and environments, most people tend to lean back into their old habits, not develop new ones.

After years of begging, cajoling, and threatening them to start doing things differently, I had to accept that Yayo and Banks were not capable of doing much more than what they were used to. You can lead a horse to water, but you can't make it drink. Those guys had been standing by the well for years and were still going to die of thirst.

It was extremely disappointing, but I had to accept that many of their dominant character traits—recklessness, resentment, and a lack of discipline—were always going to impede their progress. It was just who they were.

It might not sound like it, but I worked very hard to ensure their success. As I've said, I would have loved for Yayo to have become the next 50 Cent. If Yayo had been able to capitalize on his opportunities, it would have opened so many doors and empowered me to move even faster. I could have transitioned to focusing on other opportunities a lot earlier. Instead, I ended up having to be 50 Cent for a lot longer than I ever intended.

It wasn't just Yayo who I wanted to elevate. The idea was for everyone associated with G-Unit to eventually become bosses in their own right. All they had to do was follow my example. I had set them up to succeed by putting them on my records and letting them share the stage with me on tour. Once they were established, all they had to do was replicate the same formula with new acts that they had selected, repeating the process all the way down. They never did it. Either they didn't want to, or they just didn't know how to identify new artists that they could then own a piece of.

My intention was for G-Unit to be the first branches in a family tree that started with me and would go on to launch generations of rappers. Instead, I created a family tree that lived for one generation before dying. It shriveled up. I birthed my sons, but they didn't bear me any children. It all stopped with them.

THE WRITING IS NEVER ON THE WALL

Back in the days of the Old Testament, there was a Babylonian king named Belshazzar. He led a decadent lifestyle, even by ancient standards. I'm talking about keeping a harem filled with beautiful women and throwing drunken orgies that would last for days.

One night he decided to really push the royal envelope. He usually held his parties in his palace, but on this night, he decided to host one in the city's holiest temple. The king got so drunk that at the height of the party he started drinking wine out of sacred cups that had been brought to the temple from Jerusalem. They were only supposed to be handled by the temple's priests, but Belshazzar was on a mission to prove that there wasn't any taboo he wouldn't break.

Almost immediately after he finished drinking from the cups, the king suddenly saw a disembodied hand writing the following phrase on the temple's wall:

Mene, mene, tekel, upharsin

At first he probably thought he'd had too much wine, but when he took a closer look, he saw the words were really on the wall. That sobered him up quick. He called his wise men over to explain what the hell was going on, but they couldn't understand what the words said either. Then he called over the Hebrew prophet Daniel, who was able to translate what the words meant: "God has numbered the days of your kingdom and brought it to an end. You have been weighed . . . and found wanting."

It was a serious warning, but Belshazzar wasn't worried. He was the king of Babylon, after all. No Hebrew God was going to tell him what to do. So he kept the wine flowing and his party going. He should have listened, though. Fed up with the disrespect, that Hebrew God struck Belshazzar dead that very night and left his empire in ruins.

I share that story because it represents the origins of the phrase "the writing's on the wall." Back then, it was about a king who defied God. Today we use it to describe a moment where it should be obvious that a situation is about to take a turn for the worse.

In a business context, you might say that the writing was on the wall for BlackBerry once the iPhone came out. Or that the writing was on the wall for Blockbuster once everyone started ordering movies from Netflix.

Of course, in hindsight, it's easy to look back at what happened to the BlackBerries and Blockbusters of the world and identify when their fortunes were about to take a turn for the worse. To actually identify when that turn is happening in real time, especially when it's happening to you, is a much harder task.

That's because the writing is *never actually on the wall*.

If that were the case, it would be easy to know when to shift up your business plan, start looking for a new job, or even get out of a bad relationship.

But no one flew a plane over the Blockbuster headquarters trailing a banner that read, "Hey CEO! Renting DVDs is about to be a thing of the past! In the future, everyone will stream their movies!"

Just like you're not going to walk into your job and find a note on your desk that says, "Just a heads-up: we're going to be downsizing in the next year, and your job's going to be eliminated. Might want to start looking for something else now."

Or just like how you're definitely not going to come home one night and find a Post-it on the fridge that says, "Hey baby. Just wanted to let you know I'm having an affair with your best friend."

No, if you're the CEO of Blockbuster, you've got to have enough vision to see where things are going and transition your business to a streaming model before Netflix corners the market.

If you're that employee, you've got to have your finger on the pulse of the industry, realize your company isn't doing as well as it had been, and start looking for that new job while you still have some leverage.

If you're that wife, you need to cut that friend off and have a serious talk with your husband. Or maybe even just kick that man out of the house.

It would be great to get advanced intel whenever we're about to enter a tough period, but unfortunately, none of us will ever be warned as plainly as Belshazzar was.

You might not ever be able to read the writing on the wall, but what you *can* read is the energy around you. If you're willing to be observant and listen, you'll find the messages that energy carries are spelled out almost as clearly as Belshazzar's warning.

For example, let's go back to 2009, the year I went on tour in support of "Crack a Bottle." I had sensed that the crowds weren't responding to my music the same way, and my album sales definitely confirmed it. When I dropped the album *Before I Self Destruct* later that year, it would go on to only move a million copies worldwide. A fantastic number for most artists (especially these days), but a dramatic drop for me at the time. In contrast, 2003's *Get Rich or Die Tryin'* sold 14 million copies worldwide in 2003. *The Massacre*, which dropped in 2005, moved 11 million worldwide. My numbers were clearly moving in the wrong direction.

But when I'd visit the Interscope offices, people were still speaking to me like I was selling 10 million records. "We love you, 50," one exec might tell me, while another might put his arm around me and say, "50, we want to be in this biz with you forever." That was nice to hear, but it wasn't the truth.

The unspoken truth was that the record industry was dying. It wasn't just my sales that were falling off, but everyone's. No label was ever going to make anywhere near as much from monetizing streams as they had from selling CDs.

Unlike some of his peers, Interscope's CEO Jimmy Iovine identified the storm that was headed his way. He calculated that if in the future most people were going to be listening to music on portable devices, headphones were going to take on a much larger significance in the marketplace. Based on that intuition, he started evolving from someone who sold records to someone who sold headphones.

That foresight paid serious dividends for Jimmy, but it didn't pay off as well for the recording artists on his label. Turns out that it's not optimal to work for a record label that isn't actually focused on selling records.

That's why, if the writing on the wall were a real thing, when I showed up to the Interscope offices, there would have been a banner hanging from the side saying "SORRY 50, BUT WE DON'T FUCK WITH YOU ANYMORE." That was exactly what they felt, but again, no one was going to spell it out for me.

I had to decipher that message through the energy that was being directed toward me. I had to notice the differences between how I was handled when I was truly important to the bottom line and when they were just acting like I was. When the money was flowing in, I was treated like a franchise player. My marketing budget was unlimited. No request I made got turned down. Every flight was first class, every hotel stay was in a presidential suite. When I stopped by the offices, people waited on me hand and foot. From the receptionist to Jimmy, everyone was excited to see me and showered me with attention. Why wouldn't they? I was putting money in all of their pockets.

Once the sales started slowing, I felt the energy begin to shift, subtly at first. Contracts started to take longer to get done. My phone calls and emails weren't getting returned as quickly. I was spending more of my time meeting with junior executives than with top dogs.

Unlike a lot of artists, I try to be a student of the industry. I would read publications like *Billboard*, *Variety*, and the *Hollywood Reporter*. I was aware of the fact that music sales had dropped over 50 percent, from 14.6 billion to 6.3 billion, in the decade between 1999 and 2009. Nobody was selling like they used to.

Taking into account the energy I had detected in the office—as well as the overall trajectory of the industry—I decided to make my move.

Instead of waiting for the inevitable ax to drop, I decided to beat Interscope to the punch. I set up a meeting with Jimmy and told him I was ready to move on. "You guys aren't really in the music business anymore," I told him. "I'll be better off as an independent. Plus, I'm going to start getting more active in movies and television. That's what I'm passionate about."

"Oh, you want to do both?" Jimmy asked me. He presented it like he was surprised, but I could tell that it was more of a relief to him than anything else. I guess they wanted me out of their hair.

It would have been easy to feel resentful in that moment. Jimmy was never my boss. He was my partner. And, as partners, we'd done very, very well together. I could have taken a moment to ask why, despite that success, he hadn't always had my back. Why he hadn't done more to support my last few records—even as he'd sunk lots of money into clearly inferior projects like Puffy's *Last Train to Paris*. (Actually, I *do* know why. I'll save that for the next book.) I was already focused on the future, a future that would find me becoming heavily involved in film and television.

Instead, I read the energy in the building, sensed the way the industry was heading, and took control of my own future. Always a better plan than waiting for the writing on the wall to appear.

EXPANDING YOUR MIND THROUGH YOUR CIRCLE

Whenever I hear people say money hasn't changed them, I always think the same thing: that just means they haven't made enough of it yet!

Trust me, when you're making real money, a lot of things change. And one of the most important things is the type of people you hang out with.

I've made a lot of new friends over the last fifteen years. Many are just industry friends. People I see at events, take a selfie with, bullshit with for a couple of minutes, and then keep it moving. But there is a smaller number of people who have really had a beneficial impact on my life. Friends that have dramatically changed how I see the world through sharing their experiences, insights, and philosophies.

One of my favorite new friends is Robert Greene, the coauthor of my book *The 50th Law*. Robert is definitely not the type of person who would have been in my previous circles. He's a middle-aged white guy, and there's nothing "street" about him at all. He's a real history buff, someone who is happiest when he's reading and studying.

I didn't know anyone like that prior to my relationship with Robert. I had friends who would read a couple of books here and there (including Robert's classic *The 48 Laws of Power*), but I didn't know anyone who was a true scholar, who could speak with real knowledge on any number of different subjects and periods of history.

Before becoming friends with Robert, I'd never been too interested in subjects I thought didn't directly involve me. My attitude was, how could something that happened in ancient Rome or Imperial China have any significance for my life?

The stories Robert told me made me realize I was being very closed-minded. There was, in fact, an almost unlimited pool of strategies and techniques I could draw on from the examples of history. Robert explained to me that when you read about a Napoleon or a Bismarck, you couldn't just think of them as old white guys in dusty history books, but geniuses who understood how to match strategy to their circumstances. And this is what maintaining power is really about.

Of course our relationship is a two-way street. I educated Robert about my experience and helped draw him out of his books a little. By rolling with me, he got to see someone putting some of the strategies he studied into practice, in real time. I think that was exciting for him. One time he even told me, "You know, in America, you and I aren't supposed to be friends. People want there to be walls between us, because we supposedly come from different worlds. History and hip-hop aren't supposed to meet. Why not? We've both got a lot to learn from each other. Our friendship is a way to break down those walls."

One thing I really appreciated about Robert was how, even though he's spent his life studying the various ways people manipulate power, it's not actually the kind of thing he is obsessed with in his own life. Every year, he gets flown around the world to meet with kings, presidents, and heads of state (I can't say which ones), all of whom want to pick his brain on strategies. He shares his information with them and goes back home to his books. If anything, he can be a little too soft, especially in his personal life. There have been a few times I've had to tell him that it's okay to be a little ruthless with people. It's really not in his nature to destroy someone just because he can. He knows about manipulation, but at heart he's a compassionate guy. That's a good person for me to be friends with, because some of that energy rubs off on me and helps me be more sympathetic in certain situations.

Another person I've formed an unlikely friendship with is Deepak Chopra, the bestselling author and wellness expert. If Robert Greene is something like my teacher when it comes to history, Deepak is my spiritual teacher. One of the most valuable things he's taught me is the importance of getting my head in a more conscious and relaxed space.

That's always been tough for me. I'm someone who's constantly thinking and strategizing. I've felt that if I take even a few seconds of mental relaxation, someone else is going to catch up and overtake me.

Deepak helped me understand that the best way to ensure I stay mentally sharp is to actually give my mind a breather. The technique he taught me to help me take that break is meditation. He explained that there are a lot of different types of meditation you can practice, but the one he recommended is a mantra-based technique.

If you've never tried it, a mantra is a phrase or word that you repeat over and over again in your mind until your brain starts to calm down. A lot of times it's a Sanskrit word, but Deepak told me I could just use the phrase "I am." He said that whenever I felt like my thoughts were racing faster than I was comfortable with, I could just sit down in a quiet room, close my eyes, and repeat "I am, I am" over and over again until the noise in my head was gone.

I tried following his instruction, but I found that, after saying my mantra for a few minutes, there were so many thoughts racing through my head that I'd get distracted and forget about what I was supposed to be doing. I didn't want to quit, so I hit up Deepak for some advice, and he told me that this was normal. The purpose of meditation isn't to "stop thinking" or to make you stop having thoughts, but rather to help you lower the volume on those thoughts, so that when you're starting to feel overwhelmed by whatever is in your head, you have a tool at your disposal that you can use to slow things down and begin to think more clearly.

That made a lot of sense to me, so much so that I actually set up a little area in my apartment just for meditation. Whenever I'm feeling a little stressed, I'll sit in that room and say my mantra for ten or fifteen minutes. It's a very easy way to regain control of my mind.

Having that room is great, but I find that I do my best meditating on airplanes. Knowing that I'm going to be stuck in the same seat for several hours, I always try to spend some of the flight meditating. It's tempting to open up my laptop and watch a movie or TV show, but that's not really doing anything beneficial for me. Instead, I'll commit to saying my mantra for at least a half hour. For the first ten minutes or so, I'll keep losing track of my mantra and drifting back to whatever thoughts were at the top of my mind. But if I stick with it, after a while I get into a groove. I might not totally let go of my thoughts, but I definitely get in a much more peaceful mind frame. When I'm done meditating, I feel much more clear in my thoughts and my decision-making process. It's a great way to turn a flight into something constructive.

When I was growing up in Queens, if you had told me I'd end up being friends with a white dude who was a history buff and an Indian dude who was into meditation, I would have laughed at you. I simply didn't associate with anyone who seemed "different" from me.

Today, I can't imagine a world where I don't have friendships with people like Robert and Deepak. They've both, in different ways, fundamentally helped reshape how I see and interact with the world.

I concede that I'm in a different situation than most people. Chances are you're not going to have the opportunity to meet one of your favorite authors or a world-renowned healer.

There is nothing stopping you, however, from seeking out more well-rounded people and bringing them into your world. Not every one of your friends has to be into the same things that you are.

For example, if every time you're out with your homeboys the conversation is always only about hip-hop and the NBA, then you have to do better.

Or if all your homeboys still wear jeans and sneakers to every event, you need to do better on that front, too. I used to be like that. Growing up in my hood, suits were only for funerals or court dates. But I've adjusted as I've grown. I've accepted that there are going to be occasions where I need to wear a nice tailored suit with leather shoes. I still get people asking me, "Why are you wearing that?," but I'm not going to stay stuck in one place just because that's where *they're* most comfortable. Even if my natural instinct is to throw on a fitted with some jeans and sneakers, I appreciate people who can put me on to new designers or places to pick up great suits.

You need people in your life who are going to invite you to places you might not normally go, or send you interesting articles you might not normally read, or have you try food you might not normally order.

You must find people who are going to inject new energy into your life. Because if you keep having the same conversations with the same people year after year, your energy is going to stagnate. Your ideas are going to get stale. Your momentum is going to get stuck.

I'm not just expanding the circle of people I socialize with. I'm also committed to expanding the circle of people I interact with professionally.

In practically every corporate room I go into, I am surrounded by people who likely have had a lot more schooling than me. Who have read more than me. Who have been exposed to more culture than me.

There was a time earlier in my career when those situations might have made me a bit insecure, where I might have looked for a reason not to enter that room in the first place because I didn't want to feel stupid or uninformed.

I was able to get past that insecurity by accepting that those people weren't more cultured than me; they just had been exposed to a different culture. The culture I experienced growing up in South Jamaica was every bit as real as the culture a kid who grew up in Beverly Hills or the Upper East Side of Manhattan had been exposed to. They just had different foundations and priorities.

I also came to understand that, just as I was intimidated by what I didn't know about their culture, they might be equally intimidated by what they didn't know about mine. Their kids might go to a private school in Beverly Hills, but they were playing my music in the car on the way there. This meant that there was no imbalance, and we were on equal footing culturally.

These days, I'm not intimidated anymore. Instead I'm looking for rooms where everyone else is more knowledgeable and educated than me. I love those sorts of rooms. Not because I don't value my own experiences, but because I know that when I'm around highly educated people, I'm going to be able to extract real value out of their input. When I combine that information with my own instincts and experiences, it's the perfect formula to make amazing shit happen.

Your time is never wasted when you're gathering information. This is why I'll always prioritize information over a check. Recently, I got a very nice check to play a show in Israel. I didn't have to show up until the day of the show, but I told my people to book me to arrive a day early. "You want to see the sights?" they asked. "That's not it," I explained. "I need to meet the motherfucker who can write a check like that!" I didn't know what this guy did, but I knew I could learn something from him.

It's not only a professional priority. I love talking to anyone who can provide me with new information that can change my perspective. There could be a subject that I feel like I'm rock-solid on, that there's no way anyone could change my mind on it. Then a smart person hits me with a new perspective on it—an insight I hadn't considered before—and everything changes.

That happened to me recently. I was talking with a friend about the news that Vice President Pence said that he wouldn't meet a woman for dinner without having his wife present. People were upset with his remark, but I didn't see what the outrage was about. "What is wrong with that?" I asked my friend. "When he said that, there's a side of me that identifies with him. He's got a system that works for him. Leave him alone." But this friend wasn't willing to leave Pence alone. Or me, with my limited vision.

"Listen, 50, you need to look at this from my perspective," he told me. "I have two daughters. And I'm not having any more kids. Those two are my future. Let's say that one of them excels in school and wants to get into politics. She works her way up through the ranks, does all the right things, and gets involved with an issue. Now she has a chance to meet with the vice president for dinner. And his office tells her that his wife has to come along or she can't get the meeting. That's not fair!"

"Why not?" I asked. "He's just trying to stay focused. He's aware of his imperfections. We should celebrate that. Not attack the man for that."

"No, he deserves to be criticized," he replied. "First of all, he's going to the dinner as the vice president, not as a man. So when he says he can't meet my daughter without his wife present, that means he's looking at her as a sexual object. Not as a lobbyist, a policy expert, a senator, whatever she might be. He's seeing her as a sex object first and foremost."

He had a point. I was starting to see where he was coming from. But my friend wasn't done.

"Here's the other problem, 50. You know that the vibe is different when it's just two people talking business versus when one of their spouses is present. When it's just two people, they can get down to the nitty-gritty. Talk shit about their enemies. Conspire together. Trade notes and trade dirt. Discuss stuff they might not talk about in front of other people. That's how a lot of business gets done in the real world.

"But when a spouse is there, the vibe changes. The conversation's about kids, vacations, or what TV shows everyone has watched. It doesn't get down to the dirt.

"If my daughter is talking to the vice president, I want her to be able to get into the nitty-gritty. I want her to be able to talk about making real moves with someone in a position of power. I don't want her to be penalized for being a female. To have to limit herself to a different type of conversation than a man in her position would have. Fuck that!"

"Oh, shit. How didn't I see that?" I asked my friend.

When he put it like that to me, it was like a bomb went off in my head. I had been seeing the issue in black and white, and he helped me see it in Technicolor.

My vision was limited because I had been identifying with Pence as a single man. As someone who is familiar with lust, I could appreciate his position. I had failed to identify with the woman in the situation, with how she was losing out despite doing nothing wrong.

I live for moments like that, when I can identify where I've been wrong about a subject and start to evolve my thinking. I don't live to be right all the time or to have a bunch of yes-men tell me, "That's right, boss," when I say some dumb shit. No, I want to have my mind expanded and my perspectives shifted by as many intelligent people as possible. Every single place I go, I'm studying people. The way they say things, their attitude, information they share. I could be on the train, and I'd be watching people and taking notes. That's how I learned business, by studying people I admired and how they conducted themselves. Smart people give away so much information through their words or their actions. Grab every single one of those gems that you can.

Hip-hop has brought about a lot of positive changes in this country and improved countless lives. One area it could improve, however, is to stop putting so much of a priority on being cool. We like our rappers to be damaged, but we don't like them to be insecure or nerdy. We need to change that up, to say it's okay to admit you don't know things. That you don't have all the answers. That you feel unsure of yourself in certain situations. It's only by admitting that you have some growing to do that you can even start the process.

There are some people who always try to position themselves to be the smartest person in the room. They do that because it soothes their insecurity. They'd rather present the impression of being important than actually put themselves in the position to grow.

Never be that person. Always challenge yourself to be around people who might be informed in different ways than you are, who have had different experiences, and, most important, aren't intimidated to share that information with you. Those are the people who are going to supercharge your evolution into your best self.

CHAPTER 6

POWER OF PERCEPTION

The world will see you the way you see you. And treat you
the way you treat yourself.

—BEYONCÉ

When *Get Rich or Die Tryin'* was released, I still had one foot very much in the streets. That connection to struggle made me very relatable.

Once I achieved success on the highest level, however, that connection was lost. With fame and fortune, I stopped being human. I was closer to a comic book character than to someone with real feelings. The perception was that if you cut me, I wouldn't bleed.

Over time I've been able to let go of any resentment connected to the perception that I'm not susceptible to the same pains, fears, and disappointments as everyone else. I accepted that there were certain assumptions about me I wasn't going to be able to change. What I *could* do, however, was hustle smarter to make those perceptions work in my favor.

I've noticed a trend in how the media covers me. When I'm killing it, I'm known as "the music mogul 50 Cent." Let something go bad, and then I'm "the rapper 50 Cent."

It would have been easy to develop a negative fixation about that irregularity. Instead, I saw an opportunity. By referring to me as a rapper when I do something controversial, the press offers me a kind of freedom, one that other people in my position don't have.

We live in a climate where most people are afraid to openly speak their minds—especially those in positions of power and influence. They're worried that if they say the wrong thing on social media or in the press, they'll lose something. An endorsement. A role. Friends. Maybe even their careers. They'll be "canceled."

I never worry about being canceled. I've been transparent about my issues since day one, so the expectations aren't the same for me as they are for my peers. There's an acceptance that I was messed up to start with.

When I do say something wild, being labeled as "the rapper 50 Cent" becomes my shield. Any "cancellation" talk bounces right off it. Even the most critical voices out there will concede, "That's just 50 being 50."

That freedom to be myself, warts and all, has become incredibly valuable. One of the greatest tools at my disposal is my Instagram page, which has 25 million followers. Why do so many people mess with my page? Because it's always popping off! They gravitate to it because it's raw, unfiltered, and actually run by me. There's no publicist overseeing my posts, telling me what to take down. Or a twenty-five-year-old social media manager sitting in a cubicle trying to think of how to make a promotional post sound like me. It's a true reflection of me on each and every day. Very few of my peers can say that.

Here's the twist: the popularity of my page has been one of the driving forces behind the success of *Power* and my subsequent megadeal with Starz. When the press wrote about that deal, I damn sure wasn't "the rapper 50 Cent." My hustle had shifted the perception. Curtis Jackson, the mogul, the businessman, and the entertainment executive, is who made that Starz deal happen.

Now that I recognize the advantages it brings, I'm comfortable with being known as both 50 Cent *and* Curtis Jackson.

50 Cent is the perception.

Curtis Jackson is the reality.

That doesn't mean 50 Cent is fake. Not at all. Ninety percent of the things I've rapped about, I've lived. Not to mention that there are plenty of things I lived through that haven't shown up in my music.

I can now use the persona of 50 Cent—the persona I earned the hard way—to my advantage, to both protect and elevate Curtis Jackson.

The greatest fear that many people have is just being themselves. There are probably some of you reading this book hoping that you can become "the next 50 Cent." If that sounds like you, let go of that intention. Being me is not going to fit your journey, and neither is trying to be anyone else.

When you pattern yourself too closely after another person, you're putting weak, ineffectual energy out into the world. You're running away from your most inexhaustible power supply: being yourself.

What I want you to take from this chapter is an understanding about how presenting the best possible version of yourself is going to have an incredible impact on your success.

Influencing how people perceive you doesn't make you fake. It doesn't make you phony. It makes you someone who knows how to control energy—to your advantage.

Imagine your energy as being like water. For thousands of years, people have sought to channel the energy of water. The ancient Greeks built water wheels that used the power of rivers to grind wheat into flour. In ancient China they used "pot wheels" to lift water out of rivers and into irrigation canals. Islamic engineers in Africa and the Middle East used it to power "lifting machines." In modern times we've built colossal projects like the Hoover Dam, which took the power of the

Colorado River and controlled it to irrigate dry land, control floods, and supply power to millions of people.

None of those measures, which brought so much change to civilization, altered the basic nature of the water involved. The only thing they changed was how it was utilized.

Try to view harnessing the energy of how you are perceived in the same way. The fundamental essence of who you are doesn't change—you're just using its innate power in a smarter way.

SHAPING PERCEPTIONS

My first experience trying to shape people's perception was born out of necessity. I was around twelve years old and just starting to get into hustlin' drugs. It was clear I was going to be an earner, but I had a problem on my hands: I didn't have any free time to get out on the corner.

I was in middle school at the time, and there was no way my nana was going to let me drop out. The only possible time for me to hustle was between 3 p.m., when school let out, and 6 p.m., when I had to be home.

At the time, my nana was in the habit of walking me to and from school, which would make sneaking off to hustle impossible. I had to come up with a reason to walk by myself. I was already around 150 pounds at the time, damn near the size of a small adult, so I told Nana that people were beginning to make fun of me in the neighborhood. "There are kids in eighth and ninth grade who are smaller than me walking home by themselves," I told her. "Everyone's starting to think I'm slow or something. You gotta let me walk by myself."

It was hard for Nana to say yes to that, because walking to school had become our ritual. It was when we'd talk about what was going on in my life, or any of the questions about the world that were going through my young mind. Those walks were where we really bonded.

Still, no grandmother wants her grandson to be bullied, so she eventually let me start walking on my own. The next problem I had to overcome was how to explain why I wasn't home right after school let out. I might be able to buy an hour or so by claiming that I was playing basketball with my friends or taking a quick trip to buy candy, but there was no logical reason I'd be out every day till my curfew.

Then I came up with a solution. My school had an after-school program, where students could catch up on homework or take part in activities, that ran until 6 p.m. I enrolled in it and brought home the papers to Nana that showed I would be staying every day until six. She loved the idea of doing extra work and signed the papers. I went the first couple of days and then stopped showing up. The school was much more lax about attendance after school than during the regular day. If I didn't show up, they weren't going to send any truant officers looking for me. I was finally free to hustle every day between 3 p.m. and 6 p.m.

I even figured out a way to finesse getting out of going to church every Sunday, which was mandatory in Nana's house. Everyone followed her mandate until one year when she joined a new church. After a couple of Sundays, it was clear that the new preacher was a bit of a hustler. My grandfather, who didn't like going to church any more than I did, saw his opportunity. "I don't have to go to church on Sunday and have this guy try to tell me about God," he told Nana. "I'm just going to stay home and read the Bible on my own instead." When Nana didn't put up a fight, I made my own move. "I wanna stay home with my grandpa!" I told her. My grandpa was stunned, since I'd never showed much interest in hanging out with him. "The baby want to stay with me?" he asked. But he must have sensed that I was a bit of a coconspirator, because he quickly took to the idea and overrode Nana's objections. "No, no, let Curtis stay with me," he said. "It will be good for the boy."

We were both just looking for ways of getting out of church, but Sunday mornings ended up being where my grandpa and I really bonded ourselves. Before that, he was kind of a distant figure, someone who was at work most of the time. On those Sunday mornings, we got to know each other. We spent a lot more time watching football games or hanging out around the house than studying the Bible, but my nana didn't have to know that. We were forging a bond that's lasted to this day.

It was during this period that my grandfather demonstrated another valuable lesson about the importance of controlling perception, especially in a relationship. My grandfather worked at the local GMC factory, and he had a ritual when he got paid every other Friday. As soon as he walked in the door on payday, he would give my grandmother his check. She wouldn't have to badger or hassle him—he'd just hand it right over to her.

As a child it never made sense to me. "You work your ass off all week and then just give your paycheck to someone else?" I used to think. "What sort of system is that?"

But recently we were on a trip together (I take him on at least one trip with me every year) and I said to him, "Pop, I never understood how you just gave her all the money."

"You couldn't understand it at the time because you were too young," he explained. "But I gave her all the money to stop her from looking at things that I couldn't give her. Instead of having her head filled up with fantasies, I let her *work with reality*. Having that piece of mind at home was worth more to me than a few extra dollars in my pocket."

I finally understood his strategy. If he had been secretive about how much he made, it would have been understandable that my grandmother would have become suspicious that he was holding out on her. She might have bothered him for a nicer dress or an expensive pair of shoes. "He's probably got it," she might have thought to herself. "He's just being cheap."

By showing my grandmother exactly what he was bringing home and then giving it all to her, my grandfather had shifted the energy in the house. If she wanted the nicer pair of shoes or the more expensive dress, she was going to have to justify that purchase to herself. Not him.

And by handing her everything, my grandfather became a sure thing in my grandmother's life. Most people are always going to stick with a sure thing. When I looked at it like that, his actions suddenly made so much sense to me.

While I was happy to build a closer relationship with my grandfather during those Sundays, I didn't particularly like lying to Nana, especially about what I was really doing after school. But I was beginning to understand that in order to get what I wanted at the time, I was going to have to learn how to juggle Nana's perception of me with who I was becoming on the streets. I could have done what a lot of kids did in my hood, which was just drop out of school and say, "I don't give a fuck whether my family likes it or not." But my love for my nana was too strong. I had to let her hold on to her perception of me as her baby.

More than anyone else in my life, Nana understood me, even if I tried to keep part of my life hidden from her. After she died, my aunt was reading my nana's old Bible and saw that she actually used to write down her prayers on little scraps of paper, which she would tuck between the pages. My aunt showed me one of the prayers, in which Nana wrote, "Please keep Curtis safe from himself, because he has a temper. Lord, it's not his fault because that boy has been through a lot."

When I read that note, it was one of the most emotional moments of my life. I would have given my life to save hers in that moment. That's how much she meant to me.

My love for my nana is why I committed to keeping up two identifies. At home I would continue to be Boo Boo, the sweet kid who followed Nana's rule of no cursing under her roof. Who loved her pork 'n' beans with franks. Who was polite and showed respect.

Outside of her home, I developed a different persona. I wasn't known as 50 Cent yet, but I was becoming known as someone you didn't want to cross, as someone who was going to do whatever it took to get what he wanted.

While my nana might have seen me as her baby, outside of her home I wanted the neighborhood to notice me, to view me as someone worthy of respect. There were a lot of elements I knew I couldn't control—being poor, parentless, and maybe a little funny looking. But I was determined that the elements I could control—my appearance and presentation—were going to make an impression on people.

The first thing I set out to change was my physical makeup. As I've mentioned, as a kid I was overweight. Remember when I rhymed "I love you like a fat kid loves cake" in "21 Questions"? I *was* that fat kid. I spent way too much time on the couch watching TV while wolfing down cheese sandwiches and drinking cranberry juice. I was headed on a path toward obesity, diabetes, and so many of the issues that plague way too many African Americans.

Getting into the boxing gym corrected my sloppy physical presentation. Once I committed to putting in the work, I transformed from a fat twelve-year-old boy to a sleek and powerful young man. What surprised me most is that I began to crave the discipline of boxing more than I craved the cake, cookies, and soda. The cake made me feel good for a moment, but then that rush was gone. Training and staying in shape made me feel good *all of the time*.

Outside of the physical strength it endowed me with, I liked knowing that my body could sway how people felt about me. If other males weren't outright intimidated, they treated me with more respect. A lot of women were attracted, not only as eye candy, but to what my muscles said about me—that I was someone who was disciplined, that I wasn't averse to putting in consistent work on something they were focused on. The indication of those qualities, even more so than rubbing on a man's biceps or broad shoulders, is extremely attractive to women.

Ever since I first started shedding the pounds in the boxing ring, staying in shape has been a fundamental part of my persona. The only time I've slipped up was after I went on tour to support *Get Rich or Die Tryin'*. We were on the road constantly for over a year, and I wasn't properly prepared for challenges created by the touring lifestyle: lots of hotel room service and even more fast food. I slipped back into my bad habits from childhood and started eating whatever I wanted, while working out less and less.

Not surprisingly, I put on way too much weight. I'd started off the tour looking like the headlining artist, but by the end I looked like my own security. When it was time to shoot the cover for my second album, *The Massacre*, I had a problem on my hands. Or, more accurately, my chest.

One of the lasting defining images from *Get Rich or Die Tryin'* was a shirtless picture of me on the cover, looking muscular, with a diamond cross hanging from my neck. That's the image people associated with 50 Cent. It had a proven track record of selling records.

The reality was different when it was time to release *Massacre*. I wasn't obese, but there was flab where there used to be definition. I couldn't abandon the shirtless motif, so I came up with a solution: I used another shirtless photo, but this time I took a pen and drew in my missing muscles. To divert people's eyes from the flab, I gave myself definition around my pecs, shoulders, and arms. I also put on gloves, so that the whole image took on a cartoon-like quality.

The diversion worked—no one was talking about "fat 50 Cent." They were just talking about the music. *The Massacre* sold 1.5 million copies the week it came out and ended up moving over 10 million worldwide. Still, I vowed never to compromise myself like that again.

PROJECTING THE RIGHT APPEARANCE

Ever since I had to pull out my pen for *The Massacre* cover, my muscles have been real. I will admit, however, that there have been times when I've manipulated how people perceive me in other ways to further my agenda.

One of the first times I realized I could attract what I wanted through projecting success was when I was initially trying to make the transition from selling drugs to music.

I was doing very well on the streets, but no one was really taking me seriously as a rapper yet. I knew I needed to meet the right people if I was going to progress. With that mission in mind, one night me and a couple of my boys decided to go to Bentley's, an upscale hip-hop spot in Manhattan. Bentley's would broadcast their Friday night parties on the radio, which drew a potent mix of rappers, athletes, celebrities, and models. If you wanted to break into the game, Bentley's was a great place to do it . . . provided you could get past their doormen. They were there specifically to make sure every hood dude in the five boroughs looking for a record deal *couldn't* get in the door.

We pulled up in my 400 SE Benz, which was an extremely fly ride. Not many people had one. As I cruised slowly past the club, out of nowhere someone ran up on my car and slapped the hood. I'm someone who does not appreciate being surprised, and my displeasure must have shown on my face.

"Yo, my bad, son!" the guy quickly apologized. "I thought you was my man Kenny. He got the same whip!"

Once my alarm subsided, I took a good look at who was talking to me: it was Jam Master Jay from Run-DMC! One of my heroes!

I immediately pulled the car over, jumped out, and gave Jay a pound. I told him I was from South Jamaica and had always followed his career. He laughed and apologized again for running up on me, explaining he thought I was NBA star Kenny Anderson, another Queens native.

I asked Jay if he was about to go into Bentley's. "No doubt, I'm about to run up in this spot and see what's up," he said. I decided to decisively seize the moment. "Yo, we coming witchu," I told him. Jay looked at me, thought about it for a second, and then said, "That's what's up. Let's go." Just like that, we were past the bouncers and inside Bentley's. We would never have gotten in without him—*he literally walked me into the music business.* That night Jay and I formed a friendship, which eventually led to me signing with JMJ Records and everything else that followed.

Here's the thing: Jay never would have invited me into the club with him if I hadn't been driving my 400 SE. If I had just walked up to him on the sidewalk, he wouldn't have even stopped to talk to us, let alone take us inside. That's not a knock against him or his sense of judgment—random people approached him everywhere he went, and there's no way Jay could ever accommodate everyone.

But the moment Jay saw my car and thought I was Kenny Anderson, I was operating under a powerful perception. Even when it turned out that I wasn't an NBA player, I was still *somebody* to him—somebody who deserved his attention. Once I had it, it was up to me to capitalize on it.

Which I did.

There are certain material goods—and cars are at the top of the list—that signal to other people that you are someone who should be taken seriously. That you are different from the rest of the herd. Especially in New York City. You can't drive your fancy apartment or brownstone down Broadway, but you can damn sure roll by slow in your whip.

Picture this: an older rich white guy is driving around in a Rolls Royce, and I pull up next to him in a hooptie. Suddenly I notice there are flames coming out from under his car. If I motion for him to roll his window down, he's going to take one look at me and then just stare straight ahead. I might be trying to save his life, but he's not giving me any attention. His perception is that I'm not someone he should be interacting with.

Now let's pretend I pull up next to him in my Ferrari. I notice his car is on fire and motion for him to roll down his window. He's going to roll down that window and say, "What can I do for you?" Ten times out of ten. I could look exactly the same and be projecting the same energy, but he's only rolling down that window when I'm in a luxury car of my own. What I'm sitting in controls his entire perception of me.

It's not just cars. I was recently talking with a very famous media personality, and he mentioned that he always notices when someone is wearing a good watch. If he doesn't know who they are, it makes him want to know. "I'll start to wonder, 'What the hell does he do for a living,'" he told me. "And then I'll try to figure out a way to talk to him. Because he must be onto something."

There are some people who are that way with sneakers. If you walk into the room wearing the right kind of kicks, that person is going to notice you. You might not have said a word, but that person is immediately going to single you out as someone who's probably worth their attention.

For a lot of women, there's a similar energy around handbags. Most men couldn't tell the difference between a $20,000 Birkin and a fake Gucci bag from Canal Street. But to other women, the bag someone's carrying speaks volumes. You come into a room with an ill bag, a lot of antennas go up.

You can say, "Well, that guy should have treated you the same no matter what you were driving," or "You shouldn't be interested in someone just because of the watch they wear," but that statement doesn't align with reality.

E very time you walk down the street, drive somewhere in your car, go to the supermarket, work out in the gym, or post a picture on social media, you are being judged—by a few people you know and a lot more you'll never even meet. There's no sense complaining about it or saying it's not fair. Instead, it's incumbent on you to accept that you control how you're perceived and then prepare the best presentation possible.

I will tell you straight up that I judge every single person I meet on their appearance. As I'm shaking your hand, I'm also scanning your entire outfit for whatever clues I can glean from it. Especially if we're meeting to conduct business for the first time. Before you open your mouth, your appearance has already initiated a conversation with me. Make sure it's saying the right thing.

I pay particular attention to the people who dress casually around me. Let's say you come to our meeting wearing a T-shirt and some jeans. That tells me you're comfortable. Not necessarily a bad thing. If I sense you're going to do great work, then that comfort level is appropriate. If you don't transmit a competent air, however, then I'll view it as a liability. It suggests you're not taking the situation seriously enough. You'd be surprised how many people do that.

One time *GQ* magazine sent a reporter to interview me. He showed up in a T-shirt and jeans with scuffed sneakers. It might have been a hip outfit among his friends, but to me it signaled that he might not be totally locked in at his job. At one point we started talking about the importance of presentation, and the reporter asked me what I thought of his outfit. I told him maybe it was fine for him to interview me dressed that way, but I suspected that it was undermining how his colleagues saw him back at the office. "Look, *GQ* may send you to interview 50 Cent because you come dressed casual," I explained. "But they would send the guy in the suit to go interview George Clooney."

The reporter admitted that I might be onto something. To find out, he conducted an experiment where he wore a suit to work one day instead of his normal outfit of T-shirt, sneakers, and jeans. The shift in how people viewed him was immediate. Several co-workers went out of their way to compliment him on his appearance, and one of his editors even took his picture and put it on *GQ*'s Instagram page. That's a very big cosign at *GQ*. I don't know if they ever sent him to interview George Clooney, but there's no doubt that changing how he dressed also changed how he was perceived at his job. As I told him, when you clean up, people will notice.

When I see someone has put effort and thought into their choice of attire, it tells me that they value our relationship. Whether I like their particular style or not isn't important. I just want to see the effort. The other day I met with a TV writer to discuss a potential project. He had jeans on, but they were crisp. He had sneakers on, but they looked fresh out the box. He wore a loose-fitting cotton sports jacket and had dark-framed glasses. Everything about his outfit said "intelligent business casual." It projected the correct energy for what we were working on.

After we talked a while and I'd decided that I liked him, I told him that I was curious about his intent in picking out his outfit. Probably not the question he was expecting in a meeting about scripts, but he was cool with it. "Oh, I wanted you to take me seriously," he told me, adding, "but I also wanted you to think I wasn't too formal. That I would be a flexible person to work with." He added that the glasses were a recent addition to his look. "For a long time I wasn't wearing glasses because I thought they made me look old," he explained. "But a few years ago I decided to start wearing them because I figured they'd make me seem smart, which is probably a good thing if I want people to pay me a lot of money for my services."

"You nailed it. It does not register anything but intelligence to me," I told him. "I look at you and go, 'He's a smart guy. He put those glasses on so he can fucking see!'"

Mind you, it was not necessarily an outfit I would wear myself. The sneakers were a little plain, and the sports jacket wouldn't have felt right on me. But I didn't need to see him dress the way I do. I just needed to register that he had the right aesthetic for the job.

Some of you might not be in a position to afford stylish clothes or have a fresh new pair of kicks every time you go to a meeting. That's still not an excuse. Whatever your situation is, you can afford an iron. Even if your clothes aren't the coolest, if I notice that you ironed them and laid them out the night before, I'll register your intent. It lets me know that even if you don't have a big budget, you do have the right energy. I can work with that.

Conversely, when I see someone who is consistently sloppy or doesn't seem to mind wearing wrinkled clothes, it tells me that they don't value themselves. That they're not willing to put in a little extra work every day to present the best version of themselves. It doesn't take much to iron your shirt or clean your sneakers a bit. If you don't value your time and your appearance enough to do those little things every morning, why would I expect you to value me?

HOW TO CONTROL THE CONVERSATION

I know how most people in corporate America view me.

As a gangster. A thug. A bully.

If they have a meeting scheduled with me, their top priority going in probably isn't getting the deal done. It's leaving the room without getting shot.

I understand why, and part of it is my own doing. I won't say that I intentionally cultivate a gangster image—that sounds too calculated. But I was always very honest in articulating the type of lifestyle I was living back in Queens. And people who aren't from that sort of background tend to gravitate to those details.

When I first started taking a lot of corporate meetings, I was surprised that everyone in the room seemed so nervous around me.

What were they scared of? I was there to talk business. Not to shoot up the place.

Over time, I realized I could manipulate that nervous energy. If I wanted to truly control the room, the best thing I could do is give off the *least* gangsta energy possible.

If people were expecting me to radiate aggression and arrogance, I gave them humility instead. I smiled a lot. I even seemed a little shy.

Those execs had been mentally preparing themselves for an arctic blast, but all they got instead was a cool summer breeze. The difference between their perception and my reality disarmed them.

By controlling the energy in the room, I learned I'd have a much easier time setting my agenda. People become so amazed at how nice I am that subconsciously they grow much more agreeable and receptive to whatever I'm proposing.

E ven as I'm smiling and being sweet, I still find ways to let the room know that I'm in charge. One technique I'll employ is touching the arm of the person I'm talking to. Never in a heavy or invasive way. Just lightly on their forearm. It doesn't seem like it should matter, but it's an incredibly effective way of making an impression on someone.

I'm not just saying that; scientists have done studies proving that a light touch makes people much more agreeable to your requests. A study by the Society for Personality and Social Psychology found that waiters and waitresses who applied light touches to the people they were serving got better tips than those who did not. Another study, this one in the *Journal of Nonverbal Behavior*, found that applying a light touch made random people on the street more likely to help with finding lost objects and even signing petitions. In short, a properly applied touch gets people to do whatever you want them to do.

Why? Scientists think it's because when someone touches you

in the right (i.e., nonaggressive) way, it causes your body to release chemicals like dopamine, oxytocin, and serotonin that make your brain happy. Simultaneously, it causes the levels of stressful chemicals like cortisol (which would be triggered by an aggressive touch) to go down. The result is that one simple touch can put someone into a more relaxed mood, where they'll be more likely to agree with whatever is being proposed.

The key is applying the touch properly. First off, you can't touch people *anywhere* other than between their elbow and their wrist. This is especially true if you're a man interacting with a woman. Don't touch someone's shoulder, biceps, or face, and definitely not anywhere below their waist. Don't go out there and do some dumb shit and then try to say, "50 told me to do that!" When you apply the touch, it's on the forearm only. Zero exceptions.

Also, only apply touch if you're sitting or standing close enough to someone to do it without being awkward. If you've got to lean across a table, or reach over someone else, it won't work. The touch has to seem effortless, just a normal extension of the conversation. If you're reaching for someone, it's actually going to make them uncomfortable and therefore less receptive to you. The same is true if you try to grip their arm or try to physically control them in any way.

Try this technique out the next time you're trying to convince someone to help you with something. Instead of just asking your mother for a ride to the mall, ask while giving her a light touch on the forearm. No matter what sort of mood she was in beforehand, I promise that her energy will improve and you'll get that ride.

Or if you're at work and you're trying to convince your boss that you're the right person to lead a project, just touch them ever so gently on their forearm as you make your case. Again, it can only be on the forearm, and it should never seem flirty or suggestive. Your energy has to remain completely calm and controlled. If you can do that, no matter how difficult or reluctant your boss has been in the past, you'll see their energy change for the better. You'll get that assignment.

A nother way to subtly control the energy of the room is by talking softly. Maybe not the advice you were expecting from a rapper, but it's another trick that I've found really works.

The person who put me on to it was the legendary actor Bruce Willis. Bruce and I first met on the set of the heist film *The Setup*. One night during filming, the cast and crew went out to eat together. I was seated at the same table as Bruce, and throughout the night people would come over to pay their respects. I noticed that every time someone would initiate a conversation with Bruce, they'd have to lean in close to catch what he was saying. Similarly, whenever the entire table was engaged in a conversation, if someone asked Bruce his opinion, he'd answer in almost a whisper. The entire table would have to lean toward him to hear.

After dinner Bruce invited me to join him in the hotel lobby for a cigar. As we smoked, I asked him about what I'd observed. "Say, man," I said. "How come every time someone asked you something at dinner, you answered in damn near a whisper? You're not talking like that now."

Bruce started to laugh. "You noticed that, huh?" he said. "Very observant of you. That's something I picked up years ago. Whenever you're around a lot of people and everyone's trying to be heard, the secret is to speak as softly as possible. When someone speaks like that, our natural reaction is to lean in to them as close as possible. We don't realize it, but when we do that, we're transferring all our power to them."

"Damn," I said. "That never occurred to me before. I'm used to people trying to control the room by being as loud as possible."

"Try it," Bruce said. "You'll see what I'm talking about."

So I gave it a shot, and Bruce was absolutely on point. The more quietly I spoke, the more intently people listened. In testing the technique, I found that giving people less than they expected wasn't just effective with verbal communication, but with body language, too.

For example, I noticed that executives always respond to nonverbal cues when they're talking to a room. If they make a point, they expect something from you in return. It could be a laugh, a slight nod, a raised eyebrow, or even just a shift in your seat. Something that communicates to them, "Yes, important person, I'm receiving your information." Even if we're not conscious of it, we usually end up giving them that affirmation that they're looking for.

I decided to do an experiment when I was doing a round of meetings with TV executives. For some reason, they seem just a little bit cockier and more arrogant than other execs, and really like to control the room. I wanted to see if I could snatch that control out from under them without them even realizing it. Every time some big shot TV exec was pontificating about their plans, when they looked to me for that affirmation, I'd just sit there stone-faced. No nod. No laugh. I would not offer them anything.

It would completely throw them off. They became very flustered. Once I had them off their game, it was much easier to assert my agenda and move the conversation in a direction that was beneficial to me. I was hustling harder, but literally without moving a muscle.

Try it yourself. If you're in a meeting and your boss looks to you for affirmation, don't give it to them. That doesn't mean stare at your phone or off into space while they're talking. By all means, maintain eye contact and show that you're listening. Just don't offer them any nonverbal feedback beyond that.

I promise that if you do that, the person who's speaking will become fixated on you. Subconsciously, they will be thinking, "Everyone else is giving me verification. But this person isn't giving me anything. What's going on?"

You could be the most junior person in the room, but after that meeting you're going to occupy some prime real estate in your boss's head. They're going to be thinking, "That's a smart person. I need to pay more attention to them."

You will have made a positive—and lasting—impression on your boss. Now it's on you to capitalize on that advantage you've created for yourself. If you don't follow up that meeting with impressive ideas and a strong work ethic, the impression won't be worth much. But if you can use your boss's newfound interest to showcase the great work you've been doing, it's really going to propel your trajectory.

FAKE IT TILL YOU MAKE IT

Bill Gates and Paul Allen were computer nerds who met in high school in Seattle, where they both shared an interest in early computing systems. Several years after graduating, Allen found himself in Boston working for Honeywell, while Gates was a student at nearby Harvard.

One day Allen met up with Gates to show him the latest edition of *Popular Electronics* magazine. The cover story was about something neither of them had ever seen before—a "personal computer." Previously, computers were only for big companies or the government. The article introduced a game changer—the Altair 8800, a personal computer invented by a company out of New Mexico called Micro Instrumentation and Telemetry Systems (MITS).

Today, we wouldn't even recognize the Altair as a computer. It didn't have a screen or a keyboard. It "communicated" by little red lights that lit up on the front of its boxlike frame. To Allen and Gates, though, it seemed like something out of the future.

They also saw its launch as a potential opportunity. The Altair ran on a very slow and unreliable operating system. Allen and Gates had been working on a program they called BASIC, which they were convinced would make the Altair much more user-friendly.

They decided to contact MITS and pitch them on their program. They got MITS's CEO on the phone and explained that they'd been working on the Altair and developed a new program specifically for it. The company's CEO, Ed Roberts, was intrigued and invited them to New Mexico to give him a demonstration.

Allen and Gates were ecstatic, except they had one problem: they had never actually bought an Altair or finished writing BASIC. As soon as they got off the phone with Roberts, they ran out and bought an Altair. Then they spent the next several months frantically writing the actual script for BASIC.

Of course, Roberts ended up loving the program and even hired Allen to work at MITS. That experience led to Allen and Gates launching their own company, Microsoft, which would go on to make both men among the richest in the entire world.

Bill Gates and Paul Allen would never have set out on the journey, however, if they hadn't been willing to bullshit Ed Roberts on that first phone call. They weren't lying about their talent as computer programmers or their confidence in improving the Altair. But they damn sure exaggerated what they'd actually *done* prior to that call in order to make the best possible impression. One of the main reasons they both went on to have such legendary careers, other than their skill and work ethic, was that they both understood the importance of crafting a narrative, of making themselves appear to have already achieved a higher level of success than they were actually at. In time, they wouldn't have to fake a thing. But if they hadn't been a bit bold with the truth when they were first starting, they might never have got their own company off the ground.

One of hip-hop's favorite expressions is "Fake it till you make it," which is exactly what Bill Gates and Paul Allen did. The idea is that, even if your circumstances are disadvantaged or you lack experience, so long as you project the confidence and energy of someone success-ful, it's only a matter of time till true success comes and finds you.

It's an expression that's been used so often it's almost become cli-ché. Don't let its overuse fool you, though. I can promise you that this principle has real power, even after you "make it."

A great example is when I released the *50 Cent Is the Future* mix-tape. It was the first project I released after getting dropped by Colum-bia. I was in one of the most vulnerable spots I'd ever found myself in and knew I had to do something to grab the industry's attention.

At the time, bootlegging was a major issue in hip-hop. Industry insiders had been getting their hands on albums before their official release dates and then selling them to bootleggers. Those bootleggers would sell the disc with a fake cover on the streets for $5 to $10 a pop, instead of the $20 a CD might go for at Best Buy or Virgin Megastore. That left the artist completely cut out of the process financially.

The bootleggers wanted to carry whatever was hot that the major labels were putting out: albums like Nelly's *Country Grammar* or Nas's *Stillmatic*. Those artists—Nas in particular—would then do anything possible to keep their music from getting into the bootleggers' hands. And if they did come across some unlucky immigrant illegally selling their album, a beatdown usually ensued.

I saw the situation completely differently from those major label artists. Because I needed a buzz, I actively *wanted* my music to get bootlegged. To make it happen, I hatched a plan.

No one would give me a record deal, but I decided to put *The Future* out on my own anyway. The key was to do everything possible to give it the appearance of being a major label release. I hired a pho-tographer to shoot the front cover and a designer to create a package that looked like a regular release. I even put a fake bar code on the back cover to make it look as official as possible. Then I had my people "leak" the album to every bootlegger that would take it.

My plan worked to perfection. The bootleggers quickly started pushing my "album," not realizing they'd "stolen" something that I was actually trying to give away. All over the city, in different hoods and multiple street corners, word began to spread about a new 50 Cent album that wasn't available in stores. You had to know the right bootlegger to get your hands on it. Because it was so hard to find, it instantly became the cool thing to have. The perceived exclusivity only drove interest higher.

In one instance, the perception was too strong. One of my homies was walking down Jamaica Avenue and saw an African guy selling *The Future* on a table. Unaware of my plan, my friend thought the guy was ripping me off. He ran up on the bootlegger, flipped his table over, and punched the dude square in the face. He ended up knocking the dude's teeth out of his mouth.

Afterward, my friend reported back to me on what he'd done, thinking I'd be pleased. "What did you do that for?" I scolded him. "Fool, we need him to sell the CD because we ain't got no deal yet. We're trying to create the buzz. Don't be punching anybody else in the mouth! You messing with the whole thing, man!"

My friend was apologetic. "Oh, my bad, 50. I thought the dude was trying to steal from you."

"Nah, this is part of the plan," I told him. "In fact, go back and buy a few more copies just so him and his people know the streets really want it."

I took a much softer approach with the bootleggers. One time I was walking toward Chris Lighty's office in Manhattan when I saw a guy with a bunch of CDs laid out on a sheet on the sidewalk. "What you got?" I asked him. "Oh yeah, I got that new 50 Cent, man. It's the bomb!" he told me, obviously not realizing who he was talking to. "Oh word? Lemme see," I told him. Sure enough he had *50 Cent Is the Future*. I loved knowing that my CD was the one he was pushing first. I gave the guy a big smile and bought two copies off him. Had to keep that demand going!

One of the major values that labels offered artists was their distribution network. The labels controlled which albums got into the right stores, as well as how they were displayed and promoted. By leaking my own music, I'd figured out a way around that. Those bootleggers became my own personal distribution network. As long as there was a demand, they were gonna keep making copies and getting my music (and my name) out there.

I'm confident that the success of my bootleg "album" is what helped get me on Eminem and Interscope's radar. I wasn't content sitting around hoping that someone would decide I was hot—I lit my own fire instead. By creating the perception that I was as hot as the major label artists of the day, I basically paved the way to becoming one myself.

ACT LIKE YOU DON'T NEED IT

Another technique you can employ to get something you want is to act like you don't actually need it. It's a technique that requires finesse, nuance, and unshakable confidence. Employ it correctly, and it will get you real results.

Suppose you go into an interview for a job you really desire. It's in your ideal field and pays much better than your current job. If you get it, not only will you be furthering your career, but you'll also be able to get out of the credit card debt that's been drowning you. Not to mention your commute will drop from forty-five to fifteen minutes. It's everything you've been looking for.

When you sit down for your interview (in your ironed outfit, of course), your instinct will be to express just how enthusiastic you are about the position. You've already spent weeks fantasizing about what your life will be like once you get that job. Now you just want to spill all that energy out in front of the person who can actually give it to you.

Do not succumb to that instinct.

Do, however, express in no uncertain terms that you are interested in the job. Make it clear that, in the event you accept it, you are confident you could not only meet but exceed expectations for the position.

But do not ever give the impression that you "need" that job or that you are "dying for it"—even if that's *exactly* what you're feeling.

You must suppress that instinct because of this fundamental truth: neediness is a turnoff to everyone except the most compassionate people. The vast majority of people are attracted to the things they think they *can't* have. No matter what the setting, unattainability is the ultimate aphrodisiac.

When you're looking for someone to invest time, money, or energy in you, you can never let them think they're doing *you* a favor. You must make them believe that the favor is actually coming from you— that by being brought into your orbit, they will be setting *themselves* up for a win.

I became acutely aware of this phenomenon once I became successful. When I was struggling, no one wanted to give me a break. Now that I've made it, everyone wants to cut me in on great deals or rare opportunities. If I go to an award show, I'll get a gift bag worth tens of thousands of dollars. Billionaires invite me to fly on their private jets or stay in their luxury villas. Hedge fund managers give me investment tips. Everybody, it turns out, wants to do you a favor precisely when you *don't* need it.

When you hear about successful people who are already doing great getting $30K gift bags or free flights on private jets, it's easy to grumble, "Man, the rich always get richer," but grumbling won't change your reality. What *will* change it is figuring out how to project the energy and confidence that will make people want to treat you in a similar way.

One of the true magicians of the "act like you don't need it" strategy was the financier Bernie Madoff. He's the guy behind the Ponzi scheme that milked people out of over $64 billion. That's right, $64 *billion*.

I'm not celebrating what Madoff did. He ruined a lot of vulnerable people and organizations and even contributed to his own son committing suicide. But when I read about his story, I couldn't help but notice how masterful he was at employing an "I don't need it" mentality to get people to give him their money.

In the simplest terms, Madoff's scheme worked like this: he would encourage people to invest with his firm, but instead of actually putting their money in the stock exchange, he'd put it into his personal bank account. Then he'd make up fake stock reports that showed his investors getting an incredible return on their money. He guessed correctly that as long as people saw their money growing at above-market rates, they would keep it with him and let it ride.

The only issue would be when people asked for their money back. Since Madoff never actually invested the money, it would be impossible for him to cover those asks. The money wasn't in his account anymore—he'd already spent it on homes, cars, planes, all that good stuff. In order to keep the scheme going, Madoff would have to constantly bring in new investors and keep the finances flowing.

Because he needed as many new investors as possible to prevent his scheme from collapsing, you'd probably think Madoff would be very aggressive in going after potential targets. Especially in cultivating the big-money folks he met at galas and parties in Manhattan, Hollywood, and the Hamptons. You'd assume he'd be wining and dining them, gifting them front-row seats at sporting events, flying them around on his jets, getting the guys call girls, whatever he could do to get in their good graces.

Nope. Madoff did the exact opposite. Whenever one of those deep-pocketed people approached him about investing with his firm,

Madoff would turn them down. He would tell them his fund was full, that there was no possible way he could take on any new investors. Sorry, he just couldn't do business with them.

That would drive those rich folks crazy. Remember, these were power brokers who were never told no. Instead of walking away, it made them want to work with Madoff even more. They became convinced that Madoff was sitting on a more lucrative situation than they'd originally thought.

Let's say a rich guy offered to invest $5 million when he first approached Madoff, a level of investment most managers like Madoff would jump at. After hearing no, the guy might come back to Madoff with an offer to up their investment to $10 million. Nobody says no to a $10 million investment! But Madoff would still act like he wasn't interested. The rich guy would be flipping his wig. He'd get pushy. He'd have their mutual friends call Madoff and lobby on his behalf. Instead of being courted, the guy would start courting Madoff. He'd be determined to get as much of their money to Madoff as possible, because his attitude convinced them that he had to be some sort of mastermind. After all, who else would turn down all that money?

Finally, only when the number got high enough for him, Madoff would pretend to give in. "All right, fine," he might say. "You can come in for $15 million. But don't tell anyone else I did this. It's just for you." Just like that, he'd take the guy to the cleaners. The guy might as well have said, "Bernie, would you please steal my money?"

Madoff did this to very bright people. Hollywood directors. Owners of professional baseball and football teams. Actors and actresses. People who were extremely shrewd and successful in their own fields. None of that mattered. They all got finessed by someone who acted like he didn't need it.

Madoff pulled this off in high society, but I've seen it work in street situations, too. On the street, people are used to constantly being asked for things. "Yo, lemme hold something." Or "My man, can you spot me till next week?" Folks are always on guard to make sure no one plays or gets over on them.

People who understand this instinct can use it to their advantage. Let's say a con man bumps into one of his old homies at the bar and senses the opportunity to work some of his magic. First, he'd buy the guy a few rounds. Top shelf, no well liquor. Make it seem like money was no object. After a few, he might casually mention the Benz he had parked outside or the trip to Aruba he just took his girl on. All his energy and words would project the impression that he was operating out of abundance. The exact opposite of someone looking for a handout.

Eventually the guy's friend will want to know what's funding the lifestyle. The con man will reply, very humbly, that he's doing well in real estate. He won't say much more and instead will push the conversation back to funny old stories—the time we took those girls to Coney Island, or when the fight broke out in the park.

The friend will remain fixated on the money, though. "Hey, what sort of real estate deals you doin'?" he'll eventually ask. That's when the con will make his move. "Oh, it's complicated. Basically, I'm just flipping city-owned properties," he might say. "Yeah, this thing right here I got going on is really great. I know some people in City Hall, and they've put me on to some serious opportunities. Especially this new development I just got some money together for. I think it's gonna make a killing."

The trap has been set. And more often than not, the needy person will walk into it. "Yo, my man, what's good? You gotta let me in on this!" The con man will take another sip of his drink and pretend to mull it over. "Look, because we've been peoples for a long time, if you want in, I can hook you up. But the *absolute* most I can let you put in for is $10,000. I'm sorry, but the rest of it is pretty much spoken for."

"I'm down!" the friend will say and start to make arrangements to get the money together. And just like that, he's been had. The reason he fell for it so easily is because the con man acted like he didn't want anything. If he had said, "Yo, gimme as much as you can get your hands on," or had pressed his friend for a certain amount, that would have set off the alarm bells. By applying zero pressure, he was able to circumvent all his friend's security systems. The guy was so conditioned to people asking and pressing him for things that it never occurred to him to watch for the guy who *wasn't* asking for anything.

Here's a little test to see if you're understanding how to use the power of perception. Let's say I gave you $1 million. But then I told you that in order to keep it, you had a month to turn it into $2 million. Otherwise, I'm taking it back.

What would be your strategy to double your money?

Would you try to start a business and hope it grew quickly?

Would you give it to an investor and hope they weren't the next Bernie Madoff?

Would you buy ten kilos of coke and try to flip it that way?

I hope not, because none of those represent the easiest path to that $2 million.

All you'd have to do is put that money in your bank account and then walk over to your local branch. In this situation, I even give you permission to dress casually. When you get there, ask the branch manager to open up your account.

Their eyes are going to get wide when they see all those zeros on the screen. They're going to become super friendly, very eager to help you in any way they possibly can.

You just stay poised and confident. After they ask you what they can do for you, calmly say, "I'd like a loan for a million dollars, please."

It might seem like an insane thing to ask for, but they're actually going to give you that million so fast you might get whiplash. Fill out a few forms, make some small talk, and in an hour or two everything will be official. And just like that—*BAM!*—you've done it.

Why would the manager be so quick to give you the money? Because they saw that you already *had* a million dollars. They didn't care whether you got it from a rapper, a dead relative, or a drug deal. They just knew that you had it. You might have walked into that branch as just another customer, but all those zeros made you an instant VIP.

(If you've really got the heart of a hustler, you won't stop there. Once you have your two million, you'll stroll over to another branch and turn it into three.)

I'm making it sound simple, but I've seen people successfully apply this technique in other situations. They might not start with a million dollars, but they know how to give off the perception of being a millionaire. Maybe they dress like one. Or vacation like one. Or convincingly drop the names of enough people who are rich until it sounds like they are one, too.

Hell, this is how half of Hollywood made their fortunes. People will get their hands on something of relatively little value—a verbal commitment from an actor, a treatment for a movie idea, or an option on an obscure book. But they act like they're sitting on a pile of gold. Then they keep flipping and flipping whatever they're holding until they're the producer of an actual movie.

The most important character trait they'll demonstrate is confidence. Every time they hit a hurdle, or seem to be on a dead-end road, that confidence will be what gets them through.

They also never seem to be asking for anything. They always project that air of someone who already has what they need. That actor might have said, "Sure, I'll star in your movie," when he was drunk and barely remembers the conversation, but that Hollywood hustler will act like they've got a signed contract with him. That movie treatment might only be three pages long, but the hustler will project the energy of someone who has a finished script.

I'm being honest, I've even had someone do this with me. Several years back, I decided to go into business with a movie producer I met named Randall Emmett. He had experience producing films, so when I decided to create my film production company, Cheetah Vision, I hired him to help run it for me. I paid for everything, including an office, staff, expenses, the whole thing. I even acted in movies we produced for significantly reduced quotes, all for the greater good of building something new.

Randall was an employee of Cheetah Vision, but he positioned himself differently publicly. He allowed people to believe that he was my new "production partner." That was a very smart perception for him to cultivate. It allowed him access to people and places he wouldn't have had otherwise. It also led people to write checks that would have never been written if he was on his own. Ultimately, he went off on his own with one of the people who raised money for projects.

I was okay with it initially, since I understood how the "Hollywood" game works. But I started having a big problem with it when Randall attempted to take credit for *Power* and my overall deal with Starz. Randall might have been pretty good at getting movies made, but he had never been able to get anything going on TV. He was not involved creatively with *Power*, and he had absolutely nothing to do with my overall deal at Starz. Actually, while Randall was involved, my original deal at Starz was terrible. I ultimately learned that was the case after my attorney contacted Starz to renegotiate and build my first overall deal.

Randall had overplayed his hand. For years he'd actually owed me around a million dollars of profit brought from the company, but I hadn't stressed him to pay it back. After a long time passed with him running his mouth, though, my patience had run thinner than Wiz Khalifa. I had my attorney call him up and ask for my money while (unbeknownst to Randall) I was sitting right next to him, listening.

Randall started off the conversation very aggressively. "Are you kidding me? Get the fuck out of here," he told my lawyer. "After all that I've done for 50? After I got him a $150 million deal with Starz? You're going to sweat me for a lousy million? Fuck off."

I had planned to stay quiet, but I couldn't believe my ears. "What is wrong with you, Randall?" I calmly interjected.

There was no reply. "I'm curious. What's with the tough talk?" I continued. "We both know that's not who you are. I'm not dealing with you anymore after this, but before this gets any worse for you, I strongly suggest that you agree to the payment plan we're offering."

Randall must have run out of tough words when he realized he was talking to me, because he got off the phone quick. Then he started texting me excuse after excuse of why he couldn't get me the money right away. I had planned to handle the situation privately, but I was so disappointed in his attitude that I decided to air him out in public. That's how the "I'm sorry, Fofty" text got out there (more on that later). And, of course, I ended up getting all of my money.

It's always a balancing act when you're trying to project an "I don't need it" energy. If you're not forceful enough in your conviction, no one is going to believe you. But you also can't start believing your own hype. Randall was stupid enough to do that. Even as you're telling the world you don't need a thing, you can never forget there are certain people who you are always going to need on your side. Don't try to run the game on them. Always have a select few you remain honest and humble with.

WHAT I'M ATTRACTED TO

Ever since an early age, I've been what you might call a ladies' man. I don't say that to brag. It's just the truth. I don't look like a Ken doll, but I've never had an issue connecting with the opposite sex. It's likely because I've always been comfortable with myself, which is a very attractive trait.

Men, however, don't become truly sexy until our success is publicly noted. So when I started doing well, my perceived attractiveness shot up to a new level. I was cute before, but once I was actually famous, I became one of the sexiest men alive. (Hey, I'm not saying that! *People* magazine said so!) Women are attracted to the stability that comes with money and fame. They looked at me and saw someone reliable who could provide them with everything they needed.

I'm not talking about gold diggers or groupies, either. I was pursued by some of the most incredible women in the world. Not just physically attractive women, but women who were also incredibly successful in their own right. Lawyers, doctors, actresses, and entrepreneurs. Women with the complete package.

I remember back when I was touring for *Get Rich or Die Tryin',* I found myself in a hotel room with an extraordinarily attractive and intelligent woman. Just before things started to go down, I excused myself to use the restroom. As soon as I shut the door, I started doing a little jig and grinned from ear to ear at myself in the mirror. I was so excited I even jumped up in the air and clicked my heels. I just had to take a moment and celebrate. I literally couldn't believe the caliber of woman who was waiting for me in the other room.

Today, I'm a little more laid-back in those sorts of situations. But I've never lost sight of the reality that as much as I enjoy women's company, my sexiness will always be tied to my success. Even if a woman presents differently at first, I still suspect it's part of her motivation. This makes it very difficult to determine who I want to pursue a deeper connection with. I'm always wondering, "Does she want 50 Cent? Or Curtis Jackson?"

This is why I am definitely most attracted to women who don't seem to care about my success, who aren't overly impressed by the persona of 50 Cent. In other words, the ones who act like they don't need 50 Cent, but could be interested in Curtis Jackson.

For example, a lot of people have been curious about my relationship with the comedian Chelsea Handler. I guess we seemed like an odd couple.

I didn't care about what anyone else thought. Chelsea and I met on her talk show, and I started pursuing her right after. I sent her fifty white roses. I'd call her office and ask to speak with her. She didn't hit me back at first, but finally I got in touch with her when she was about to go to Nashville for an event. I asked if I could fly down and meet her, and she said okay. We met and had a great time together. After that we ended up hooking up whenever we were both in LA. I even made plans to go on vacation with her and her family. (Don't worry. I'm not putting her business out there. She's talked about all this publicly.)

We had fun times when we were together, but what really attracted me to her was how she moved professionally. In addition to a talk show, she also had a reality show and was writing bestselling books. She was a real boss. With all of her various hustles, she was probably pulling in over $30 million a year. *That* was sexy as fuck to me.

Most important, she made it very clear she didn't need *anything* from me. Chelsea had way too much going on to ever look to me for making something happen for her. If anything, I was probably trying to soak up a little bit of her energy.

Ultimately, it never went anywhere serious. There was a bit of a miscommunication before my ex-girlfriend Ciara was scheduled to appear on Chelsea's TV show, and we stopped talking after that. I still think she's amazing, though. She's achieved so much success, and what makes it even more impressive is that she's done it on her own terms.

I've never been a big proponent of marriage. Maybe I'm jaded because I've spent a lot of time in Hollywood, where I've learned "husband" is really just another way of saying "My serious boyfriend." At the end of the day, I view marriage as a business deal, and not a particularly good one for the person coming into the relationship with the most money.

Yet as I get older, I start to find myself being more open to the idea of settling down and building a more stable family life. When I go through the mental checklist of things I'd look for in a potential wife, I'm not starting with looks or fame. Those qualities aren't as important to me anymore. The most critical quality for any woman I'm going to be interested in is self-sufficiency, both financial and emotional. Otherwise, I'm always going to think that they're just trying to get me to sign one of those bad contracts. As I was telling a friend the other day, "Taking care of a woman is not a bad concept. But taking care of a woman who has to be taken care of is a *terrible* concept!"

Once I keep going down the checklist, I'm going to have to see qualities like compassion, sense of humor, love of family, and ambition (okay, being cute won't hurt, either). But it's that absence of neediness that's going to make me receptive to the possibility in the first place.

That's how powerful putting out an aura of self-sufficiency can be. It can even get a jaded bachelor like me to talk about putting a ring on it and settling down.

OWN YOUR NARRATIVE

We've been talking about why it's so important to craft your own identity, and now I want to share some examples of people who have been hurt by letting other forces control how they are publicly perceived.

I often think about my close friend, the late Prodigy of Mobb Deep. The duo, which included his partner, Havoc, was legendary for their gritty depictions of life in Queens' notorious Queensbridge projects. Prodigy was an incredible artist, and without a doubt one of the best rappers of his generation. But, for a lot of people, the defining moment of his career came in 2001, when Jay-Z infamously mocked him by "putting him on the Summer Jam screen."

If anyone isn't familiar with the story, Jay-Z and Mobb Deep were involved in a public beef at the time, which led to Jay rapping the following about Prodigy: "When I was pushin' weight, back in '88, you was a ballerina / I got the pictures, I seen ya." It was a reference to the fact that Prodigy used to be a dancer at the ballet studio his mother ran in Queens. And yes, Jay actually had gotten his hands on a picture of Prodigy in ballet tights, which he later infamously put on the screen at Summer Jam.

The implication was clear. Prodigy talks about how much of a gangsta he was in his music, but at heart he was really soft. In hip-hop, you can't get much softer than being a "ballerina."

Prodigy clapped back at Jay, but it didn't really reverse the damage. That picture of him in ballet tights on the Summer Jam screen was a major blow—one that he never truly recovered from.

I never felt it should have been that damaging, though. Yes, it was true that Prodigy's mother ran a ballet studio. And that he used to take classes there. What was so embarrassing about that? He had a mother who raised him in the arts. He was cultured. To me, that sounds like an amazing childhood, and nothing to be ashamed of.

If anything, I felt like Prodigy's arts background made him more prepared as a performer than the rest of us. He was a force in the studio, always coming up with new hooks and concepts. I even remember going to his house one day and noticing several movie scripts lying around. "Man, when did you learn how to write scripts?" I asked him. "Oh, I read some book that showed me how to do it," he answered casually. "I've been writing them ever since."

That's the kind of ability he possessed. He could pick up a book, digest it, and then start churning out scripts like it was nothing. Most rappers struggle to write twelve bars, let alone a movie. They just didn't have the same artistic tradition to draw from.

I felt Prodigy should have embraced his background more. It's what made him special and would have allowed him to create more significant art. Instead, he felt pressured by Jay and others to live up to the persona he had cultivated in his music.

Tupac found himself in a similar dilemma. Like Prodigy, he had a cultured mother who raised him to be incredibly informed about the arts and politics. Tupac didn't grow up writing raps. He grew up writing introspective and revolutionary poems. He was exposed to the same kind of energy as Prodigy.

I always felt 'Pac and Prodigy were art students who adopted thugging as a theme. Instead of embracing all the culture and pride they'd been exposed to, they tried to run in the opposite direction. By doing that, they ran into a trap. In Prodigy's case, it meant getting lured into a battle with Jay-Z he could never win. Once Jay sniffed out that Prodigy was only representing a theme, he knew how to batter his public perception.

'Pac paid a much heavier price. By raising the thug flag so high, he sent out a very dangerous signal, one that attracted all the real thugs to him. Once they were present, there was no way he could control that energy. It would have been difficult for a true gangsta, but for an art kid like 'Pac, it was outright impossible. It was that energy that ended up getting him killed.

Prodigy and I were close friends, and I miss him a lot. He was such an interesting and well-rounded dude. Every conversation I had with him taught me something new. If I have one regret, it's that I didn't push him harder to let go of the thugging theme and get closer to his true roots. If he had done that, it not only would have revived his career but also enhanced the overall state of hip-hop. It would have shown a new generation of rappers that it was okay to embrace their backgrounds, no matter where they came from.

LET PEOPLE BE HONEST ABOUT THEMSELVES

There was a time I didn't understand the importance of letting people be themselves. Back in the early 2000s, G-Unit's in-house DJ was a guy named Whoo Kid. In addition to playing, one of Whoo Kid's jobs was putting out mixtapes, which were extremely popular at the time and played a very large role in creating G-Unit's buzz. One day Whoo Kid was talking to an A&R guy at Atlantic Records and happened to notice the unreleased new single from Fat Joe's Terror Squad on the guy's desk. Whoo Kid knew it was a valuable exclusive, so when the A&R guy wasn't looking, he stole it!

Of course, Fat Joe, Big Pun, and the rest of the Terror Squad were not happy when their song leaked on Whoo Kid's next mixtape. They wanted blood! So when they saw him at a club a few weeks later, they immediately tried to grab him and stomp him out.

Whoo Kid was from Queens, but from Queens Village, which isn't quite as tough as Southside. Someone from Southside would have taken that ass kicking just to make sure they got in a few licks themselves. Not Whoo Kid. When he saw Terror Squad coming for him, he ran away as fast as he could. Those Terror Squad guys didn't even lay a finger on him. (Whoo Kid couldn't run forever, though—eventually Big Pun caught up with him and actually threw him in the back of a van. Whoo Kid managed to talk his way out of it, though.)

Usually, hearing that one of your crew had avoided an ass whipping would be a cause for celebration. Not in the G-Unit. Instead, I was outraged when I heard what Whoo Kid had done.

"Yo bro, they're telling me you ran from Terror Squad," I said.

"Yeah, I did," he replied.

"*What?*" I asked incredulously. "Are you a pussy?"

"Yes!" Whoo Kid quickly replied. "Yes, I am!"

I was floored. I literally didn't know how to respond. Where I was from, you never, ever wanted to admit you were afraid. Once you did that, you were food. Everyone was going to come and take a piece of you until there was nothing left.

Being a coward ran counter to everything I'd been taught growing up. It was like telling a kid who'd been raised in the church that there was no God. Or telling a kid who grew up in Chicago in the nineties that Michael Jordan was a bum on the court. Nothing short of blasphemy.

Evidently Whoo Kid's experience was a little different than mine. He didn't mind being seen that way. The difference in perspective left me at a loss. How could I possibly have someone representing G-Unit who had no problem being thought of as a pussy? My initial reaction was to fire him on the spot. To give him the proverbial bus ticket home.

I might come across as reckless sometimes, but the truth is I don't like to make rash decisions unless my environment forces me to. No one was pressing me, so I took a moment to consider the possibility I was overreacting. What exactly was Whoo Kid's job with G-Unit? Was it to fight? No.

His job was to play music. To get the crowds hyped. And he was great at that. Whoo Kid was a pro at getting the energy turned all the way up.

His job was also to put out mixtapes that would keep G-Unit buzzing in the streets. Obviously he took that job *very* seriously. What did it really matter if he was afraid to fight?

Not much at all, I had to admit.

Whoo Kid never got that ticket home. In fact, I came to respect him for being honest. It would have been easy for him to say something like, "Nah son, I'm no pussy. They just sayin' I ran. I was about to light those guys up, but they dipped before I could get at them."

A lot of people have lied to me over the years like that, claiming that they were about to handle things they never had any intention of touching. They talked tough because they thought that's what 50 Cent wanted to hear. Not because that's what was in their hearts.

Sure, 50 Cent wants to be surrounded by guys who aren't intimidated. Those kinds of people have always been around, and always will be.

Curtis Jackson, on the other hand, has come to understand that he needs different types of energy on his team. People who don't always seek out conflict, but can get things in other ways. I want both types of people on my team. All I need to know: who is who.

The situation with Whoo Kid is when I learned that, as a leader, I have to empower the people under me to be who they are. If people feel there's only one energy that I'll respect, that limits what we can do collectively. Whoo Kid gave me his truth, and because of his honesty, we've enjoyed a very fruitful relationship for damn near twenty years.

Another person who was very honest with me was Jimmy Iovine, who ran Interscope when I was selling millions of records. Jimmy was comfortable working with gangstas and making music that reflected their lifestyle, but he was very clear that he was no gangsta himself. If the conversation ever turned to serious street business around Jimmy, he'd quickly tell everyone, "Hey, watch what you say around me because I'm a rat. Don't tell me anything, because I'll definitely rat you guys out if I have to."

A lot of people used to laugh when he said that, because it sounded so ridiculous to those of us who grew up on the street. We were taught that snitching was the very last thing you ever do—let alone admit to.

But I appreciated Jimmy's candor, even if some found it a little hypocritical: "Hey, be a gangster in the songs, just not around me in real life." I'd rather know where a man stands and adjust accordingly than think I'm operating under a certain set of standards when I'm not.

Some people said, "Fuck Jimmy if he's cool being a rat." My reaction was, "Then just don't tell your business around Jimmy." Seems pretty straightforward. He and I were selling tens of millions of records together. Why would I walk away from that or the money because he said something that was unacceptable in another context? That would have been foolish.

Instead, I filed it in my mental Rolodex and went on conducting business with him. And when he eventually made decisions that were good for him but not necessarily for me, I was prepared for that.

Whether you're the boss, a partner, or just a worker, you have to create an environment where people can be honest about their character with you. Otherwise, you're going to build unsustainable situations.

That's what ruined Ja Rule's career.

Ja grew up as a Jehovah's Witness in a better part of Queens than I did. The only time he came to my part of town was when he would knock on the door and try to sell copies of *The Watchtower*. A nice religious boy. There's nothing wrong with that.

But the people around him, like Irv, tried to turn him against his true nature as a gentle guy and transform him into a gangsta. Instead of accepting his blessings—his talent for fun, female-oriented music—they were hell-bent on turning him into something negative.

When they got a record deal with Def Jam, what did they call it? Murder Inc. Records. They had an open road in front of them, but they decided to paint themselves into a dangerous corner. Since none of them were actual murderers, they started seeking out people who had that energy. They eventually found what they were looking for, and it almost brought the whole company down.

If you take a close look at guys like Ja Rule, you'll see that they walked with a crutch. In his case, it was the image of a gangsta. He took DMX's flow, dressed up like Tupac, and tried to rap about other people's lifestyles. It worked for a second, but as I've said, when you're walking with a crutch, there's a limit on how far you can go.

If the people around Ja had understood this, and had given him the confidence to embrace his true nature, things would probably have turned out much better for all of them. They could have kept making feel-good, female-friendly records for years. Those records never go out of style. Instead, Murder Inc. hasn't put out an album in over ten years, and today Ja Rule is best known as the fraud making a fool of himself in the Fyre Festival documentaries.

It's always better to empower the people around you to live their truth. When you force them to perpetuate a role, eventually people will see it.

One of the main reasons I'll always be relevant is because no one can be a better 50 Cent than me. They can be younger than me. Have a better sense of style and a better ear for beats.

But they can never be a better 50 Cent than me (though that hasn't stopped a lot of people from trying). As long as I'm always myself, no one can beat me at that.

As long as you're comfortable walking your truth, no one will ever beat you at being you, either.

CHAPTER 7

IF WE CAN'T BE FRIENDS

Disagreement is something normal.

—DALAI LAMA

For years I didn't like Oprah Winfrey.

She's not the type of person (tough, smart, and powerful) you'd want to have an issue with, but I felt a type of way about the things she said about hip-hop music in the past.

It seemed like every time Oprah would go off about how hip-hop was misogynistic and ruining America's youth, she was talking about the same things on my album.

What actually bothered me was being kept off her show. I wanted to be on it.

Oprah was where A-listers would go to promote their projects. Sell books. Move albums. Hype movies. I considered myself an A-lister, so how does that look that I'm not there, too?

I felt I had to explain my absence to my audience. So, as I tend to do, I kept it real about the situation. I did a few interviews where I said the reason Oprah wouldn't have me on her couch is because she's a reflection of her audience, which is made up of middle-aged white women. That audience finds me scary, so it would figure Oprah wouldn't be into me, either. (I also named one of my dogs after her, which I admit was a bit much.)

After I made those comments, I didn't spend a lot of time worrying about how Oprah might take them. She'd already made it clear I wasn't coming on her show, so why did I care about upsetting her? She had her business to run (for the record, I think she should have kept her afternoon TV show after she started OWN), and I had mine.

Then one night I was at a fundraiser in New York City for the NYRP, a nonprofit founded by Bette Midler. It's a fantastic organization that sponsors a lot of renewal programs for parks and neglected areas of New York City.

It wasn't my normal crowd—a lot of older white people in tuxedos—but I love Bette and respect the cause so I bought a table. At one point in the evening, I bumped into Gayle King, Oprah's best friend. Now, Gayle is the real deal—a very sophisticated, secure, and smart lady. She's never afraid of a situation (as she showed with her R. Kelly interview), so she marched right up to me and basically said, "Why you talkin' shit about my girl?" I had to explain to Gayle that I didn't have a true beef with Oprah.

"Listen, I'd love to be Oprah's friend," I continued. "But if we can't be friends, could we at least be enemies?"

When I said that, I saw Gayle arch her eyebrows and look at me a bit differently. It registered with her that, while I might have been talking trash about her friend, there was a method to what I was doing. "Okay, you're different than I thought," Gayle told me. "I'm going to tell Oprah she needs to meet you. You two need to talk."

True to her word, Gayle set it up for me to be on Oprah's show. It was a great episode. She came to my old house in Queens, met my grandmother, and walked around the neighborhood with me. Eventually we got to our relationship.

"Did you say things to be proactive?" she asked. "Or did you just not like me?"

"I would see moments where you would discuss your feelings on the culture—rap culture—and everything that was wrong with the culture was on my CD," I said with a smile. "And I was like, 'Ah, she doesn't like me.'"

"You're talking about the N-word?" asked Oprah. "Misogyny?"

"All of those things."

"Views against women. Violence. . . . You know, just things like that," Oprah replied, not backing down.

"Just those little things," I said, laughing.

"In that moment, I'm thinking, 'She don't like me,' because there are so many different impressions . . . and not to say those things were wrong, but it made me say, 'If I can't be a friend, at least let me be an enemy' . . . so I can coexist," I said, before adding, "I just use it as a strategy."

"Ohhh. *That's* interesting," said Oprah, looking at one of her producers off camera.

The reason Gayle and Oprah were so intrigued by that phrase was because it shattered their preconceived notions about me. Before meeting me, they had bought into the 50 Cent persona—that this was someone who got into beefs and drama because he just couldn't help himself.

But when I said "at least let me be an enemy," they understood that when I got into a beef, it was never driven by emotion. Instead, I was moving off of strategy.

My strategy was pretty straightforward: I'd always prefer to be friends with someone, but if they're not interested, then I consider being enemies the next best option. Why? Because if you hate me, you're more likely to talk about me.

If you feel passionately about me in a negative way, at some point you'll probably say to your friend, "Man, I can't stand 50 Cent." Your friend is going to ask you "Why?" and just like that, I've become the subject of a conversation. That's all I'm asking for.

Now I've got a foot in the door. Maybe after hearing about me, your friend won't feel quite as negative. Maybe they'll think, "This guy sounds kinda interesting. I'll check out his music. Or watch *Power*." Maybe that's even how you got to this book in the first place. Through a friend.

That conversation would have never taken place if you felt neutral about me. No one asks their friends if they've listened to a song they feel neutral about. No one mentions a writer or a designer that doesn't elicit a strong reaction in them.

We only bring up things we love. Or things we hate.

I'd always prefer the love. But if I can't get that, I'll take the hate.

There's always a chance I can turn that hate into something positive.

The ancient Greeks believed in a concept called "agon," which roughly translates to the idea of people coming together for purposes of a contest or competition.

To the Greeks, the most basic energy in the world was a battle between two forces. A debate was a fight between two people over an idea. Exercise is a fight between energy and fatigue. Study is a fight between you and the material. Every new day is a fight between light and darkness.

The Greeks didn't shy away from those fights. They believed that competition, in any form, was beneficial. Their most famous example of putting that belief into action was the organized athletic competition they created, which today we know as the Olympics. The Greeks valued the Olympics so much that they would actually stop battles in the middle of the fighting so that contestants could walk through unharmed and make it to the games on time.

Today the Olympics give out silver and bronze medals to contestants who don't win. The ancient Greeks didn't believe in participation trophies. Each competition had only one winner. The victor went back to his village a hero, and everyone else went home a loser.

The ancient Greeks' attitude toward competition reminds me of hip-hop culture today. Since day one, every rapper who picked up the mic has wanted to be acknowledged as the best whoever did it. No rapper is competing for a silver or bronze medal. Every single one of us got into the game to take home the gold.

That mind-set was born in hip-hop's roots in the streets. That dynamic, for better or worse, keeps the culture youthful. Unless you can keep your grip on the throne, it's out with the old and in with the new.

Because of my upbringing, I'm extremely comfortable with the concept of competition. I don't care if it's music, TV, clothes, liquor, or sneakers: if I'm looking to get into a space that someone else is already occupying, watch how fast I turn it into a competition.

Some people shy or even run away from challenge, but I always stroll confidently toward it.

It's a sensibility that's earned me a reputation as a bully in the minds of many. I rarely dispute the title, but it's an oversimplification. I don't wake up in the morning looking to pick fights with people. I don't celebrate conflict. Again, I'd rather be friends. But if someone says they want a problem with me, I'll respond, "No problem."

Because it's never a problem for me to compete.

COMPETITION BRINGS OUT THE BEST

Ever since he was a teenager growing up in Italy, Enzo Ferrari had a passion for car racing. In 1922, at the age of twenty, he began working as a test driver in Milan and later joined Alfa Romeo as a driver. He spent a few years on the racing circuit but retired after the birth of his son. Race car driving was dangerous business back then, and he decided that instead of risking his life every week, he would focus on the development side of the car business. In 1940 he founded his own manufacturing company, Ferrari, which would go on to become one of the best known and respected brands in the world.

Around the same time, another Italian car enthusiast, Ferruccio Lamborghini, was establishing a manufacturing business. But unlike Ferrari, Lamborghini was making tractors, not race cars. He enjoyed racing, but his larger passion was focused on the internal workings of machines.

After purchasing a Ferrari himself, Lamborghini recognized a number of flaws in the design. The cars were too noisy and had a notoriously touchy clutch, which had to be repaired. When he took his car in to have the Ferrari mechanics fix it, they wouldn't let him personally observe their repairs, which pissed him off.

Since Ferraris were already considered the best luxury sports cars on the market, Lamborghini saw these flaws as inexcusable. He decided to bring his critiques to Enzo Ferrari himself. Ferrari was deeply insulted that this "tractor mechanic" thought he could teach him something about race cars and rejected the advice.

The moment created a deep-seated rivalry between the two. Stung by Ferrari's snub, Lamborghini decided he'd turn his interest in cars into a professional pursuit. He wasn't playing around, and four months later the Lamborghini 350 GTV debuted at the Turin Motor Show.

Enzo Ferrari had a head start over Ferruccio Lamborghini in this budding rivalry. He had already been in the business for a number of years, was older, and had far more racing miles under his belt. Not to mention he'd already made a ton of money.

Lamborghini, on the other hand, had technical know-how on the inner workings of cars, an insight that Ferrari's founder lacked. It was said that Lamborghini's office building was even intentionally built next to their manufacturing facility, which allowed him to take a quick trip to the factory and work on the cars in person when a problem arose. He had a willingness to get his hands dirty, literally, to see his dream shine.

As competitive rivals, Lamborghini and Ferrari would bring out the best in each other's work. Ferrari was never too interested in making street cars, as his passion lay in racing. Lamborghini was more focused on practicality and everyday use. If he hadn't been pushing the market in that direction, Ferrari might have never come off the racetrack and into the street. The sense of competition forced both companies to evolve into stronger, more versatile versions of themselves. As it's said, iron sharpens iron.

The results of that competition were innovation and the building of dynasties. Ferrari and Lamborghini could have been friends, but a peaceful and gentle first meeting may never have inspired the creation of some of the best cars in the world.

I've personally been a supporter of both brands over the years. I've had a few Ferraris and a few Lambos too. And while both are incredible cars, I've got to crown Lambo the winner of this particular competition. A couple of years ago, I bought a beautiful Ferrari 488. The dealer told me the car had to be plugged into an outlet in the wall of my garage when it wasn't running so the battery would charge. I followed the directions, but every time I'd try to start it up, nothing happened. The car looked great, but what am I really doing with a car that won't drive anywhere? That thing was a lemon, so it had to go back. Ferruccio Lamborghini wasn't lying back in the day—those Ferraris don't always run right!

Ferruccio Lamborghini and Enzo Ferrari used their competition to push themselves to heights neither of them ever dreamed of when they were starting out. Forget about just being successful companies—a hundred years later, each of their last names has become synonymous with quality and luxury. That's making an impact!

I really believe that the better your opponent is, the better you become. It was true in the luxury auto business, and it's true in almost every field. It's certainly at the front of my mind whenever I start working on a new project.

Take music. Whenever I'm about to hit the studio, I try to think about all the great musical moments I've experienced from different artists. I say "great moments" because I don't necessarily have a favorite artist. But I do have favorite moments. Usually it's a song that jumps out to me and captures a feeling I find inspiring. Black Rob's "Whoa" was like that to me. I can't say Rob was one of my favorite artists across the board, but for the four minutes and seven seconds that song was playing, no one else was better to me. Same way with Boogie Down Productions' "The Bridge Is Over." Even though KRS-One was dissing Queens, his aggression was so contagious that I loved that song. Listening to it even thirty-five years later always puts me in an aggressive, confident mood.

When I'm trying to get in the zone creatively, I'll catalog ten of those moments in my head. It doesn't even have to be a complete song; it could just be a great hook or a catchy chorus. I'll collect all those moments and label them my creative competition.

The entire time I'm recording, I'll refer back to those moments. If I'm listening to a verse I just laid down, I'll ask myself, "Was it as fire as 'Whoa'"? If the answer is no, then I need to go back in the booth and give it another shot. Same thing with each chorus or hook that I compose. I'll compare it to those great moments I've cataloged. If I feel like it's falling short, I go back and do it again. I keep holding up what I've done against those moments I've cataloged and ask myself, "Is it good enough?"

Now, is every song I record going to be a classic like "Whoa" or "The Bridge Is Over"? Of course not. But by forcing myself to measure up against a song like that, I bring out the best in myself. It's like the old saying, "Shoot for the moon. Even if you miss it, you will land among the stars."

But in order to push yourself to be great that way, the first thing you have to be able to do is appreciate the greatness in others. You cannot go around believing that no one is as good as you and therefore you don't have anyone to measure up against. That's bullshit. No matter what you do, or what your field, there is someone else great in it, too. So instead of believing your own hype, identify that individual and make them your competition.

People like to say I'm a hater, but nothing could be further from the truth. What I am is an appreciator. I'm always appreciating what other people are doing. Competing is not hating. It's actually putting appreciation into action.

You must be an appreciator no matter what you do. Let's say you're a novelist. Identify whoever the writer you think is the best and measure whatever you write against them. If you're an architect, walk around your city and measure yourself against the most beautiful buildings you see. You need to stare at those buildings and say, "You know what? That staircase was really fucking good," and then store it away in your mind. And if you really think your work is nicer than anything you see, compare yourself to whoever built the Eiffel Tower or the Taj Mahal. No matter how confident you are in your own abilities, there's still someone out there for you to compete against.

Never think you're above competition. One way I see people fall into this trap is by listening to the individuals around them. This happens with rappers all of the time. A guy will get in the booth, spit a verse, and one of his homies will say, "Yo, that was a hot line." Bam! That's all it takes. Now in the rapper's mind he's already the greatest of all time.

His friends will go on to tell him he's better than whatever Sound-Cloud young boy is hot at the moment. The rapper will eat it up and grow even cockier. But notice what his homies are *not* saying: that he's better than Jay. That he's better than Kendrick. That he's better than me. Those are the standards you need to hold yourself up against before you start thinking you're the GOAT.

If you only compare yourself to inferior opponents, you'll feel like you're doing something when you're really not doing much at all.

This is why a lot of rappers challenge me prematurely. Their friends make them think they're ready when they haven't achieved anywhere near what I have. That's fine with me. I just have to knock them back down to size a bit.

No matter what you've accomplished, you're never done competing. I've sold over 30 million records, but every time I step in the booth I know I'm about to be measured up. Not against anyone else, either. Against myself. Whenever I put a new song out, people are going to say, "That's cool, but it's not like when you first did it." I used to get frustrated with that response, but now I accept it. I'm not going to get another chance to make a first impression. Until I put down the mic for the final time, I'm going to be locked in a rivalry with myself. That doesn't frustrate me anymore. I'm dope. Why would I be mad at the comparison? Now I just need to go out and beat myself.

THE BEARSVILLE BOOT CAMP

Roughly two hours north of New York City, just outside of the town of Woodstock (near the home of the famous music festival of the same name), you'll find the Bearsville Studios. The recording studio, which kinda reminds me of a barn, was founded in 1969 by Albert Grossman, a legendary music industry promoter. Grossman is best known for once being Bob Dylan's manager, as well as the man who guided the career of Janis Joplin and folk stars like Peter, Paul, and Mary. Grossman's dream was to build a studio in a rustic setting close to New York City where rock artists could escape the noise and distractions of the city. For many years, the studio was considered one of the finest rock and roll music recording spaces in the country.

In 2000, Grossman was long gone (though his wife, Sandy, still ran the place), but he and Dylan were replaced by another type of artist: New York City rappers. Responding to the same impulse that had motivated Grossman over thirty years earlier, the hip-hop production team the Trackmasters had decided to rent Bearsville out for three months. The duo, comprised of producers Tone and Poke, took over the studios and then invited a mixture of established and unknown rappers and producers to travel up to Woodstock and record with them. There wouldn't be any clubs to go to, or entourages hanging around. It was basically a hip-hop boot camp where the only agenda was music, music, and more music. Here's how I wound up there with them:

One day I saw Cory Rooney, a producer and songwriter from Sony, and Markie Dee from the Fat Boys at my neighborhood barbershop. I had just finished a demo tape, so I asked Cory if I could play it for them. Cory said okay, then led us to his black convertible 500 SL Benz parked out in front, and we all piled into the car to listen. A couple of seconds into the first song, Cory's phone rang and he picked it up. I didn't like that. He kept talking through the second song. Meanwhile, Markie seemed disinterested.

After a few more songs, Cory turned to Markie and said, "I dunno, what you think, man?"

"It's cool," replied Markie, but I'd already seen enough. I knew I was a nobody to them, but I wasn't going to sit there and be disrespected.

"Gimme my tape back," I growled, popping the demo out of the stereo. "Y'all old school." I grabbed my tape and jumped out of the ride.

It was a pretty brash, some might even say stupid, way to treat two industry veterans. I figured I'd never hear from them again. Then a few days later I got word that they were looking for me. It turns out Cory had been listening (guess he was a good multitasker after all) and had passed along the tape to Tone and Poke. They'd liked what they heard, Cory told me over the phone, and wanted me to come upstate to work on some music with them.

I was excited they liked my music, but it also sounded like a setup. I'd just insulted these two, and now they wanted me to take a ride upstate with them? Seemed like a trip I might never come back from.

I was torn. My street instincts were on high alert, but Tone and Poke were respected producers who had had a string of hits with Nas, Will Smith, and R. Kelly. I really wanted to work with them. I invited Cory and Markie to come back by the barbershop so I could take their temperature before committing to anything. When they pulled up, they didn't seem pissed. In fact, they seemed really eager for me to come upstate with them. My instincts told me I'd be safe. I packed a small bag and took off with them that very afternoon.

I ended up staying in Bearsville for eighteen days. Albert Grossman might have envisioned the studio as a retreat, but my time there was one of the most competitive—and creative—periods of my life. I arrived at Bearsville as an MC whose reputation barely extended past my neighborhood. Suddenly I found myself surrounded by some real industry heavy hitters. Not just Tone and Poke, but established producers like L.E.S., Al West, and Kurt Gowdy, as well. Pros who really knew their way around a studio and made beats to the highest standard. There were also rappers there, like N.O.R.E., Slick Rick, and later Nas, who were already very established in the culture.

It would have been very easy—even understandable—for me to be intimidated by the environment at Bearsville. I was far away from home in some studio out in the middle of the woods. Most of the other artists there were way ahead of me in terms of success. A lot of rappers in my situation would have looked around, gotten unnerved, and taken the first bus home, fled back to the safety of their neighborhood instead of subjecting themselves to the intensity of being locked in a building with their competition for two weeks.

I wasn't going anywhere. Bearsville was like heaven to me. I loved that we were in the middle of nowhere and there was nothing else to focus on except the music. I was completely locked in. I wasn't the most polished rapper there, or the best lyricist, but I was determined no one there was going to outwork me.

Other guys might start their day hung over or sitting in their rooms getting high, but I didn't hear those sorts of distractions. Once I woke up, the only thing I was doing was going for a jog in the woods. Then it was time to hit the studio. I'd usually be the first one there.

Once checked in, I'd go from room to room, asking each producer to let me hear the latest beat they were working on. Once I'd listened to it a couple of times, I'd go sit down in a corner somewhere and try to write a verse for it.

Once I finished, I'd go back to the studio and ask the producer if I could record whatever I had come up with. It was a very tough crowd to impress, but I was determined to stand out. I wanted to hear someone say, "Nah, he's got some shit," every time I finished a verse.

I was a total beast, day in and day out. It got to the point where I had spit verses on every track Tone and Poke had come up with and I still wanted more. I ended up rhyming over unfinished tracks—basically just drums—because my creative juices were flowing so strongly and I was overflowing with material.

I recorded over thirty-six songs in Bearsville, many of which would go on to appear on *Power of the Dollar*. I'd come into the boot camp a relative unknown, confident in my ability, but also unsure about where I stood as an MC. After those eighteen days, I knew damn sure that I belonged.

It is extremely powerful to meet your competition head-on and walk away from the confrontation knowing you have what it takes. That confidence stays with you for a long time.

M y time in Bearsville left me with more than enough material for what was supposed to be my debut on Columbia. We submitted the music, and the label gave me a release date. I started preparing for what I knew was going to be a major launch. But as the release date started getting closer and closer, it became clear to me that I was the only one doing any real preparations.

Columbia didn't really understand me as an artist. I could see that they were just going to throw the album out there and hope that something popped. If it did, great. If it didn't, then I'd be gone.

That might have been how they did things, but it wasn't an acceptable approach to me. I'd thrown everything I had into the time in Bearsville, and I knew I had the right material. My entire life was riding on the album being a hit. If you're just going to throw me up against the wall and hope I stick, then I'm going to turn into your friendly neighborhood Spider-Man.

I didn't have a plan B for my album not working. So I started looking around for a way to make myself a priority. I was going to create my own glue.

At the time, hip-hop was in a cautious state because of the recent deaths of Biggie and Tupac. Everyone was afraid of a new war popping off, and it became taboo to mention another rapper's name in your song. If people did take shots at each other, they were subtle ones that only a hard-core fan would ever catch. For instance, when Nas wanted to diss Jay-Z, he didn't do it by name at first. Instead, he rhymed something like, "20 G bets I'm winning them / threats I'm sending them / Lex with TV sets, the minimum / Ill sex adrenaline." To the outside world it didn't sound like anything, but those of us in the culture knew that Jay-Z rode around in a Lexus with a TV set. So that was a subliminal shot at Jay.

Nas might have been subtle in his attacks, but in the void created by that unspoken truce among rappers I saw a golden opportunity. I hadn't signed any truce. There weren't any rappers out there who had value to me as a friend. But as enemies . . . well, that was a different story.

I knew if someone had the confidence to come out of the shadows and reembrace hip-hop's tradition of firing direct shots, the buzz would be deafening. I decided to be that person.

"How to Rob" wasn't intended to just diss one person, it was a diss to the entire industry. It was as if I was saying, "If none of y'all want to be my friend, then we're all going to be enemies." I let almost everyone have it—Jay-Z, Wu-Tang, Big Pun, Missy Elliott, Will Smith, Jada Pinkett, Slick Rick, DMX, Bobby Brown, and Whitney Houston all got called out by name.

In order to signal that I was only interested in competition, not real hostility, we threw in a line ("I've been scheming Tone and Poke since they found me") directed against the Trackmasters, too. Just to show that even my guys weren't above being dissed. Then we added the Mad Rapper in the chorus, saying "This ain't serious / Being broke can make you delirious," to bring a little levity to the situation.

Even with those disclaimers, the record created an uproar the moment it dropped on Hot 97, New York City's premier radio station at the time. Most of those artists weren't prepared for someone saying their name in a song. Throughout the culture, everyone was asking, "Whoa! Who is this new guy? Because he's sayin' everyone's names and don't care about nothin'!" Some of the biggest ones, including Jay-Z, Big Pun, and Wu-Tang, had responses for me. Which was exactly what I had hoped for.

I needed something that was going to create attention around me, and "How to Rob" got me noticed immediately. Columbia snatched up the song and put it on the *In Too Deep* soundtrack, which exposed me to a wider audience. Everything was going according to my plan . . . but then I got shot, which essentially derailed everything I'd put into motion.

It would end up taking a few more years to experience the hit debut I'd worked so hard toward. But I still learned a valuable lesson with "How to Rob": people always respond to a competitor. When you're viewed as someone who is going to run into the fray, as opposed to running from it, you'll always have eyes on you. Whether it's rap, sports, politics, media, or business, there's always going to be an audience for someone who isn't afraid to mix it up with their rivals.

All you have to do to capitalize on that appetite for action is to keep your emotions out of the process. I didn't have a problem with most of the artists I mentioned in that song—I respected the hell out of guys like Jay, Pun, and Raekwon. But being respectful wasn't going to put me in the position I needed to be in to realize my dreams. I had to demonstrate my competitiveness to make the industry take notice of me, so that's exactly what I did.

They haven't stopped paying attention to me since.

CURTIS VERSUS *GRADUATION*

If "How to Rob" announced my competitive streak to hip-hop culture, my competition with Kanye West is what introduced it to mainstream America.

Our battle took place in 2007, when Kanye's third album, *Graduation*, was due to come out a week after my third album, *Curtis*. When I saw that the dates were so close to each other, I realized that we had a chance to do something special by turning our releases into a head-to-head competition.

I pitched Kanye on the concept of each of us dropping the same day. Being an independent thinker himself, Kanye saw the value in my vision and agreed to move his release up. He understood we could collectively generate much more buzz by hyping our battle than being out on individual promo runs.

The media loves a spectacle, and few things were more of a show than Kanye and me going head-to-head. We both played it for all it was worth, doing appearances together and adopting the role of two prize-fighters before a big fight. To be clear, there was no actual beef between us. Kanye had never expressed any discomfort about the success

I'd had, and I respected him as an artist. It was truly just a case of two people being comfortable with the concept of competing against each other.

Personally, I knew competition was what I needed at that point in my career. I was in the most vulnerable state an artist can reach: confusion. So much had happened to me in such a short period of time that I had lost touch with my sense of self. Competition would help take me back to my roots. In order to regain that spark, I even moved back to my grandmother's house in Queens for a bit so I could soak up some of my old energy.

Kanye was in a different point in his career at the time, but he took the competition just as seriously as I did. In the weeks leading up to the release, he locked himself away in his studio, redoing mixes and trying to make his album sound as tight as possible. He reportedly mixed "Stronger" over fifty times before he was finally satisfied. Neither of us were treating it like a stunt. Both of us were playing to win.

In the end, Kanye took home the gold. *Graduation* sold 957,000 units its first week, while *Curtis* moved 691,000 units. It marked the first time two artists had moved over 600,000 units in the same week since 1991.

Today, selling 691,000 units your first week would be considered a massive success, but at the time the narrative was that Kanye had soundly defeated me. Of course he did beat me, but what the public couldn't see was that I'd still earned a major victory.

The truth was that by the time *Curtis* was ready to drop, Interscope was already starting to pull back from me. I was in the green with them financially, as my first two albums had each sold a combined 20 million copies. But despite that success, it was still their discretion whether to continue spending marketing dollars on me. Despite all my success, they decided to slow down the cash flow.

Even more damaging than holding back on the marketing dollars, they were undercutting my promotional strategy for the album. My plan had been to build up a street buzz with the song "Straight to the Bank," which spoke to my core audience. Once that song was bubbling a bit, my idea was to release "Amusement Park," which had more of a pop feel. It was the same strategy I used when I released "Wanksta" before "In Da Club." Get your core audience engaged first, and then drop something for a wider audience.

Interscope should have supported my plan—it had worked in the past—but when "Amusement Park" did not hit number one as fast as they expected, they started to second-guess the strategy. That threw off the energy I was trying to build. To make matters even worse, when the record when to print, the whole album leaked prematurely. Those records should have come out after *Curtis* dropped, instead of in the weeks leading up to it.

Once those leaks happened, I was in a bad spot. The public was none the wiser, but I knew Interscope had already severely damaged my launch. Thankfully, I knew just what to do. Instead of sitting around and moaning about my label, I took matters into my own hands. Just like I had seven years earlier when Columbia was dropping the ball, I created a competition that would generate the buzz my label wasn't capable of creating.

Even worse, I was competing against an artist whose label was doing everything—and I mean everything—to make sure he beat me. Jimmy Iovine might not have cared about beating Kanye, but Jay-Z, who was the head of Def Jam at the time, damn sure cared about beating me. Jay had been extremely uncomfortable with my run in NYC for years. So he did everything under the sun to make sure he could beat me through Kanye.

I realized what I was up against in the weeks leading up to the release when Kanye and I both agreed to do joint appearances on BET. I had planned to bring Eminem with me, but BET told Interscope we couldn't have guests. Interscope said fine, and told Em not to come. Then the day of the show, I get there and Jay is performing with Kanye.

So clearly Jay had gone to some length to get around the "no guests" rule, whereas Interscope had just let it go. They simply weren't as motivated as Jay.

Jay took a lot of pride in Kanye's victory. I think that's one of the reasons he's so disappointed in Kanye today. Jay knows how much he supported Ye during that period, but it still wasn't enough for Ye. That probably hurt Jay.

Jay even mentioned my battle with Kanye in his book *Decoded*, taking a little shot at me when he wrote, "Rappers who use beef as a marketing plan might get some quick press, but they're missing the point."

I congratulate Jay for doing the right thing by his artist in that situation, but I think he was the one who missed the point. First, like I mentioned, there was no actual beef in that particular competition. Second, without that competition, I have little doubt that due to Interscope's missteps, my sales would have been much lower. Our competition actually turned what would have been a tough first week for me into a very respectable one. If I had just left Interscope to their own devices, I might have only sold 400K that first week. Instead, I managed to salvage a tough situation and create a historic moment. As I later told an interviewer, "Kanye West gets the trophy, 50 Cent gets the check!" That's no shot at Kanye (he made a lot of money, too), but it's a trade I'll take every time.

CURTIS LANNISTER

Sometimes, as in the case of *Curtis* versus *Graduation*, you can create your own competition. Other times, the world will try to choose your opponent for you. When that happens, you need to be hustlin' at your smartest. Because while you should never run from competition, you do have to dictate who your opponent is whenever possible. You can't allow yourself to get into a battle with someone just because that's what the media, or fans, want to see. You have to put yourself against the opponent who not only gives you the best chance of winning, but also leaves you in a more favorable position if you do end up losing.

When *Power* first came out on Starz in 2014, it didn't seem to have any direct competition. Then *Empire* dropped on FOX in 2015, and suddenly everyone wanted to stack the two shows up against each other. On the surface, the comparisons seemed reasonable. Both shows were set in the world of hip-hop. Both had black casts and plots that revolved around strong female characters. Both featured soundtracks that were central to the energy of the show. Both shows had black executive producers. I understood why people wanted to pit us against each other.

At first I was happy to play into that perception. FOX was spending a lot more money on *Empire* than Starz was allocating for *Power*, so it was advantageous for me to tie into their marketing. I also noticed FOX trying to co-opt some of our narrative when they put out a promo that said, "Empires are built on power." They even did a promo photo that was almost identical to an old one I'd done with G-Unit. That resulted in Taraji P. Henson and I having a fun little back-and-forth on social media.

While I was comfortable manipulating *Empire*'s early momentum, I didn't want to be associated too closely with the show long-term. First of all, I was wary of being pitted against another show just because we both had a black cast. Second, despite the cultural overlap, I viewed *Empire* and *Power* as fundamentally different kinds of shows. *Empire* was on FOX, which meant it was free network programming. There was a limit to the type of content it could contain. *Power* was on Starz, which made it premium cable. And because of that, we were able to present a much more edgy and graphic package to our viewers. As I wrote on Instagram, "EMPIRE is some s— you should get for free. Now that power is worth paying for, STARZ premium cable."

Why would I compete against a free show on FOX when I was putting out a show on premium cable? If I was going to compete against a show, it had to be on the same playing field I occupied. So I took a look around and decided to go up against the biggest kid on the block.

If you're going to compete, do it against the best. And there was no one better on premium cable at the time than HBO's *Game of Thrones*. So I made it a point to come for *GOT* time and time again.

I wouldn't miss any opportunity to put *Power* in the same conversation as *GOT*. After someone cleverly superimposed my face on Tyrion Lannister's body, I went on the offensive on IG, saying, "This shit ain't nothing but hating ass game of throne fans sit there with too much time on there hands mad because POWER is #1 fuck you and your flying dragons. We on some real life shit hoe."

People ate it up. What I didn't mention was that the clever trickster was actually an artist I keep on payroll precisely to create viral moments like that.

People like to say I'm a bully, but I have zero problem poking fun at myself if it helps build buzz. An actual bully doesn't possess that sort of self-awareness. Their skins are way too thin to post those sorts of pictures of themselves. But I'm not moving off emotion. My skin is tough enough to do whatever it takes to keep my brand poppin'!

Everything I posted concerning *GOT* was a calculated exercise to make sure that fans, foes, and media outlets knew that our intentions with *Power* never had anything to do with quietly succeeding. The critics might not have put *Power* in the same conversation as *GOT*, but I had managed to steer the public conversation to put us side by side.

The impact was substantial. HBO had the larger paid subscription base and a much, much bigger budget, but *Power* still managed to slay the dragon a few times in the ratings. Even better, since the fantasy series hit its finale in 2019, *Power* viewership has been steadily outperforming anything else HBO is bringing to the table. I'm confident that our show's word of mouth is so reliable because of my expressed passion and support for the fans.

Looking back, it's unlikely that *Power*'s reduced resources and smaller footprint were ever going to topple America's oldest paid-subscription cable network, but that's how competition works. You can join a losing fight and still come out of it with something valuable.

I mentioned I didn't want *Power* to be labeled as a "black show." There's a good reason for that. The longest, and most celebrated, competition in America is black versus white. It's also the one competition that I choose to sit out. It's the one I know is rigged against me.

That doesn't mean I'm not proud to be black or supportive of black artists. None of that. *Power* is, without question, at its core a black show. I'm the executive producer. Courtney Kemp, a black woman, is the showrunner and writes the scripts. The stars are all POC, with the exception of Joseph Sikora. The show has employed a lot of talented black people and people of color, as do all my TV shows.

I still do not want it to be known as a "black show."

Basically, doing so would be to put it in a box—one that's almost impossible to break out of.

It's what happened to me with *Get Rich or Die Tryin'*. Think about that movie. It starred me, a black man, and was about a rapper fighting his way to the top. It was directed by Jim Sheridan, a feisty little Irish dude who'd helmed award-winning films like *My Left Foot* and *In the Name of the Father*. The score was by Quincy Jones, someone who's been able to connect with Americans at every level. The script was written by Terence Winter, a writer and executive producer on *The*

Sopranos and *Boardwalk Empire*. It was shot by Declan Quinn, an award-winning Irish cinematographer.

In its bones, *Get Rich or Die Tryin'* was a mainstream movie . . . but that's not how Hollywood saw it. They saw it as a black film. And black films don't get to open in the same number of theaters as mainstream ones. This is why when *Get Rich* came out, it only opened in about 1,700 theaters.

Now compare that to another movie about a rapper fighting his way to the top, *8 Mile*. That movie had all the same elements as *Get Rich*, with the major difference being that Eminem was white. *8 Mile* opened in about 3,000 theaters.

That means *8 Mile* had almost twice the opportunity in its first week at the box office as *Get Rich* did.

I have zero beef with Em over that situation, but I have a big beef with the system that decides my film would only appeal to a black audience. The reason they gave me a movie deal in the first place wasn't because I was black. It was because I was a superstar.

And the reason I was a superstar was because tens of millions of white kids had bought my album. And the reason they bought my album was because they were fascinated with my life. So how does it stand to reason that a movie about my life would not appeal to those same white kids? There's no reason. It's an illogical system that prevents artists from being able to compete on a level playing field.

So I try to stay off that field.

I'm always going to hire black actors, black directors, and black showrunners. But I'm not blind to the realities that are still out there. When they made the poster for *Power*, I made sure that Joe Sikora's character, Tommy, was on it—just as Russell Crowe was on the *American Gangster* poster, despite it being Denzel Washington's vehicle. My goal is never to be the best in one category or niche. My only goal for *Power*, as with everything I do, was to make it bigger and bigger and attract the widest audience possible.

DON'T KEEP YOUR COMPETITION AFLOAT

One of my imperfections is that I can enjoy competition too much. Sometimes I'll actually help my opponents by bringing them into my orbit for longer than they deserve.

There have been a lot of artists who I've publicly beefed with who have benefited more from those encounters than I did. They remind me of those parasitic organisms that live off a larger host. As long as they're attached to the host, they're okay. But as soon as the host moves away or they lose their grip, they die.

That's how I view my relationship with artists like Ja Rule, Rick Ross, Jim Jones, French Montana, and the Lox. None of them ever came up with a long-term way to generate interest in themselves outside of getting into a war of words with me.

They've all tried to branch out into different endeavors, but their primary function is to sell records. And they know that saying something to me keeps the record-buying audience watching them. So they come at me.

I understand why they do it—everyone wants to stay relevant— but it's a flawed long-term plan. If all your shine comes from somebody else's sun, what happens when that person moves away? Because once I get off them, it's like they don't even exist anymore. People will say, "Where the Lox at? Did they fall off the planet?"

That's what happened to all those guys. Once I shifted my focus to film and television development, it was like their careers hit the block of ice that sank the *Titanic*. Without me as a foil, they were sunk.

Gianni Versace once said, "It is nice to have valid competition; it pushes you to do better." I agree with that. The problem is when you're engaged with inconsequential competition. There are no wins for the more established party in that sort of battle.

What I need to work on is being more disciplined at not taking the bait. Just the other day, Rick Ross tried to lure me back into an engagement by saying that I'm not relevant to the culture anymore. It was easy to see what he was trying to do. *He* is the one who's irrelevant, so he needed to reengage me to get that relevancy back.

Even though I identified his strategy, I still threw a couple of light jabs his way. Nothing emotional. No real tension. I just pointed out that artists like him need to position themselves next to the guys who have that momentum and try and survive off that. Just pointing out what should be obvious.

I shouldn't have even give his comments that much consideration. I've got to do better at removing myself from competitions like that earlier. The longer I stay engaged, the longer they stay relevant. Why would I allow myself to be locked into a competition with Rick Ross? He's trying to sell records. I'm trying to sell TV shows and build networks. He wants to compete, but we're playing two totally different games.

S ometimes the right move is to disengage with competition that's inconsequential. In other situations, you've got to be very firm in establishing your dominance.

A lot of people wonder why I went so hard on Teairra Marí on social media when she was a seemingly inconsequential opponent. Well, let me explain what happened and why.

Teairra, a one-time singer and reality TV star, sued me for allegedly conspiring with her ex-boyfriend to put their sex tape on social media. I never did that. A judge saw what she was up to and not only dismissed her case but also ordered her to pay $30,000 to cover the legal expenses I incurred defending myself. In fact, as of today the awards continue to increase.

Teairra cried broke, and all across social media people were calling on me to forgive her debt. "Aww, 50. She ain't got it," one person might say. "Oh, just let it go, cuz," another would write. "You don't need that thirty grand."

Those people were missing the point. Or multiple points. First off, I didn't tell her to pay me thirty grand—the law did. It's not for me to forgive the debt. Because people could identify with not having $30,000, the compassion was directed toward her, even though she was the one who had done the wrong.

She also wouldn't be "giving" me anything—she was simply being told to put the money back into my pocket she had already wrongly removed.

Second, I had to send a strong message in how I responded to that particular situation. In my heart, I have no doubt the only reason she sued me in the first place was because I had a gigantic bull's-eye on my back. That's the reality in America. If your pockets are deep, someone will take a shot at you legally and see if they get lucky.

So yes, I'm sorry she was broke, but I still planned to collect every last penny of the $30,000. Not because I needed it, but because I needed the larger public to understand that if you want to take a frivolous shot at me, you will pay for it. I'm not just going to shrug that sort of action off. I'm going to win, and then I'm going to collect.

Speaking of collecting, I was trying to send a similar message with my "Pay Me by Monday" IG campaign. If how I handled Teairra Marí was a warning to the public, then "Money by Monday" was a warning to the people I knew directly: don't try to borrow money from me and then just forget about it.

The message was received. Trust me, for as many people as I outed for owing me money, there were a lot more that I didn't put on blast. But after they saw me outing Randall Emmett and comedian Jackie Long, they made sure they got on a private payment plan quick.

What's interesting is that people didn't respond to me going after Randall the same way as when I went after Teairra. No, they loved that I had him so shook he was calling me "Fofty" in his text messages. They loved that he was begging me to take my foot off his neck. Why? Because everybody understands the feeling of being owed money by someone disrespectful. Especially someone who has the money but *still* chooses not to pay you back. That's something we can all relate to. No matter who you are, there's probably someone out there who owes you some cash but doesn't seem to be in any rush to pay you back. They might give you a hug and a smile every time they see you and never even bring it up. Hell, they might even sit in your house with their feet up on your coffee table and act like they don't have a debt in the world. Meanwhile, your head is about to explode from the disrespect.

So when I put my foot down and say, "Screw that! I'd like to have that money back, please!" that's a sentiment that almost everyone can support.

KEEP A BOOK

At some point in your life, you might have owned a Lacoste shirt. You know, the ones with the alligator on the front? But you probably aren't familiar with the history of the company. Lacoste was founded in the 1930s by a French tennis player named René Lacoste. His nickname as a player was the Crocodile, because he was so tenacious on the court. That's how the shirts got their insignia.

Lacoste was an international tennis star by the time he launched his brand in the thirties, but only a decade or so earlier he wasn't considered a top player. He was getting served (literally) by most of the players he was going up against. He decided he needed to come up with a new strategy to compete.

He realized his best chance for an advantage would be to create a "book" on his opponents. Every time he went up against an opponent, or observed one as a spectator, he would write an entry about the person in his book. He would list their strengths and their weakness. He would note their temperament and how they seemed to react to different scenarios.

Lacoste's book became his secret weapon. In an era before TV or highlight clips, most tennis players were operating in the dark when they took the court against a new opponent. There was no way to know about someone's tactics or habits. Their strengths or their vulnerabilities.

Thanks to his book, Lacoste had a unique advantage for his matches. With his combination of knowledge and tenacity, he went on to become one of the best players of his generation, winning twenty-four titles, including Wimbledon and the French Open.

Today, Lacoste's technique of creating a "book" on opponents is the norm in sports. Almost every team, from Pop Warner football to Major League Baseball, keeps a "book" on their opponents. We might call those books "scouting reports" today, but it's fundamentally the same concept. It's keeping a record of your opponents' strengths and weaknesses so you can put that knowledge into practice if you ever meet them in competition.

Books, or scouting reports, are now ubiquitous in sports, but they are barely utilized in other competitive situations. What's proved to be effective in baseball or football could work just as well in film, TV, fashion, marketing, etc., if you applied it the same way.

I certainly keep a mental book on the individuals I consider my competition. I follow all of the moves they make carefully. If someone does something I consider smart, I make note of it and try to think of ways I could do something similar. If I see my competition do something I consider foolish, I make note of that, too. And then I look for a way to leverage that vulnerability against them down the road.

The key is that I remove emotion from the equation when I make my mental notes. I don't get jealous when I see someone make a smart move, just like I don't get excited when I see them stumble. I just make note of what happened and file it away for later.

I'll do that with my hip-hop competition like Puffy or Jay, but also in film and TV. I always watch successful executive producers like Shonda Rhimes, Dick Wolf, Tyler Perry, and Ryan Murphy. I note which writers they like to work with and what sort of material they focus on. I'll observe how they roll out new shows and identify the messaging that's effective, as well as what doesn't seem to hit. I'll study how they navigate their relationships with the various networks and how they create leverage for themselves.

When I sit down at night and hit the power button on my remote control, I am not watching as a casual fan. I'm studying each show the way René Lacoste studied tennis players back in the day. Or the way an NFL scout watches his team's opponent for the following week. That's the level of commitment that's required to separate yourself from your competition. If you want to be a writer, you have to take notes on every author you read. If you want to be a chef, every time you eat a meal at a restaurant, you have to be thinking about how your competition works with flavors, texture, presentation, and ingredients. If you want to be an ad executive, you just can't walk past a poster on the subway platform. You have to study every poster, supermarket sales display, and bus wrap that you see and make note of what's catching your attention and what doesn't hold your eye.

Don't complain that it takes the fun out of eating in a restaurant or watching a mindless TV show at the end of a long day. If you're truly passionate about your dream, you'll want to analyze as many TV shows as possible, or visit as many cutting-edge restaurants as possible. When you're hustling at your hardest, you're going to observe and engage with anything that gives you even the slightest advantage.

I keep my notes in my mind, but a powerful exercise is physically writing a book on your competition. If someone in your company has a senior position you'd like to occupy, write down the book on them. Try to identify what constructive things they do every day that has them in that position. Do they come in earlier than you do? Do they have a better relationship with the boss? Are they more outgoing? Do they have a tendency to get ahead of issues? Are they confident in presentations? Faster to respond to emails? Anything you think they do well, write it down.

Then take note of their weaknesses. Do they tend to overpromise? Do they like to leave early at night? Do they trust their underlings to do too much of their work for them? Play a little fast and loose with their expense account? Get caught up in interoffice relationships that they probably shouldn't?

Write all those down, too. And then study that list. In it you have the information for improving your performance—as well as the information that will reveal the most opportune places for you to strike when you're ready to make your move on that job.

Whenever you write something down, it promotes a more focused way of thinking. When ideas only live in your mind, it's easy for you to lose track of them. Even if they're extremely powerful, they get lost in the stream of new information that's constantly entering your head. You could have an incredible idea for how to earn yourself a promotion, but it could get dislodged by the thought of what you might get for dinner. Then that idea that had so much promise gets swept back into the piles and piles of other ideas that we all have crowding our consciousness. Maybe you'll get back to that great one. Or maybe you won't.

Writing those ideas down protects you against that idea getting lost. Once it's on paper or your computer file, it's there forever. Staring you back in the face whenever you look at it. Whether or not you act on it is still up to you, but at least you won't forget it. Once you have it down on paper, you're setting yourself up to make something valuable happen.

CHAPTER 8

LEARNING FROM YOUR Ls

Mistakes are a fact of life. It is the response to the error that counts.

—NIKKI GIOVANNI

Ever since he was a young child, Soichiro Honda was obsessed with cars. (I know the feeling.) Honda grew up in rural Japan, where he learned about making bicycle and engine parts in his father's blacksmith shop. Honda wasn't much of a student, never making it past elementary school. He spent almost all of his time tinkering with spare parts and trying to build things in his father's workshop.

In 1922, when he was just fifteen, Honda left home by himself to take a job at Art Shokai, one of Tokyo's first auto repair shops. Lacking a formal education, Honda had to start off sweeping the floors, but over the next few years he developed a reputation as a serious and creative worker. One of the ways he proved himself was helping design one of the first racing cars made in Japan, which was named—I'm not making this up—the Curtis!

After a few years, Honda was put in charge of a new branch of Art Shokai in the city of Hamamatsu. Honda's branch did very well, and when he felt like he'd finally earned his bosses' respect, Honda decided to pitch them on an idea that had been brewing in his head. Drawing on his experiences in his father's blacksmith shop and working on the Curtis, Honda approached his bosses with a new way to design car pistons. Their feedback was negative—they told him his idea wouldn't work and refused to support him.

Honda was sure he was on to something, so he quit his job and launched his own company, Tokai Seiki, to produce the pistons. He sunk everything he had into his company, even going so far as to pawn his wife's jewelry. He spent nights sleeping in his workshop until finally he felt the pistons were ready. He packed 30,000 of them into several trucks and traveled to Tokyo, where he presented them to the buyer at a new auto company called Toyota. The buyer looked over the pistons and then delivered some bad news: Honda's design was substandard. After reviewing the pistons, Toyota decided that only *three* out of the entire batch were up to their standards. They refused the shipment.

Honda was in an extremely tough spot. He'd sunk all his money into making his own pistons, and they'd just been declared worthless. Most people in his situation would have cut their losses and closed up shop. Not Honda. Instead of walking away, he decided to take a hard look at what had gone wrong. If his pistons were being declared DOA, he was going to perform his own autopsy on them before he gave up on his dream.

When Honda reviewed his design, he was able to identify where he'd screwed up. He had relied too heavily on his firsthand experiences in his father's shop and later at Art Shokai. He hadn't spent enough time actually studying the engineering theory behind his designs. Passion wouldn't be enough—he'd need education, too.

Instead of shutting his company down, Honda committed himself to becoming more educated about both design and manufacturing. He spent the next several years traveling around Japan, taking engineering classes and visiting steel factories, trying to soak up as much new information as he could.

After years of study and observation, Honda felt ready to go back to the drawing board. This time he was able to overcome the design and manufacturing issues that had tripped him up and produced a batch of working pistons. It won him a new contract with Toyota.

Honda's difficult times weren't over, though. In 1944, toward the end of World War 2, one of his piston factories was destroyed in an American bombing raid. Then, only a year later, a massive earthquake destroyed another of his factories.

Having two factories destroyed in two years would have been the final straw for most people. Even the most hardened hustler might not be able to get back up from that, but Honda still refused to stay down. He sold what was left of his company to Toyota for just 450,000 yen. With the proceeds of that sale, he set up a new company, which he called the Honda Technical Research Institute.

That company, known as "Honda" for short, would go on to become one of the most profitable car manufacturers of all time. Honda himself would become internationally known as the "Henry Ford of Japan" and would be credited as one of the most innovative businessmen of the twenty-first century.

When asked toward the end of his life what had been the most important lesson in his journey, Honda pointed back to the moment he'd delivered the flawed pistons to Toyota. He had failed, but his determination to learn from his failure transformed him into a much more potent entrepreneur. "Many people dream of success. To me, success can be achieved only through repeated failure and introspection," Honda said. "In fact, success represents 1 percent of your work, which results only from the 99 percent that is called failure."

Soichiro Honda's story really connects with me. I know how hard it was to accomplish what he did.

A lot of people have great ideas. Only a small percentage of them have the passion and work ethic to actually follow through and put it into motion.

Of that select second group, every single one of them will still make a mistake or experience some sort of failure during the struggle to bring that idea to fruition. How that person responds to their failure is going to determine the outcome of their journey.

Are they going to let it kill their passion? Is that perceived failure going to make them settle for something less risky, like a nine-to-five working for someone else?

Or will they experience a reaction to that obstacle that's even more severe? They might become so dejected that they go off the deep end and start drinking or getting high every day. Or they might get so stressed that they find God and walk away from it all.

Those are the reactions that the majority of people—even the most driven—have when they encounter failure. Don't let yourself have that reaction. Approach failures the same way that Honda did: as a tool that can help you get things right the next time.

We treat failure like the scariest thing out there, like it's Freddy Krueger, Pennywise, and Michael Myers rolled into one. Just mention its name, and people start running.

Don't look at failure as something you need to distance yourself from. Try to embrace it instead. Wrap your hands around it and examine it. Believe that you can use it to rebuild your idea and take it to an even higher level than you'd originally conceived.

That's the approach all true winners take. It's the attitude Honda possessed when he said, "My biggest thrill is when I plan something and it fails. My mind is then filled with ideas on how I can improve it."

Think about that. He didn't look at failing as a setback or a defeat. He called it a "thrill." Something to be excited about. Imagine if you could view your own life that way. Nothing would ever be able to get you off your game.

There could be a myriad of reasons why your plan didn't manifest. Your timing could have been off. You might not have executed your plan the right way. Someone you were depending on might have fallen through. A market could have shifted. Hell, someone might have dropped a bomb on your factory.

The bottom line is that whether you started from shit or were born with a silver spoon in your mouth, you're going to encounter resistance. Every successful person has scars from those encounters—you just can't see most of them. I certainly have those scars. Some of them I'm just starting to share with the world.

For many years in the hood we've labeled failures as "Ls," short for "losses." The term has become a symbol of something you don't want to have associated with you—"Man, he gotta take that L."

What we need to do is flip the concept. Instead of worrying about "holding that L," focus on "learning from that L" instead. Because your Ls are where your greatest instructions will always be found.

It rarely feels like it in the moment, but experiencing setbacks, losses, and disappointments will absolutely make you stronger in the long run. I've determined this based on my experiences and observations, and now science is even starting to back me up. A recent study published in the scientific journal *Nature Communications* found that people who experience failure early in their careers actually have more long-term success than people who don't initially experience any setbacks.

"We realized we may have succeeded in understanding success, but we've failed at understanding failure," Dr. Dashun Wang, one of the study's authors and a professor at the Kellogg School of Management, told the *New York Times*. "We know success breeds success. Maybe we just haven't looked at people who fail closely enough."

ADMIT THAT YOU'RE WRONG

The first and most important step in learning from your Ls is identifying that you made a mistake in the first place. Maybe that seems painfully obvious, but it's actually the step that a lot of folks are unwilling to take.

Let's say you and I go out for a drive. If I make a wrong turn and find myself in some neighborhood I'm not familiar with, I'm going to turn to you and say, "Yo, my bad. I dunno what I did, but we're lost. Lemme plug the address into Google Maps and figure out where we gotta go."

I'm not embarrassed to say that I made a wrong turn. I'm not worried that it reveals me as stupid. I've identified that I'm in an uncharted area and I want us to both get to our destination. I'm going to do what I need to in order to correct my mistake.

A lot of people don't share that response. They will drive in circles for hours and never admit that they're lost. You could be looking out the window and thinking, "I *know* this isn't the right way," but that person will keep telling you, "Don't worry, I got this." That individual will keep driving in the wrong direction, past all sorts of landmarks and signs, until they literally run out of gas. You'll both be stranded and calling AAA simply because that individual didn't want to own up to their mistake.

I know people with this character trait. I've literally been in the car with people who drive for an hour in the wrong direction just because they don't want to admit they are lost. Try to tell them that, and they'll become even more adamant about not turning around.

It's very difficult to learn from your mistakes if you have a bunch of yes-men (or women) surrounding you. This is why it's very important that your friends and associates feel like they have the freedom to offer constructive criticism, to tell you about yourself a bit.

That is why you never want to be a boss or a leader that screams at or intimidates the people under you. Doing that might make you feel powerful in the moment, but it will cost you dearly in the long run.

Floyd Mayweather is a person I've observed doing this. He has a guy working for him—let's call him Bobby out of respect—who he constantly belittles in front of everyone. Floyd is generally respectful toward the people who work for him, but he says crazy shit to Bobby. Something relatively minor can come up, and Floyd will smooth cuss him out. "What the fuck, Bobby" he'll yell for everyone to hear. "What the hell is wrong with you? Get that shit right!" Bobby will just mutter, "My bad, champ," before slinking off to "fix" whatever is allegedly wrong. The two of them are trapped in a dysfunctional relationship. Floyd never fires Bobby, and Bobby never quits. They both just stay locked into a pattern of Floyd embarrassing Bobby and Bobby taking it.

The issue is that while Floyd might only be addressing Bobby, everyone else hears him. They register that, even though Floyd claims to be mad, he never actually does anything about it. That tells the other employees that Floyd doesn't actually care about performance or productivity, he just wants that whipping boy around. "I better keep my eyes down and focused on what's in front of me, because I don't want to get treated like Bobby" is how they will start thinking. "And I damn sure won't tell Floyd when I think he's making a mistake."

That's the absolute worst attitude your employees can have. Walking around on eggshells and hoping that they're not your next verbal victim. You want them to feel respected, to feel free to offer opinions and insights. You have to remember they're around you every day and see things that you might miss, which means that they might be able to identify certain mistakes before you do. Empower them to express those opinions to you. If you can promote dialogue and encourage feedback, you might gain some valuable information that could help you avoid obstacles before you hit them yourself.

On the other side of the coin, if you happen to be that employee who's screamed at all the time, you need to do some self-evaluation. Look in the mirror and ask yourself, "Why did I get singled out for this role?" You didn't apply for the position of whipping boy, but that's the position you found yourself in.

(A quick note on the term "whipping boy." You might think it comes from slavery, but it actually refers to a practice with young princes in Renaissance Europe. If the prince failed a test, his tutor wasn't allowed to whip him, which was the punishment back then. You couldn't put your hands on a prince, so the tutor would whip the prince's servant, or whipping boy, for the mistake instead. Now *that's* a shitty job!)

You have to ask yourself how you got there. What sort of energy did you project to your boss that told them *you're* the one they can be most comfortable yelling at? Did you come off as someone who seemed timid and wouldn't push back? Or did you register as the type of person who would be looking for a confrontation? (Remember, a lot of folks, even if they're not conscious of it, seek out people they can have drama with.)

Whatever sort of energy you're able to identify, you need to change it. Try projecting a more strong-willed, or less acquiescent, energy, depending on the situation. If you don't notice a change in your boss's attitude in thirty days, that's when you start looking for a new job.

Once you have been cast in the role of the whipping boy (or girl), it's very hard to rebrand yourself. It's not like Floyd is going to start treating Bobby differently and then promote him to a better position. Bobby fills some sort of emotional need, and Floyd is going to keep him right where he is.

Don't let yourself become the Bobby of your workplace. Admit that you made an error in the type of energy you initially presented, and then look to move on. But still, make sure to learn from the situation. The next time you sit down for an interview, make it clear that you're there to produce, not have someone's emotional baggage dumped on you.

N ow, the boxing promotions game is one of the most ruthless ones out there. I was in it for a while and can attest that it's as cutthroat as hip-hop or even drugs.

Take a look at Mike Tyson. He is not the type of guy you take money from. Mike is the furthest thing from a sucker. But even he got taken by Don King. It's just very hard to avoid as a fighter.

Boxing isn't like other professional sports where there's a league overseeing the business side of things. If you're an NBA rookie and hire a crappy agent, you're still going to get paid. Same with the NFL. The league puts all sorts of provisions in place—rookie contract scales, minimum salaries, etc.—to essentially protect you from yourself. Not to mention, they tell you who to play and when to play them. They don't leave any of the thinking and planning to you. You just gotta show up and play.

Boxing doesn't provide that sort of infrastructure. You're essentially an independent contractor, and it's on you to make the deals happen. To determine who you're going to fight and when. And for how much.

For guys who usually don't have much in the way of business experience, that's a lot to consider. It's not that boxers are dumb—fighting requires a tremendous amount of mental focus. You can take a few plays off in basketball. Or jog a couple of routes in football. But take even a half second off in boxing, and you're liable to get knocked the hell out. Boxers have to pour everything they have into what happens in the ring. They just don't have the bandwidth to focus on the details with the same intensity outside of it. They feel like they need someone else to orchestrate the business for them.

And this is why people like Don King and Bob Arum have such an easy time stepping into that void. Boxing is the only sport where the lions become afraid of mice. Fighters earn the money, but they don't trust themselves to get the deal done, even if that's how they present themselves publicly. They depend almost completely on someone else to figure out the money.

One time Floyd asked me to go with him to a meeting with a company that wanted to start a boxing equipment line for him. They were going to put his name on gloves, cups, boxing shorts, and other gear and sell it in outlets like Walmart. It was a very professional presentation, and the whole time Floyd seemed engaged. He gave the company's executives positive affirmations when they addressed him, and he asked small questions from time to time.

But when we got back into his car after the meeting, he turned to me and asked, "Yo, 5 . . . What them people was talking about?" It struck me that even though he seemed to be concentrating and staying engaged, he didn't trust that he'd understood what he'd heard. He needed someone he trusted to confirm the information for him.

It was safe to ask me, because we were friends at the time. He could trust me not to try to steer him in the wrong direction or try to slice off too big a piece of the deal myself. I had my own money and didn't need to eat off my friend. Most people aren't in my situation . . . and most people aren't his friend. That means that almost every other time Floyd walked into a meeting, he was depending on someone else to confirm what he'd heard. That's an extremely dangerous position to put yourself in.

You might be wondering, how does a guy in Floyd's position not have someone to watch his money? The answer is that someone *is* watching. It's just that it's in that person's best interest to watch the money go away. Why? Because if it were up to Floyd, he'd probably never fight again. He's got an undefeated record, something he's extremely proud of. So if you see him talking up a bout that doesn't seem to make sense—like fighting the MMA star Conor McGregor, or the Japanese kickboxer Tenshin Nasukawa—it means one thing: the money is gone.

That's why it's in the manager, promoter, and accountant's best interest for him to stay broke. Otherwise, he's never going to lace those gloves up again and bring in another massive paycheck.

CHAPTER 9

THE ENTITLEMENT TRAP

There is joy in work. There is no happiness except in the realization that we have accomplished something.

—HENRY FORD

I never had much in the way of expectations for middle age.

As a teenager, I figured I'd either be dead or in jail by the time I hit forty.

Even after I experienced success as a rapper, I assumed by forty I'd be completely washed. Maybe chillin' out on a tropical island somewhere eating cookies with my belly hanging over my swim trunks.

That island definitely sounded better than the grave or a cell, but I can't say I was excited about the prospects of growing old. Everything exciting in my life, I assumed, was going to happen in my twenties and early thirties.

And yet, here I am today, staring middle age square in the face, and I feel as enthusiastic about what's ahead of me as I have at any time in my life.

I can feel that I'm on my way up again. And I'm going to rise higher than I ever have before.

This is why I *refuse* to carry deadweight anymore.

My public persona can come across as gruff or callous, but behind the scenes I've always been something of a softy. I've had a bad habit of tolerating counterproductive characteristics in people because I feel bad for them. It's almost as if I somehow blame myself for them not realizing their dreams. Pity apparently makes for foolish allowances.

But, as I grow older, the one thing that becomes clearer to me each and every day is that I don't owe anyone a thing.

And neither do you.

S ome people are not built to make it.

That might sound harsh, but all my experiences have taught me that it's true.

No matter how much support you provide them or love you show, their lowest habits are going to pull them right back to whatever struggle they came from.

That's why one of the keys to being able to hustle smarter is learning how to identify these kinds of people before they drag you back down to the bottom with them.

One of the first rules of lifeguarding is to never get too close to a drowning person. Why? Because when you reach them just before they go under, that person is just going to jump on your back and cause you both to sink. You always want to try to keep something—a float, a board, or a piece of wood—between you and the person you're trying to rescue. If they get too close, punch them dead in the face and get them off you. Otherwise you're both going to die.

Life can be like that too. You want to save people, but in order to do it without you both getting pulled under, you need to keep a little distance.

That is not to say you should never try to help. Does it feel good to put a person on to a new opportunity? Of course it does. I've spent my whole career trying to do exactly that. When I've played basket-ball I've always gotten more pleasure out of an assist than scoring on my own.

But if someone keeps missing the shots you set them up for, it's not your responsibility to keep feeding them the ball. There are a lot of players out there; your job is to win games, not keep running back up and down the court with the same clowns who can't get the job done. Time to call for a sub.

M ost people, of course, don't like to be subbed in for. They feel they should get to stay in the game no matter how many shots they've missed or turnovers they're made. They feel like they're entitled to that playing time.

I've seen a lot of people pollute their potential after sipping from the well of entitlement. This is certainly true of many of the people I've been associated with over the years.

Even my own son.

What they need to understand, and what I want to relay to you in this chapter as well, is that you should never feel like the world owes you anything.

It doesn't.

There is no version of hustling harder or smarter that involves re-lying on the assumption that someone is going to do anything for you. You must accept that it's all on you.

That might seem like a very cynical way to view the world, but I would argue that it's actually liberating.

You can only feel betrayal when you feel like you're owed some-thing from someone.

You can only feel resentment when you had expectations for as-sistance.

When you accept that it's *all* on you, only then can you finally be free to focus 100 percent on being the best version of yourself.

THE TWENTY-YEAR VACATION

When I first got together with Shaniqua, neither of us had much. We were both living in what we perceived to be the bottom. Our goals didn't extend much past having a decent place to stay and fresh clothes to wear.

Then my situation changed, and I suddenly had resources at my disposal. A lot of resources. And I wanted to share them with Shaniqua. We weren't together anymore, but she was the mother of my son. She was with me before the fame, and I acknowledged and respected that. She saw me rise, and I wanted to help her find her own success.

With that in mind, I would ask her, "Whatchu want do with your life?" Did she want to go to school? Did she want to learn interior design? Fashion? I kept asking her to identify the occupation that would provide her with some kind of purpose that could provide both wealth and personal satisfaction.

Not only would this be good for her personally, but I also wanted our son to be raised by someone who had a career of her own. But no matter how many times I asked, Shaniqua never had an answer for me. I'd bring up different possibilities and scenarios, but there was never a connection.

It was incredibly frustrating. I didn't like sending a check every month to someone who didn't seem to have any interest in working. She might as well have been on welfare back in the hood. The only difference here was that she was getting a bigger check from me than she would have from Uncle Sam.

It finally came to a head one day when I was visiting her and Marquise one weekend. "So, what you want to do?" I asked her once again.

She just looked at me, rolled her eyes, and said, "Ain't nobody work if they don't have to."

"Oh, shit," I sputtered. I suspected people thought that way, but no one had ever been ill enough to actually say it out loud in front of me.

"You already did it," she said firmly. "So why should I have to do it, too? I'm good."

I don't mean to sound dramatic, but it was one of the most shocking conversations of my life. And I've had a lot of conversations people would consider shocking.

I am extremely serious about the value of hard work. I believe it creates not only success but happiness, too. You can never feel satisfied if you're not applying yourself to something you're passionate about.

When Shaniqua said, "Ain't nobody work if they don't have to," it was like she was dismissing everything I believed in. At that moment, I knew things would never be right between us. We just saw the world different ways. I was disgusted that she didn't want to work, and she was disgusted that I thought she should.

I understand that she had the responsibility of raising our son largely on her own. I tried to apply less pressure on her when he was younger because of that. But once he was in his teens and didn't need someone holding his hand every second, I hoped Shaniqua would finally start to show some ambition.

There was a period where she made some noise about getting into real estate. I thought that was a great idea—Atlanta was a growing market—and I offered to pay for the classes she would need to get her license. But after a few months, it was clear the passion wasn't there. She wasn't excited walking into a house for the first time, and envisioning all the possibilities for it, or by taking an older property, fixing it up, and flipping it for a profit. She just liked that being a real estate agent was something you could do from home. Of course, nothing ever happened.

Looking back, I can see that the moment when Shaniqua said

"ain't nobody work if they don't have to" is when our relationship hit the point of no return. Up until then, I had visions that we could still fashion some sort of partnership. Maybe not romantically, but at least as parents with a common goal. A business we could start that would benefit our son down the road.

When it was clear that she not only did not share that vision but was actually *offended* by it, my attitude toward her completely changed. I became petty. It was as if I were a fitness buff and she was obese. Every time she'd pick up another proverbial cookie, I'd be like, "Damn, you really need that cookie? It's just gonna go straight to your hips!"

I was barely conscious of it, but I was being mean in the hope it would embarrass her into some sort of action. It had the opposite effect, though. The more I homed in on her lack of hustle, the more she began to resent me. The resentment kept building up between us until it matured into hate—a hate that's still present to this day.

What's upsetting isn't just that our relationship has become so toxic, but that she passed that sense of resentment and entitlement along to our son. He'd been given every advantage in the world, far beyond most kids born in the ghetto, but he still feels like he's been somehow cheated or robbed by me.

It's a scenario I never imagined I'd find myself in with my firstborn child, but here we are.

ENTITLEMENT CREATES RESENTMENT

There have been a lot of disappointing moments in my relationship with Marquise over the past few years. But the lowest was when I saw him post a picture of himself with Kyle McGriff, the son of Kenneth "Supreme" McGriff. Without rehashing too much bad history, Kenneth McGriff was one of the biggest drug dealers in Queens and the man the authorities believe was behind the attempt on my life. So, by posing with his son, Marquise was basically cosigning the individual who might have tried to have his father killed.

I had known Marquise resented me for a while, but I never imagined that he could hate me so much that he'd allow himself to be used as a prop by my enemy. Someone recently sent me a quote from Benjamin Franklin that really resonated with me. Franklin's son had sided with the British in the Revolutionary War, despite the fact that his father was one of the leaders of the Revolution. It messed with Ben Franklin for the rest of his life:

> Nothing has ever hurt me so much and affected me with such keen Sensations as to find myself deserted in my old Age by my only Son, and not only deserted, but to find him taking up Arms against me, in a Cause wherein my good Fame, Fortune, and Life were all at stake.

Marquise might not have been literally taking up arms against me, but he was standing next to the son of someone who might have. I could recognize Franklin's pain.

I've spent a lot of time searching my soul, trying to understand what could make a son forsake his own father like that. I've tried to put myself in Marquise's shoes. Just as he doesn't know what it was like to grow up under the circumstances I did, I don't know what it was like to grow up as the son of 50 Cent. Certainly on the surface he had everything he wanted, but there must have been pressures and insecurities from being my son that I can't identify with. I accept that.

I still can't see how those pressures and insecurities would force a child to go against his own father. Especially a father who has provided everything for him. As I go over our relationship in my mind, the only answer I can come up with is that I actually might have done *too* much for Marquise.

How do you make a privileged child feel deprived or angry? I guess by getting him whatever he wants.

L ike many kids from his generation, Marquise has always been into sneakers. Because he's my son, he couldn't just rock any old sneakers, either. If a new pair of Jordans came out, he had to have them right away. If Marquise asked for a pair of Jordans on a Monday, his mother would make sure they were on his feet come Tuesday.

It still didn't make him happy. Instead of being excited to rock his new pair of Jordans, all Marquise could think about was all the retro Jordans that he *didn't* have. All the different flyways and colors that *weren't* in his closet. When he should have felt gratification, all he really felt was disappointment.

I could not relate. The kid didn't have a job, but somehow wanted to collect $300 sneakers? And then *still* felt unhappy when he actually got them? His entire mind-set was alien to me.

I have to believe his mother was behind his disappointment. He thought he could have every sneaker ever made, even though he hadn't actually earned any of them. "He's not regular," she would tell me when I would ask why he needed another new pair. "He's your son." She had already established the pattern that you didn't have to work for something to get it. Marquise was just following her lead.

I didn't want that sense of entitlement to become a core part of who he was. I was determined to help him learn that he would actually be much happier when he worked for the things that he wanted, that their value would increase exponentially.

One day I was driving through Harlem when I noticed that a sneaker store was going out of business on 125th Street. My mind immediately flashed to my son—"Marquise loves sneakers"—so I pulled over to see if I could grab him a couple of pairs on the cheap.

Being naturally inquisitive, I asked the owner why he was going out of business if sneakers were so hot. He explained that he'd picked the wrong location and never got enough foot traffic to make it work.

My mind started clicking.

"Say, how much do you pay for a pair of Air Force 1s?" I asked.

"About forty bucks," he told me.

"And how much you sell them for?"

"About eighty bucks."

That seemed like a pretty solid profit margin to me.

"What you gonna do with all these Air Forces now?" I asked.

"I dunno," he said. "Probably just stash them in my basement till I figure out my next move."

"I'll tell you what," I told him. "I'm going to buy the rest of your inventory from you right now. At cost."

The guy jumped at my offer. Suddenly, I was the new owner of a couple hundred pairs of Nikes.

I hatched a plan. Marquise was in Atlanta, where I knew storage space was cheap. I would ship the sneakers down to him so he could put them in a warehouse. Instead of opening up a brick-and-mortar shop, which would have taken a lot of investment and depended on that aforementioned foot traffic, he could set up an internet site selling sneakers, what is referred to as direct-to-consumer sales. All it would require would be for him to run the site and maybe hire a friend to manage the warehouse side of things. The idea felt like a winner.

As soon as I left the shop I called up my son. "Yo, Marquise. You know how you always been fascinated with shoes?" I asked. "Well, I just figured out a way that you can afford them for yourself and start to earn a little money of your own, too."

I broke the whole plan down for him. I explained how it was a great opportunity that would not only support his passion, but allow him to get a nuts-and-bolts understanding of how a business works. "This is a layup," I told him. "Not too many stores get to start off with free inventory. You can really do something with this. If you're truly passionate about sneakers, this is the time to show it."

Marquise said all the right things on the phone, how excited he was and that it sounded like a great opportunity. So I had the shoes shipped down to Atlanta. Then I never heard from him about it again. Weeks, then months, passed. Finally, one day, his mother called me and announced that she and Marquise had been talking.

Instead of an online sneaker store, they wanted to open a clothing boutique in Atlanta. I couldn't believe what I was hearing. The plan I'd envisioned didn't include her. I wanted our son to learn how to be responsible for himself. By injecting herself into the mix, she was just trying to keep him a boy a little longer.

I still wanted Marquise to get some experience, so I said, "Sure. Let me know when you guys want to do something," but of course their boutique never went anywhere. And the online sneaker shop didn't, either.

My issue with Marquise wasn't that he wanted all those sneakers. When I was a kid, I wanted sneakers, too. The difference is that I was willing—no, make that *determined*—to do the work necessary to obtain them. I wouldn't for a second want Marquise to ever have to resort to the type of work *I* put in to get my kicks. At the time, I perceived selling drugs as the only viable option in my environment, so I pursued it. Marquise has so many more options in front of him than I ever had. I just needed to see him pick one and put in the work.

There is nothing wrong with wanting things. That sense of "want" can be a tremendous motivational tool. Feeling like you need more than what you have is what keeps us from getting complacent.

I've pretty much got it all, but I never feel like I do. When I was younger, I always wanted more in the way of material things. Today, what I want more of is validation. No matter how many awards, accolades, or headlines I get, it's never enough. I'm still obsessed with feeling like I've got the hottest show or just dropped the hottest verse. Needing the respect of my peers and the confirmation of sales is what keeps me pushing forward. I need to feel like they're looking at me and saying, "Man, 50 did it again." That's what gets me high.

What sets me apart is that I never expect anyone else to bring me those accolades. I go out each and every day obsessed with putting in the work that will earn me whatever sort of validation I'm looking for.

When it comes to Marquise's approach to dealing with wanting something, the apple fell from the tree . . . and kept rollin' and rollin'. Sure, Marquise never following up on the sneakers might seem like a small thing—the type of irresponsibility and lack of initiative teenagers and young adults display all the time—but it was a huge disappointment to me.

Forget about being able to afford his personal sneaker collection— that online store could have ended up making us both a killing. We had that conversation years ago. Since then, online sneaker sites have become incredibly lucrative. GOAT.com is valued at $550 million, while StockX .com has a *billion*-dollar valuation. If Marquise had followed through on what we'd talked about, he could have been included in that conversation. He could be independently rich. Shit, he might be in the position to tell *me* to go fuck myself and my money if that's what he wanted to do.

I'm sure when Marquise reads about GOAT or StockX, deep down he probably realizes I was right. Maybe he says, "Why did I not listen to my father and start that fucking online shop?" Or maybe he can't bring himself to say that.

I don't think he's accepted that, no matter all our ups and downs, I still have his best interests at heart. There is nothing that would make me feel better than to see him blossom. No Grammy, no Emmy, no picture on the cover of *Forbes* would mean more to me than seeing my son turn into the person I believe he can be.

IN THE LION'S DEN

Another relative who doesn't fuck with me because of entitlement issues is my cousin Michael Junior, a rapper who goes by the name 25. Michael's problem is that he's always looked for me to make his career happen, instead of making it happen for himself. He feels like I haven't supported his dream enough, and we barely speak anymore because of that.

Michael has resented me since he was in high school in Queens. One day he told me some kids were messing with him.

"Oh, word?" I replied.

"Yeah, you know . . . ," he said and then moved on. He didn't speak on the issue again, so I let it go.

A few months later, someone told me Michael was running around with a rag in his pocket. He'd joined the Bloods gang. I told his mother, my aunt Geraldine, and the two of us had a conversation with him in which we tried to steer him away from that affiliation. Instead of taking our warnings to heart, Michael lashed out at me. "Remember when I told you I had a problem at school?" he asked me angrily. "Well, you never came and helped me. But they did."

I couldn't believe it. "Michael, it wasn't my job to come to your school to handle your beef," I told him. "If anything, having me show up would have put an even bigger target on your back. You could have handled that for yourself. If you think being a Blood is going to make things better, you got another think coming. Let's see how that works out for you."

Michael wouldn't listen to us. He even got mad at his mother, claiming she loved me better than him. His rationale was that she'd become attached to me when she used to babysit me as a child and never developed the same affection for him. It was ridiculous. Here she was, begging him to change his ways, and he was telling her she didn't care about him. Another example of how the crazy ideas you get in your mind as a kid can really stagger you as an adult if you don't change how you think.

Michael began to embrace the persona of a gang member. He would really pour it on in his music. When I rapped, I would talk about street situations, but only ones I'd experienced or observed firsthand. Michael was just making stuff up. It was a dangerous game to play.

I didn't like the direction he was headed in, so I didn't help him the way he had anticipated. Instead of accepting that rapping might not be for him, he kept looking for a record deal. That search led him to the offices of Jimmy Henchman. Jimmy's in jail now, locked up for life on two murder charges, but at the time he was a fierce enemy. His office was absolutely the worst place in the world Michael could have been.

Not being a real street dude, Michael was blind to the danger he'd walked into. He was in the mouth of the lion and couldn't even feel the fangs hovering right over his neck. "Say, you're 50's cousin, right?" Jimmy asked nonchalantly at one point. "When's the last time you guys spoke?"

Thankfully Michael kept it real with him. "Honestly, I don't really fuck with 50 like that," Michael replied. "I see him at Thanksgiving and whatnot, but that's about it."

He was oblivious to it, but it was the only correct answer he could have given. There were serious people in the room that would have hurt him badly if he had said anything that would have made it seem like we were tight.

Michael hasn't been able to create any buzz for himself as a rapper, but he could never look in the mirror and admit that it just wasn't the right calling for him. Sometimes he says he can't get ahead because people resent him for being my cousin. Other times he'll say his lack of success is due to my lack of support. Whatever theory he's running with, it never has anything to do with his lack of hustle, ambition, or talent. Someone else is always to blame.

WHEN DID I BECOME RESPONSIBLE?

When you pray for success, you don't add an extra little prayer asking for jealousy or entitlement. But when the success does come, jealousy, envy, and entitlement often still turn up as by-products.

When you reached the level I have, people will always feel like you owe them. If you buy them a car, they'll take the keys from you . . . but they might also say, "That was cool, but damn, you could have bought me a house."

When I hear that, my reaction is "Wait a minute. When did I become responsible for your entire life? I never agreed to that, and why did you expect it?"

Someone can say, "50 was my man. I held him down." But when you hold that statement up under the light, what does it really mean? You didn't get into any altercations when people were out to get me. You didn't bring me any new business deals. You didn't write the hook for my new song. . . . So what exactly *did* you *do*? Provide moral support?

I'm asking because I don't know how to compensate someone who *would* have done something. I only know how to take care of people who *did* do something.

I've noticed one of the main reasons people feel entitled is because their friends gas them up. I've seen it happen so many times. Let's say someone was friends with me back in the day, maybe even went on the road during one of my early tours. They didn't distinguish themselves in any way—mainly they just stood around looking tough and tried to meet girls after the shows.

That might have been the extent of their involvement, but every time I'm in the headlines with a new deal or project, that person's friends will bring me up. "Damn, son. You been down with 50 forever. You shoulda been taken care of. He can't hook you up with something on that TV show?" And that guy will say, "Yeah, no doubt, I need to talk to him about that." He'll start to think there could be a possible angle that he wasn't considering before. Even if that individual hadn't actually felt like he was owed anything, his friend on the outskirts of the situation hyped him up into feeling that he was.

That's when I find myself in awkward conversations. A guy who I've known for years will reach out and ask to meet. We'll link up, and after some small talk he'll start mumbling, "Yo, son, I'm just sayin', you know, we've been down since forever, and I was just thinkin', you know . . ."

No, I don't know.

Finally, he'll spit it out. He wants a job. A loan. A car note paid. A bill taken care of. A role on *Power*. Bail money for his brother. It could be anything. I've heard it all.

Sometimes I'll even give the person what they want. Other times I'll tell them I can't help them and keep it moving.

One thing is always constant: those conversations leave me feeling depressed. On the one hand, I know I don't owe anyone a thing just because I took them on tour almost twenty years ago or we once sold drugs together. But, on the other hand, I'll start to think, "It is true we've known each other a long time . . ." And then I might start to waver. I might wonder if maybe I *am* being selfish.

When those thoughts start to creep into my mind, that's when I need to take a deep breath and regroup. If I was feeling shaky, then I try to find some strong mental ground to stand on.

I remind myself that while it's okay to feel conflicted about a situation, depression is a luxury that I can't afford. I cannot allow another person's lack of success to start undermining my own.

I understand that, technically, depression is something I *could* afford. Of course I could pay to go see a therapist and talk all this out. But I'm not talking about depression in a clinical sense. (If you feel like you are clinically depressed, by all means go see a therapist.)

I'm describing the feeling of my energy being sapped. My enthusiasm being dampened. My passion being depleted by someone else and their proven lack of hustle.

Sorry, but I simply can't afford that sort of confusion in my life. I don't care how long I've known you. I am going to remove you from my life forever if I start to feel like you're holding me back.

EMBRACING RESPONSIBILITY

Sigmund Freud once said, "Most people do not really want freedom, because freedom involves responsibility, and most people are frightened of responsibility."

Well, I must not be most people then. You already know how I feel about freedom. And I absolutely love responsibility, too. I want as much of it as I can possibly get my hands on. I believe taking complete responsibility for your life is the best way to make sure you never fall into the entitlement trap.

In order to be a true hustler, you have to chase the gratification that can only come from making things happen yourself, when you have a vision that no one else can identify with and pour everything you have into it. You find yourself in valley after valley and can't ever quite catch a glimpse of the mountaintop. But you keep pushing forward, until that one day when you finally do make it to that peak. Man, that's going to be the best damn view you ever saw in your life. You're going to soak up every bit of that mountain air and enjoy every inch of the panorama spread out in front of you.

But if someone just drove you up to the top of that mountain? If you just sat your butt in a car, turned on the AC, and cruised up to the top? It would not be the same. You didn't sweat and sacrifice to get up there. The drink of water you took on the mountaintop wouldn't taste as invigorating. The air wouldn't feel as amazing. The view wouldn't be as inspiring. You can only get true fulfillment and happiness from enjoying the achievement you made happen yourself.

H ere's another scenario. Let's say you've started a marketing business with a close friend. You agree to split the equity and responsibilities in the business fifty-fifty. You're going to handle the client side while your friend is going to handle the bookkeeping and paperwork. You guys start with very little in the way of capital but work day and night to build up the business. You start taking on clients and create a strong reputation. After a couple of years of toiling, bigger firms start to sniff around and make inquiries about acquiring you. It seems like you're on the verge of the success you've been working so hard for.

Then one day your friend comes to you with a confession. The business is out of money. Say what? Revenue had been growing every year. You've got several big-name clients. How could you be broke? Your friend breaks down and explains. He's had a drinking problem he's hidden from you. He hasn't been looking after the books. He hasn't paid certain bills in years. The creditors are already coming after you both. The only thing to do is pay off what you can and shut the whole thing down.

How would you react to that scenario? Sure, your immediate reaction might be to scream at your partner. You might even want to lay some hands on him, but what good would that do? It feels good for a second, but it's not going to get the money back. It would only make things worse.

Would you start assigning blame? Go around complaining to all your clients and everyone you know about how this person ruined your life? That would also be a natural reaction, but it wouldn't solve anything, either.

Would you be consumed with resentment? Would your mind constantly be clouded with thoughts of how this person had done you wrong? Ruined your dreams. Sabotaged everything you've worked for?

No one could blame you for feeling that way, but it still wouldn't fix anything.

No, you need to take the following actions in a situation like that:

Take whatever money you have left, and go somewhere to relax for a few weeks. That might sound impossible considering what happened, but force yourself to take a break. You're not going to recoup what you just lost in the next few weeks, anyway. Instead, give yourself those weeks to clear your energy. To let all that anger, resentment, and confusion get out of your system. You must do that to create space for new energy to come into your life.

Once you feel like you've created that space, go back home and start the process of putting your dream back together again. If you're broke, work on your new company during the day, and drive an Uber at night. Or deliver pizzas. Don't think those jobs are beneath you. Never allow your mind to start obsessing over the idea that, a couple of months ago you were talking about an acquisition and now you're driving an Uber. Understand that you won't be driving an Uber or delivering pizzas forever. They're just stepping-stones you're going to have to utilize to get back to where you were.

Don't let the thought of starting all over again make you depressed. Understand that most successful people end up chasing the same dream multiple times before it ever comes to fruition. Accept that what seemed like a disaster was really just a temporary hardship that every hustler goes through. You're no better or worse than any of them.

Keep saving and grinding until you're in a position to start that business up again. This time, you'll be a little more thorough in choosing a partner. You'll be a little more careful in overseeing the books and making sure everyone is doing what they're supposed to do. Your new model will be stronger, with better infrastructure. And when those bigger companies come sniffing around again, you'll be in a position to sell on much better terms than you were with the first one.

When you do sell, if you're petty, you can invite your old partner to the celebration you're going to throw. But I wouldn't advise that. He'll probably already know how badly he messed up without it coming from your lips.

Here's the key: that scenario I just laid out can only happen if you take full responsibility for what happened with the first company. Yes, *you* didn't screw up. Your friend did. Yes, *you* didn't fail to pay the bills or develop negative habits that you hid. Your friend did those things.

Those problems, however, are yours and yours alone to correct. If *you* don't immediately get back on the grind and take responsibility for fixing what happened, *you* are the one who's going to suffer.

You can't allow yourself to fall into the resentment trap, even when it seems to be the most natural thing to do. The only way you're ever going to experience that freedom Freud was talking about is to accept complete and total responsibility for creating it.

IMPORTING HUSTLE

I doubt there's anyone reading this book who has been set up for success the way Marquise and G-Unit were.

Did your father buy out the inventory of a brick-and-mortar store in order to help you launch an online site?

Did you make your debut in front of 80,000 screaming fans?

I didn't think so.

But, even without the advantages they enjoyed, you might still experience some of the same sensations of resentment or entitlement that have tripped those guys up.

This is especially true if you're still in your twenties or early thirties. There is a growing perception that millennials don't have the same work ethic as previous generations. A poll by Reason-Rupe found that 65 percent of American adults think the younger generation is entitled.

That might be what the polls say, but I can't lay the blame solely at the feet of the internet babies. Shaniqua isn't a millennial. Neither are the guys in G-Unit. They're from the same generation as me. We were all raised with the same expectations.

There's also a perception that entitlement is a specific by-product of being a spoiled white kid. I don't believe that either. My son's rich, but he sure isn't white. None of those dudes who grew up with me in Queens were white, either.

I don't view entitlement as an issue that's about young versus old or black versus white. If anything, it's become an American issue.

In this country, it seems like we resent having to hustle for success. We celebrate glamorous jobs or high-profile positions, but the nine-to-five grind seems beneath us. We suck our teeth stocking the shelves at Target or collecting tickets at the movie theater. Unless a job reflects exactly what we think we deserve—which, let's be honest, most jobs never will—we act like it's a waste of our time.

You don't feel that energy nearly as much in other countries. I've probably lapped the globe three or four times by now. I've eaten in a thousand restaurants overseas, stayed in a thousand hotels, and ridden in the back of a thousand cars. I can report that the attitude toward work is usually different abroad. People take their jobs seriously—no matter what level they're on. I see this in Asian places like Japan, Taiwan, and Singapore. From the street sweepers up to the entrepreneurs I meet, it seems like everyone is hustling *hard*. No one is acting like they resent their job. Everyone seems to be trying to get ahead.

It's the same way in the countries I've visited in Africa and the Middle East. From the dudes selling water on the street corners to the women working in the hotel shops, no one is slacking. Everyone seems dialed in to whatever task is in front of them.

Remember the hypothetical peanut stand I wrote about earlier?

The one I'd open if I ever went broke? Well, when you're overseas it seems like everyone has the same approach. They accept that they have to hustle relentlessly. And, if they do, day after day, year after year, they believe that they can hustle their way to a better life. Despite all the opportunities we enjoy, I'm not sure people have the same confidence in this country.

Over here, the sense of entitlement is found at every level of society. I certainly feel it among the rich. It seems like the people in the million-dollar penthouses feel like they have a right to live there. Everything about their identity is tied up in not losing that position. They believe their lifestyle is their birthright.

At the same time, the people in the low-end housing feel like no matter what they do, they're never going to get one of those penthouses themselves. So, instead of hustling harder, they stop caring. That's one of the real lasting effects that slavery has had on African Americans. If, as a people, you work for 300-odd years and never see yourself move even a centimeter up the success ladder, it impacts you. Hell, forget about 300, it probably had an impact after five years. That sense of "no matter how hard I work, it's not going to matter" becomes ingrained in people's mind-sets. This is part of the reason a lot of folks in the hood have lost that ambition to keep pushing for themselves. They have to battle with a different type of entitlement—feeling like you're never going to make it happen for yourself, so someone else is going to have to do it for you.

An immigrant isn't going to identify with either of those mentalities. From their perspective, there's no difference between the bricks in a skyscraper and the bricks in a housing project. The entire country looks like the most beautiful place in the world, compared to where many of them are coming from.

This is especially true in my hometown of New York City. There's a reason tens of thousands of people are trying to get here every day. Even from halfway around the world, they can see shining opportunities that we've largely become blind to. They understand that it really is "Big Rich Town," and they want in!

I consider immigrants to be the backbone of New York. They keep its hustler spirit alive. We always celebrate the Wall Street guys or the tech CEOs, but the immigrants are the ones making it happen, day in and day out. According to a study from the Center for American Entrepreneurship, 56 percent of all Fortune 500 companies in the metro NYC area were founded by immigrants. That African guy who got his teeth knocked out for selling my bootleg back in the day? There's no way he wasn't back selling CDs the very next day. He probably kept selling and selling until he opened his own chain of stores. Today he might even have one of those big companies. Or perhaps he went back to his home country and opened a chain of stores there.

We've been very successful in exporting American culture across the globe. But at the end of the day, all we make in America is people. We're exporting a lifestyle. A dream. We're not creating anything real anymore.

That's why it's time we import some of the hustle that seems to be so abundant in the rest of the world. Then we can stop feeling like people owe us something and start realizing that our hustle can lead us to whatever we want in life!

ARE THEY MAKING A DEPOSIT?

There is one question you must ask about every person in your life, no matter how long you've known them:

Does he or she ever make deposits into my life, or do they only make withdrawals?

If the answer is "withdrawals," then that's someone you need to distance yourself from immediately. Remember, no one only makes one withdrawal. Would you only go to an ATM that kept spittin' out free money just the once? Hell no. You would go every single day until the bank figured it out. Well, people are the same way. Until you shut them down, they will keep taking and taking until there's nothing left.

I'm getting rid of all the people who only make withdrawals. I've already lost people who meant the world to me—namely, my mother and grandmother—and I'm still doing just fine. There is zero reason I can't cut all the other people who are trying to drain me instead of fill me up.

This is why I don't particularly care if my father ever makes himself known to me. At this point, he would only be coming to make withdrawals from my life. There's nothing for him to deposit.

I already have enough people like that in my life. Every day they look to make withdrawals from the Bank of 50 Cent. I've already discussed the people who are straight up looking for a monetary handout, but just as frequently it's people seeking my association on its own.

"Hey, we got this phenomenal idea that can be a hit and make us some big money," they'll say, before getting to the catch. "We just need *you* to make it work."

I'm not looking to partner with people like that anymore. I want to be associated with concepts and ideas that could work with or without me. I want to be around talented folks who can lift me higher, not people who want to piggyback off my success.

The first time I ever met Mark Wahlberg was at a dinner with a group of people I'd just met. I ate my food, hung out a bit, and then went to the restroom. On the way back, I decided I'd been there longer than I needed to be, so I paid the check. When I got back to the table, I told the group, "Yo, I'm running out. See you guys later. Great to meet everyone. And don't worry about the bill. I took care of it." I didn't do that to be a big shot, it's just a role I've gotten comfortable in.

Mark couldn't believe it. "What? You did what?" he said almost jumping out of his seat. "Wait a fucking minute, wait a minute. I finally found a guy who can find his fucking pockets and he's leaving? Bro, we gotta get together. We gotta hang out." He was excited because *he* was always the guy who people would expect to pay the tab. Now someone was finally willing to make a deposit. That caught his attention.

We've ended up becoming good friends after that night, and Mark's made plenty of deposits into my life. He's someone who already did the rapper-turned-TV-executive thing with *Entourage* and *Boardwalk Empire*, and he's given me a lot of valuable advice and insight.

I would have never made that connection with him if I hadn't reached for my wallet that night. I know everyone reading this isn't in the position to pay for a fancy meal in an LA restaurant, but you are in a position to make deposits with the right people.

Professionally, you can always contribute to morale no matter what position you're in. If you're part of a team, it doesn't cost a cent to be the one with a positive attitude. That doesn't mean you have to kiss your boss's ass or be fake. You just have to stay upbeat about things. Be the person who doesn't bitch or moan when you get a tough job or assignment. Be the person who is smiling and open to interacting with co-workers instead of putting on headphones and hiding behind a computer screen. Be diplomatic, and try to identify a resolution when your co-workers aren't getting along.

The easiest deposit you can make at work, but one that will pay off in the long run, is to just show up on time. You have no idea how aggravating it is for a boss when employees just roll in whenever. It might be tempting to think, "Well, if it were my company, I'd get there early, but why should I rush over there to make these guys money?" If that's your attitude, you're never going to get your own company.

This is definitely an issue I struggle with concerning my own employees. As I said earlier, one of my weak points is that I like to be comfortable in the workplace. I like to be around people I know and trust. Unfortunately, the comfort that I'm looking for can make the entire environment too relaxed. After some time, people start to forget that they have real responsibilities I'm paying them for.

That's when they start making their own schedules. They might think I don't notice, but I do. And I won't comment on it so long as everything's rolling the right way. But if you're strolling in at 10 or 11 every morning and the work we're producing is not tight, then we are going to have a problem. I was giving you rope in letting you come in when you wanted, but now you just hung yourself with it.

Unless you are directly contributing to your company's bottom line in a significant way, please do not trick yourself into believing you can just go in when you want. Instead, make sure you're the most consistent person in the office at just showing up. It might be as simple as setting your alarm fifteen minutes earlier in the morning. But if you can get into the habit of just being on time, that is a recognizable deposit your boss will value.

As long as you are making consistent deposits, it's okay to approach your boss and ask to discuss a raise. But whatever you do, do not start that conversation by pointing out how long you've been at the company. If someone comes to me talking about how long they've been around, all they're doing is giving me confirmation that it might be time for me to get them the fuck out of there! If you have been around forever but I'm not proactively giving you a raise, there is probably a reason.

Instead, when you have that talk, keep the focus on what you've been contributing. Revenue, of course, is the best thing to be able to point to. But it can also be some of the nontransactional things we've mentioned: upbeat energy, helpful diplomacy, punctuality, and creativity. If you've been making those deposits on a consistent basis, it's probably going to stand out. And you'll be rewarded a lot quicker than the person who has been at the company a long time but is only interested in drawing their paycheck.

It is important to remember that not every deposit someone puts into your life is going to be monetary. A person might never give you a dime, but still bless you in all sorts of other ways.

My aunt Geraldine and uncle Mike deposited a lot of affirmative energy into my life without asking for anything in return. A rare trait in my family! The three of us must have been drinking different water than everyone else. We all understand that no matter what happens in your life, there should never be a moment when you feel like it's okay to stop working and start looking for a handout.

Uncle Michael and Aunt Geraldine proved that when they won a million dollars from a scratch-off ticket Michael bought. I remember being so excited for him when he told me. "What are the odds of that actually happening?" I asked him. "That's incredible!"

It was a nice little layer of comfort to add to their lifestyle. He and my aunt bought a bigger house and traded in a couple of their cars for something nicer. But that was it. All they did was upgrade.

What they didn't do was quit their jobs. They didn't say, "Okay, we've made it" and try to go on one of those twenty-year vacations. They were wise enough to understand that while the extra money was a blessing, in a few years it would be gone and they would have to keep living.

It is very easy to run through a million dollars in this country. And they did. Thankfully, they never quit their day jobs, so they're fine.

With their strong sense of self-sufficiency, we've never run into some of the issues I've had with other members of my family. My aunt and uncle are not looking to get anything from me, only give.

It's been like that forever. Even now, Aunt Geraldine still buys me socks for Christmas and tries to cook me a meal. I don't need the socks and I've got a personal chef, but that's not the point. They just symbolize the love she has for me. She's wanted to provide for me, to give me things, since I was a little boy. She's the person who gave me the nickname Boo Boo. Might seem like a small thing, but to a kid who lost his mother, that term of endearment was very important. To this day, the people I'm closest to still know me as Boo Boo (and are the only ones allowed to call me that!).

My son Sire has brought that sort of positivity into my life, too.

Everything is in place for us to have a healthy and loving relationship. Whenever I see my little guy, it's nothing but happiness and excitement. He's not looking for a thing from me. He just wants to show me where his front teeth just fell out, or a picture he drew in school. There's nothing better than sitting on the couch watching TV and having him come into the room and without a word snuggle up next to me. He's not looking for a thing—no money, no favors, no handouts. He just wants to be close to his father. Being on the receiving end of that sort of unconditional love is something I'm not used to but need to become better acquainted with.

GIVING BACK

I'll admit that there are times when I don't feel very charitable. If I walk down the street and see a guy with a funny sign and a cup begging for change, my immediate reaction might be, "I don't feel the need to help this guy because his spirit is already broken. Whatever bill I put into his cup is not going to make the slightest difference." If someone has the ability to write something so humorous that it's going to make a calloused New Yorker reach into their pocket, then that person has talent. Unfortunately, he's only comfortable using that talent to ask for a handout instead of going out there and applying it in a more constructive or productive way. I don't want to support that.

Over the years, however, I've come to understand that this attitude isn't always helpful. Yes, an individual would rather prey on people's sense of compassion than put in the work. But that doesn't mean there aren't many, many more people out there who really do have the work ethic and hustler's spirit I promote, yet have been caught in circumstances beyond their control. They do require some sort of help.

Being in a position of abundance, I'm becoming more and more focused on using my money to help those kinds of people. When you've experienced success and validation over a sustained period of time, it allows you to take the focus off yourself a little and become more conscious of what's happening in the different communities around you.

The older I get, the less I'm impressed with people who amass money, and the more inspired I am by the people who are committed to giving it away. I never realized it before, but now I can see that the givers are going to be the ones with the strongest presence in their absence. When they're dead and gone, people are still going to speak about them in reverential tones. Fifty years from now, people will remember Bill Gates more for the work he did supporting sustainable agriculture around the world than for whatever he figured out with computer chips. Just like the music mogul David Geffen isn't going to be remembered for making hit records. He'll be celebrated for the advances he supported in medical fields. Warren Buffett may be incomprehensibly wealthy, but he's committed himself to donating 99 percent of his fortune to charities by the end of his days. He's been following that oath and has made philanthropy his new calling, pushing other billionaires to do the same with the Giving Pledge.

Their examples made me become more conscious of my own legacy. I've had to ask myself, "Do I want to be mainly remembered as a person who sold a lot of records and made a lot of hit TV shows?" At one point the answer would have been "Hell, yeah!" I still value that experience, but now it's more important that I'm also thought of as someone who did something positive with the money he made.

It's not enough anymore for me to say, "Well, I'm giving back by showing people that it's possible to go from the bottom to the top." I need to do even more. I'm committed to take the money, resources, and connections I've gained on the way to the top and invest them directly back into the bottom, so that the people living there might have an easier time making a similar journey.

One of the first times I became really interested in the concept of philanthropy was after I traveled to Nigeria. I didn't know much about the country, but Heineken was paying me $4 million to do four shows, so of course I packed my bags and got on a plane.

One of the first nights there, I was chillin' in my hotel room in Lagos and ordered room service. The hotel brought all this food into my suite, and I was about to dig in when I noticed that the chicken wasn't de-veined. Something about that made me queasy. My appetite was spoiled, and I wanted to get out of my room and into some fresh air.

Suddenly an idea popped into my head. I told my road manager, Barry, to grab $15,000 out of our per diem money, put it in a bag, and get a car ready. Once Barry had the cash, I met him downstairs, got in the car, and told the driver, "Just take us to the hood."

I have definitely seen some rough neighborhoods before, but I'd never seen anything as harsh as the neighborhood the driver took us to. Forget about housing projects where the elevators smell like piss. These people were living in little huts made out of sheets of corrugated metal. No AC, no windows, no running water. If that wasn't bad enough, there was a river of piss and shit running in front of the huts. The Baisley projects in Queens looked like the Four Seasons compared to what these people were living in.

As we were driving, I also noticed that people were carrying on their heads anything heavy they needed to transport. If someone had a thirty-pound package they needed to get across town, they weren't calling FedEx. They were getting it up on the tops of their domes and walking it across town that way. The sight really blew my mind.

At one point we had to slow down because the street wasn't anything more than muddy alleys. I took some money out of the bag, rolled down the windows, and started handing out 100s to people who came up to the car.

Once the folks in the hood realized what was happening, the energy was ridiculous. More kinetic than at any concert I've ever performed at. This was a country where picking up an extra $40 might change your life for the next few months. And I was handing out Ben Franklins like candy at Halloween.

Word began to spread that I was throwing money, and by the time I got back to the hotel, there were probably 3,000 or 4,000 people waiting for me. The scene was insane. Even after all the money was gone, people just wanted to touch me. Not in a negative or threatening way, either. They just wanted to share the energy they were feeling with me. One guy pulled my do-rag off my head so fast that it didn't even knock my baseball cap off. It was incredible.

My actions ended up causing such a disturbance that we had to cancel the final show of the tour and go home. There were just too many people trying to show up and see if I was going to throw some money their way.

It felt great to know that I had helped so many people in a short amount of time, but I also realized that driving around the slums throwing bills wasn't the smartest or most effective way to use my money to help people. I needed a better plan.

I used to think I was from the bottom, but my trip to Africa was a wake-up call. It turns out that I didn't have any idea what the bottom actually looked like. My African brothers and sisters were struggling in a way I wasn't even remotely familiar with.

People in the hood might not understand this. When I tell them about Africa, they'll tell me, "Yo Fif, we're hungry here, man." No, you *think* you're hungry. But across Africa, hundreds of thousands of people are dying every year due to starvation. That's true hunger.

My understanding of how bad the situation is got even deeper in 2012 when I teamed up with the World Food Programme and traveled to Kenya and Somalia to witness the impact the hunger crisis has had on those countries. I thought my experience in Nigeria would have prepared me, but I couldn't believe what I saw in Kenya and Somalia.

In Kenya, I visited a school where all of the 500 kids there were orphaned and forty-eight were HIV-positive. They each got to eat one meal a day: cornmeal with protein powder dumped on it. There wasn't anything else on the menu. That's all they got each and every day.

I'd never seen anything so desperate. But these kids still had the most incredible energy. I'd ask them what they wanted to be when they grew up, and they'd say, "I'm going to be a doctor" or "I'm going to be a lawyer." They'd been dealt some of the worst cards you could possibly get, and they were still optimistic and upbeat about the future.

Their total lack of resentment made me think about how I used to bitch that I had to wear KangaROOs instead of Nikes. Or Marquise feeling sad because he wasn't wearing the right Jordans. If every kid in America could spend five minutes in a school like the one I visited in Kenya, they'd all be ashamed that they ever acted so entitled. I know I was.

After that trip, I committed myself to working with the World Food Programme to fight global hunger, especially in Africa. At the time, I had just launched the energy drink Street King. I pledged that, for each drink purchased, I would donate a portion of the earnings to feed one hungry kid. To get the program off on the right foot, I wrote a check that covered the cost of 2.5 million meals.

We were able to feed a lot of hungry kids through that program, but there's obviously so much more work to be done. My hope is that programs like the one we did with Street King can create a template for what I call "conscious capitalism." That means, instead of hitting a billion-dollar lick and then just sitting on it, these CEOs start to make giving a fundamental part of their business plans. The World Bank says that if the top Fortune 500 companies donated just 1 percent of their earnings to charitable organizations, it could alleviate extreme poverty across the globe. Just 1 percent. I don't think that's too much to ask of any corporation.

I'm as focused on the bottom line as the next entrepreneur, but none of us need that 1 percent so badly that we can't use it to help these kids out there. It's just that a lot of these richest folk aren't conditioned to give things away. Their mentality is similar to the one I used to have when I walked by a homeless guy: "Well, *I* worked for it. These other people just sat around not concentrating on what they wanted for their lives. So why should I have to come up with the solution?"

My answer is to take a little bit of your money and fly to Africa to visit the kids I spent time with at that school. Or meet with the kids in the Middle East, Asia, or South America who are living in similar situations. When you experience the energy these kids have in the face of so much oppression, you'll realize how it's not about your work ethic versus someone else's lack of one. It's about recognizing that you've been blessed to be able to apply your work ethic in a country with as many opportunities as America has.

When I think about those kids, it makes me question the motivations behind a lot of the decisions I made earlier in my career. Everything I once did was meant to prove that I had more than the next man. But now that I've grown and experienced more, that sort of mind-set doesn't match my sense of morality anymore.

I don't want to give the impression that I'm only focused on helping kids in Africa either. When I sold my mansion in Connecticut, I donated all of the $3 million I earned to my G-Unity Foundation. The money went to support programs that provide academic enrichment in poverty-stricken areas in America. I've also given a lot of money, almost a million dollars, to help restore public parks near where I grew up in Queens. I want kids coming up there today to have green spaces where they feel comfortable playing outside and getting familiar with nature.

It all feels like the right thing to be doing with my money. Once I've provided for the future of myself and my kids, how many more toys do I really need? Not many. What I need to do is figure out more ways to give back.

In the past I tended not to talk about the charity work I was doing because I didn't want to foster a sense of entitlement around me. I didn't want people thinking that it was my responsibility to give them money on either a personal or organizational level.

I'm not worried about that pressure anymore. In fact, I welcome it. I want to be known as someone who will write a check for a charity that merits it. I want to be associated with philanthropy. I've made a lot of things cool in my days. Using a singsong flow in my raps. Bulletproof vests. Paying your debts back by Monday.

Now I want to make charity cool, too. If I could do that, *that's* what would go down as my greatest accomplishment.

REMEMBER:

BE FEARLESS

Most people run from what they're afraid of. I run toward it. That doesn't mean I think I'm bulletproof (I've learned the hard way that I'm not) or that I'm unaware of danger. I experience fear as much as the next man.

But one of the greatest mistakes people can make is becoming comfortable with their fears. Whatever is worrying me, I meet it head-on and engage it until the situation is resolved. My refusal to become comfortable with fear gives me an advantage in almost every situation.

CULTIVATE THE HEART
OF A HUSTLER

Hustlin' might be associated with selling drugs, but it's actually a character trait that's shared by winners in every profession. Steve Jobs was as much of a hustler at Apple as I was when I was on the streets.

The key to building up that trait in your own personality is accepting that you're never hustling toward a certain goal. Hustlin' is a motor that's got to be running inside of you each and every day. And its fuel is passion. If you can keep that motor running, it will take you everywhere you want to go in life.

BUILD A STRONG CREW

You're only going to be as strong as the weakest person in your crew. That's why you have to be extremely conscious of who you have around you. Betrayal is never as far away as you'd like to believe.

That's why it's imperative to find a balance between establishing trust and discipline in the people you work with and giving them the freedom to be themselves. If you can establish that equilibrium, you will be in the position to get the very best out of your team.

KNOW YOUR VALUE

One of the cornerstones of my sustained success is that I don't rush into deals. Even though I've become synonymous with "getting paid," I never chase money. I evaluate every new venture based on its long-term potential, not on what the first check I get is going to look like.

The reason I do that is I have supreme confidence in my own value and ability. I'm secure that as long as I'm betting on myself, I'm always going to win.

EVOLVE OR DIE

If I'd been unwilling—or unable—to evolve as an individual, I'd be dead or in jail right now. One of the keys to my success is that at every stage of my life, I've been willing to assess any new situation I find myself in, and make the necessary adjustments.

While I'll always draw from the lessons I learned on the streets, I've never been limited to them. Instead, I'm always looking to absorb new information from as many sources as possible. I don't care where you come from or what you look like—if you've created success, I want to learn from you.

SHAPE PERCEPTION

Everything you share with the world—your words, your energy, what you wear—tells a story. You must make sure your narrative always presents you as the person you want to be seen as, even if your reality tells a slightly different story.

One of the secrets to getting what you want in life is creating the perception that you don't need a thing. That can be a difficult energy to project—especially when you're struggling—but committing to that perception will make you more attractive professionally, personally, and even romantically.

DON'T BE AFRAID TO COMPETE

Some people try to portray me as a troll, or a bully, but that's not accurate. My first instinct is always to build positive and mutually beneficial relationships with people. But if someone isn't interested in being friends with me, I'm more than comfortable being enemies with them.

The reason is I believe competition is healthy for all parties involved. Whether it's taking on established rappers or hit TV shows, I've always experienced my greatest success when I've met my rivals head-on and without any hesitation.

LEARN FROM YOUR Ls

As many victories as I've racked up over the years, I've experienced many more losses. That doesn't make me the exception among successful people—it makes me the rule. I don't know an affluent rapper, mogul, executive, or entrepreneur whose losses don't far outweigh their wins.

What separates those people from the pack is that instead of complaining about or hiding from their losses, they actively seek to learn from them.

AVOID THE
ENTITLEMENT TRAP

N othing was ever given to me in life. I've had to fight for everything I've earned. That's why the concept of entitlement has never seeped into my mentality. But almost everywhere I look—from the streets to the boardrooms—I still see a lot of entitled people.

You're never going to find lasting success until you take full responsibility for what happens in your life. No one owes you anything. Just as you don't owe anyone else. Once you accept that fundamental truth and accept that you control your journey, so many doors that seemed closed are going to open up in front of you.